A Photo Tour of Northeastern Minnesota

NORTH SHORE
DULUTH

David Barthel

ADVENTURE PUBLICATIONS
Cambridge, Minnesota

DEDICATION

This book is dedicated to those who know Lake Superior and continually feel its inexplicable allure.

CREDITS

All photos by David Barthel

Cover photos: Honeymoon Bluff (*front, top*); Duluth waterfront and lift bridge (*front, bottom*); Lake Superior shore near Grand Portage (*back, top*); US-Japan Peace Bell in Enger Park (*back, middle*)

Cover and book design by Jonathan Norberg

All rights reserved. No part of this book may be reproduced in any form, or by any means electronic, mechanical, recording, or otherwise, without written permission from the publisher, except for brief quotations used in reviews.

10 9 8 7 6 5 4 3 2 1
North Shore–Duluth: A Photo Tour of Northeastern Minnesota
Copyright © 2019 by David Barthel
Published by Adventure Publications
An imprint of AdventureKEEN
330 Garfield Street South
Cambridge, Minnesota 55008
(800) 678-7006
www.adventurepublications.net
All rights reserved
Printed in China
ISBN 978-1-59193-833-0 (pbk.)

A Photo Tour of Northeastern Minnesota

NORTH SHORE
DULUTH

PREFACE

The idea of publishing a book—whether a coffee table-style portfolio, educational text, or location guide—crosses the minds of many landscape photographers throughout their professional careers. As a photographer who had become deeply rooted in the business of making fine art prints for the walls of clients' homes and businesses, my own thoughts of producing a photography-based book sat patiently on the proverbial back burner, waiting for the moment when I would have enough time, the right images, a double-dose of courage, or some other epiphany that would indicate that it was the "right" time. When the folks at AdventureKEEN approached me with a proposal for creating a photo-based guidebook showcasing the region I had become intimately familiar with, I knew it was the nudge I needed. And the timing was excellent. While guidebooks for Duluth and the North Shore of Lake Superior already existed, a publication sharing some of the most notable sites to experience, with an emphasis on high-quality photography and concise, interesting information, was long needed.

My journey as a landscape photographer and associated appreciation of Lake Superior's North Shore began in the early 2000s. It was a time when serious photography was a rather peculiar pastime often practiced by nerdy old guys, with film still by far the most popular means of capturing imagery. In those early days, it was not unusual to be the only person toting a tripod along the shore below Split Rock Lighthouse on a lovely autumn afternoon. Much has changed in the nearly twenty intervening years, and now photography is more popular and accessible than ever. With that has come substantially increased visitation to many of the North Shore's treasured landmarks and a greater need to preserve them for future generations to enjoy. Therefore, it has become increasingly important to observe ethical principles that minimize our impact on the land, such as staying on established trails and packing out all waste. These principles also extend to social media, where it is good practice to avoid tagging or otherwise disclosing precise locations when publicly posting photos of delicate, seldom-trod places. Throughout the world, viral imagery from social media has led to vastly increased foot traffic in once-obscure locations, resulting in damage to fragile terrain and ecosystems. Simply put, a little common sense can help preserve the region's stunning landscapes and historic landmarks for everyone to fully experience.

This book is intended for anyone with an interest in Duluth and the North Shore, from first-time visitors carefully planning their itineraries to lifelong residents appreciating the photography and fascinating facts pertaining to their favorite locations. For ease of use, the sites are geographically organized in the book, beginning in the southwest at Jay Cooke State Park and running northeast along Lake Superior's shore to Grand Portage State Park at the Canadian Border. An alphabetical index at the end of the book provides quick access to location and contact information for each site.

ACKNOWLEDGMENTS

I want to thank the many people who have made not only this book possible but also my ongoing career in landscape and nature photography. This includes my parents for introducing me to Duluth and portions of the North Shore at a young age, the outdoor photographers who came before me for instilling in me a greater appreciation of nature and art, and the crew at AdventureKEEN for giving me the opportunity to write this book and believing in my ability to do so amidst a daunting schedule. And, of course, I cannot forget my brother, Daniel, who has accompanied me on countless trips to the North Shore and beyond.

INTRODUCTION

From the bustling port city of Duluth, Minnesota, to the wild and rugged terrain surrounding the world's largest freshwater lake, Minnesota's North Shore of Lake Superior exemplifies the natural, cultural, and historic beauty for which Minnesota is renowned. Known for his distinctive fine art landscape photography of the North Shore region, professional photographer David Barthel shares 96 of the best locations and opportunities to experience Duluth and the North Shore for yourself. Each page is filled with stunning photography and location information to help you make the most of your trip and, quite likely, return trips to this amazing region.

FASCINATING FACTS ABOUT THE NORTH SHORE AND DULUTH

- Despite its northern location and relatively cold climate, Duluth was once home to the most millionaires per capita of any U.S. city and, for a brief time, was America's busiest port in terms of gross tonnage. Numerous examples of exquisite architecture from the late nineteenth and early twentieth centuries provide evidence of a once-affluent industrial port city that continues to thrive thanks to a growing tourism-based economy.

- Lake Superior, known to the Ojibwe as *Gichi-Gami* or "great sea," is the world's largest freshwater lake by surface area. The lake contains enough water to cover both North and South America to a depth of one foot. The large body of water also affects the weather adjacent to the shore, often keeping summertime temperatures much cooler than surrounding areas. In the winter, easterly winds can produce lake-effect snow in Duluth and on the North Shore.

- The average daytime high temperatures in Duluth during the months of January and July are 19°F and 76°F, respectively. Average annual snowfall is 86.1 inches.

- In Grand Marais, where the climate is further moderated by Lake Superior, an average January day sees a high temperature of 25°F. Due to the delayed warming of Lake Superior, August is Grand Marais' warmest month with an average high temperature of 72°F. In a typical year, Grand Marais receives about 45.7 inches of snow.

- The fierce *Mataafa* Storm of 1905, which sank 29 vessels on Lake Superior, prompted the construction of Split Rock Lighthouse. The lighthouse's beacon was lit for the first time on July 31, 1910. There were no roads to the site until construction of the North Shore Highway in 1924. Therefore, all building materials and supplies had to be shipped by boat and hoisted to the isolated clifftop by crane.

- In a typical autumn season, the North Shore experiences two distinct fall color phases. During the first phase, the maples on the ridges a few miles inland turn bright orange and red. This typically occurs during the last week in September or first week of October. The second phase typically begins a week or two later when the birch and aspen closer to Lake Superior finally change color and create a sea of yellow-orange along the shore.

- The Grand Portage is an 8.5-mile footpath once used by fur-trading voyageurs in the eighteenth century to bypass large rapids and waterfalls on the 20 miles of the Pigeon River nearest Lake Superior. These voyageurs were the first Europeans known to visit the area. The Grand Portage trail still exists today and is open to hikers wishing to experience the once-bustling trade route for themselves.

- Established in 1856, Beaver Bay is the North Shore's oldest permanently settled community. Just a few miles north on Highway 61 lies the North Shore's youngest city, Silver Bay, founded in 1954 as a company town for the nearby taconite processing plant.

- Stretching nearly 150 miles from Duluth to the Canadian Border, Minnesota Highway 61 is the North Shore's main thoroughfare. The roadway never ventures more than a mile inland from Lake Superior, providing unparalleled access to the lake's scenic views and recreational opportunities.

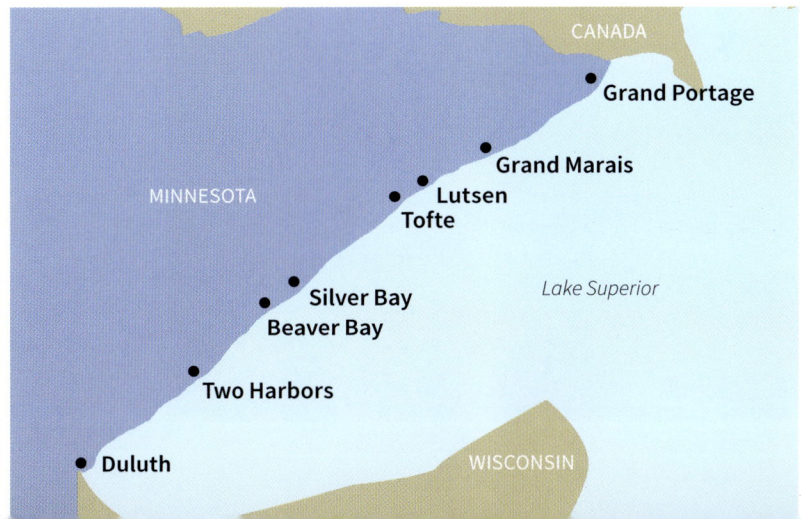

JAY COOKE STATE PARK

Jay Cooke State Park's rugged terrain includes some of the most tumultuous rapids of the St. Louis River, as it makes its way toward St. Louis Bay and Lake Superior in Duluth. The rapids are so dangerous that the park also includes part of what was once a grueling 6.5-mile portage used by Native Americans and European fur traders, who were using parts of the St. Louis River to connect the Great Lakes with western routes.

The park is named for Pennsylvania financier Jay Cooke, who envisioned Duluth as the "next Chicago" and financed the development of the Northern Pacific Railway and Thomson Hydroelectric Dam. The St. Louis Power Company, later owner of the hydroelectric dam, donated unneeded land to the State of Minnesota in 1915 for the development of a park.

Many of the park's amenities, including the swinging bridge over the St. Louis River and River Inn Visitor Center, were constructed by CCC camps during the 1930s and early 1940s. The park also contains more than 50 miles of hiking trails, a modern campground, picnic areas, and trails for bicycling, mountain biking, and cross-country skiing.

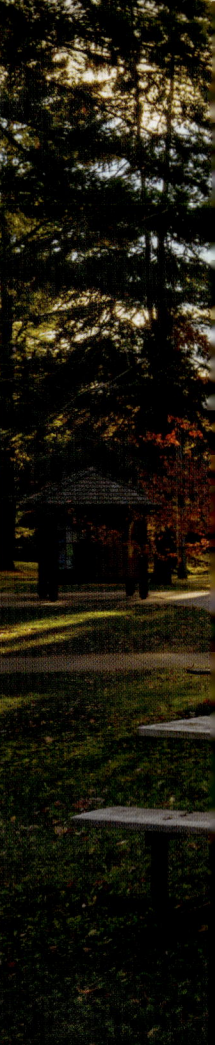

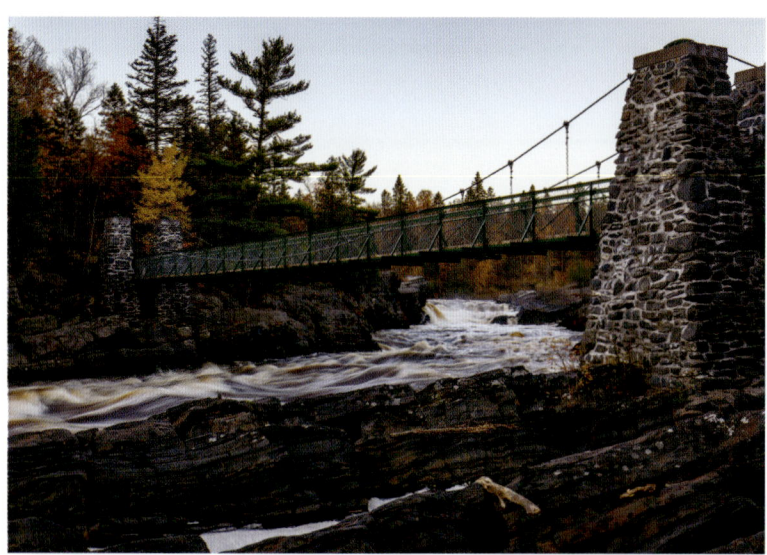

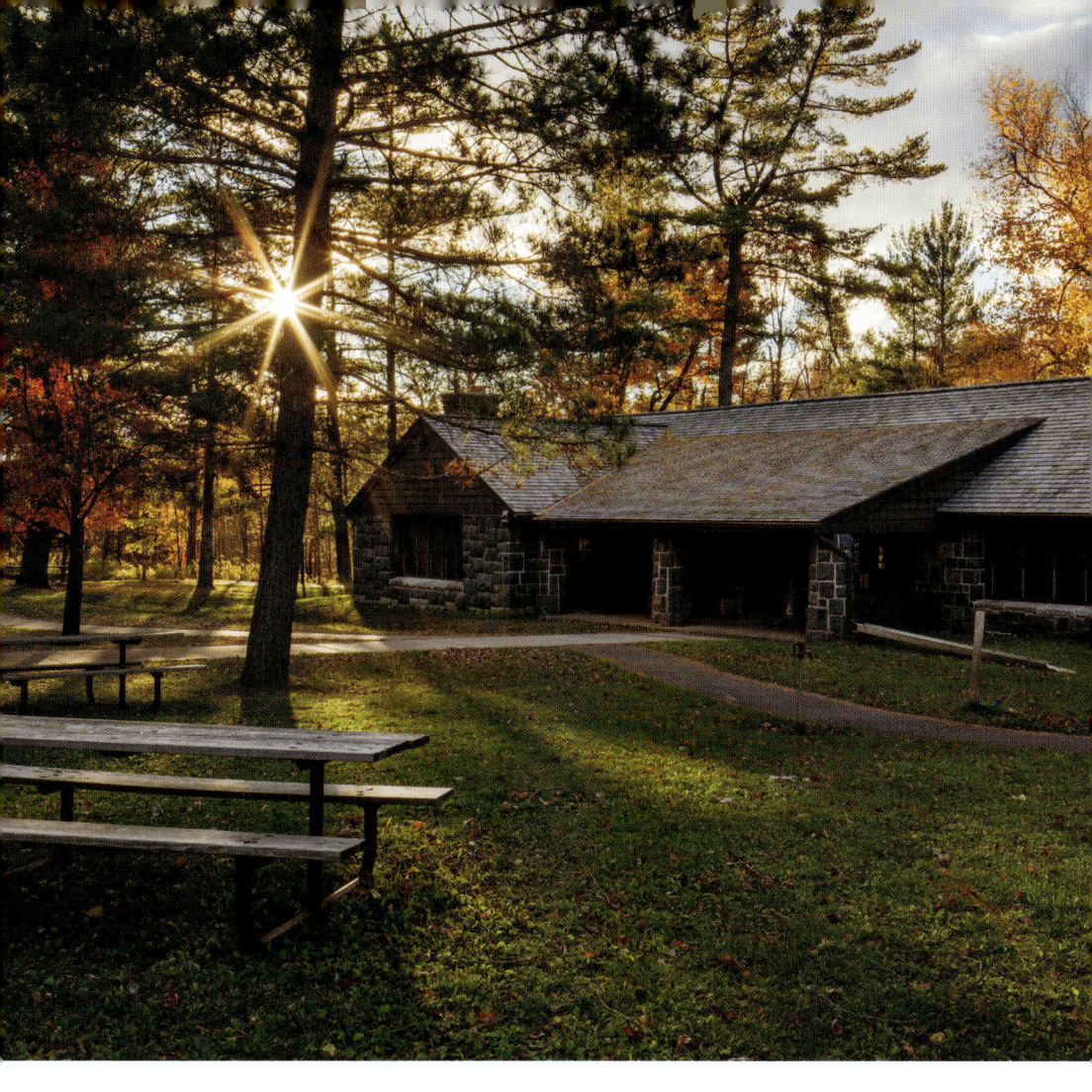

SPIRIT MOUNTAIN

Envisioned by local Olympian George Hovland and developed by the City of Duluth in 1974, Spirit Mountain Recreation Area opened for the first time in December 1974, bolstering winter tourism in the region. Its vertical elevation drop of 700 feet makes it the second tallest ski area in Minnesota, providing panoramic views of St. Louis Bay and the city of Duluth.

Spirit Mountain currently boasts 22 ski runs (the longest at 5,400 feet), a large terrain park, and summer activities ranging from camping and mountain biking to riding an alpine coaster.

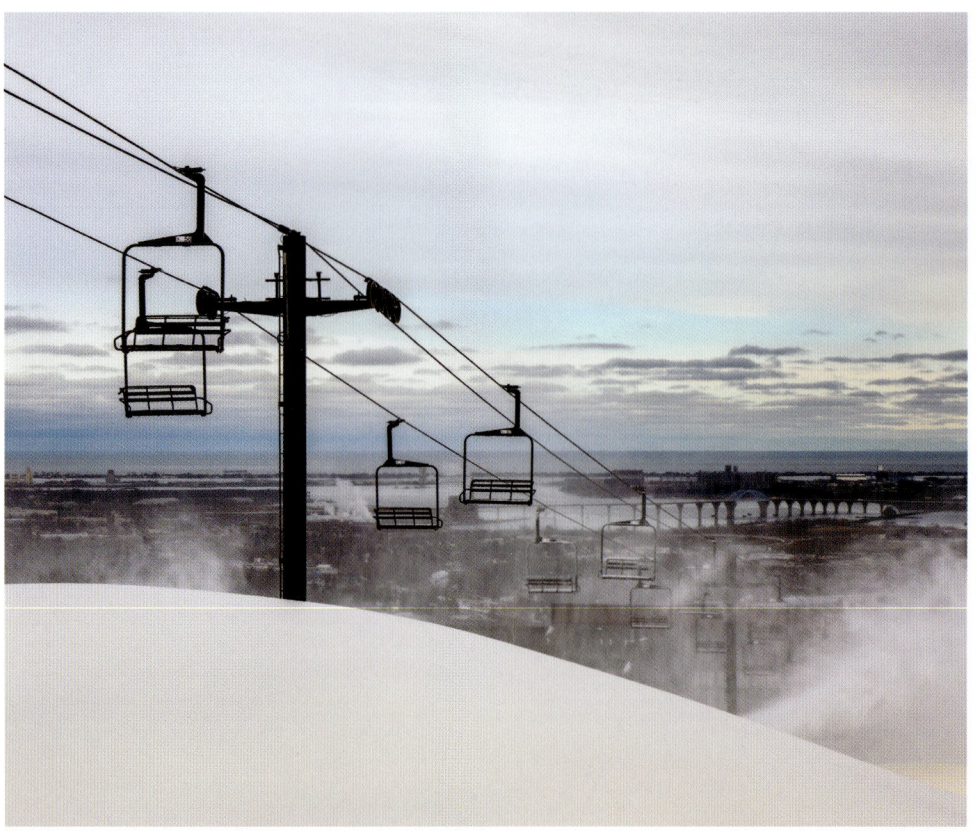

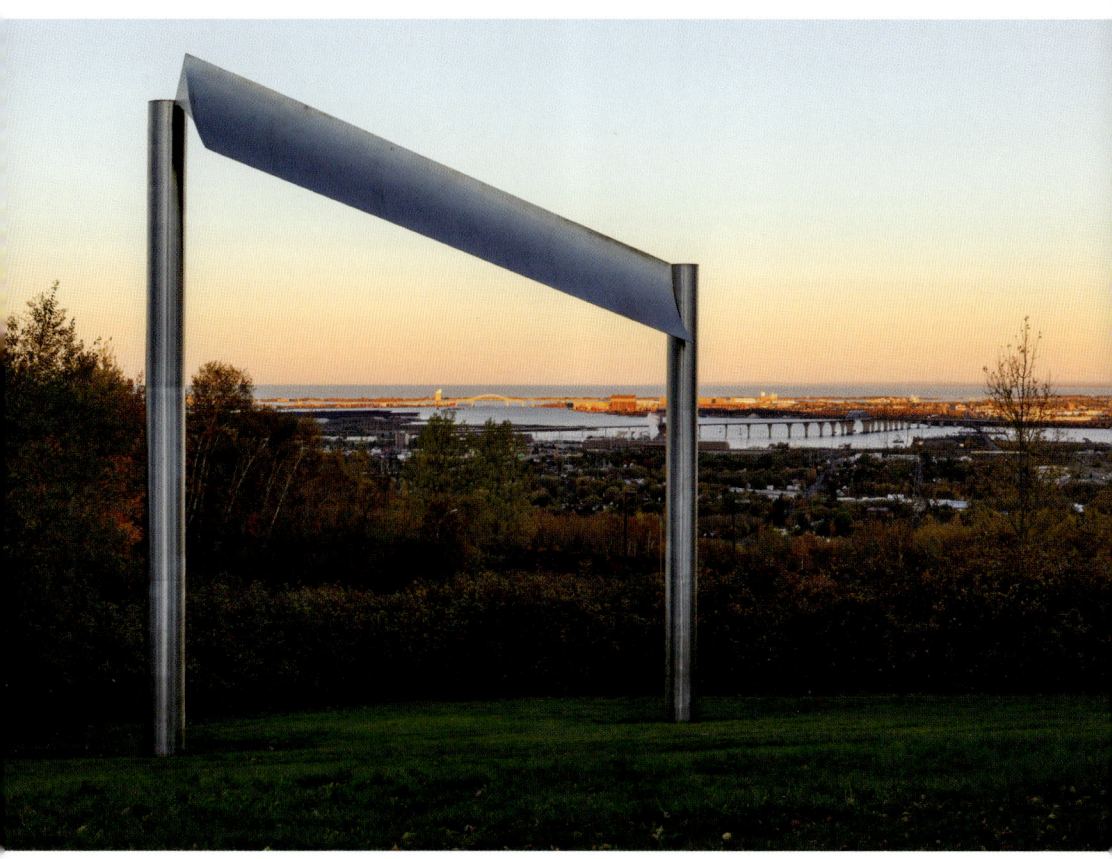

THOMPSON HILL WELCOME CENTER

Providing the first panoramic overlook of Lake Superior and the Twin Ports of Duluth, Minnesota, and Superior, Wisconsin, Thompson Hill Welcome Center is the first stop of many northbound travelers on their way into Duluth or up the North Shore. It was built in 1973 and replaced a nearby existing overlook, alongside former U.S. Highway 61, remnants of which can still be seen beside the northbound lanes of present-day Interstate 35.

Thompson Hill contains a modern rest area and Minnesota Travel Information Center. On the grounds of the center, visitors can admire the large stainless steel public sculpture *The Gate*, created by artist David von Schlegell in recognition of Duluth's status as a gateway to the North Shore and to the world via the Great Lakes Waterway and St. Lawrence Seaway.

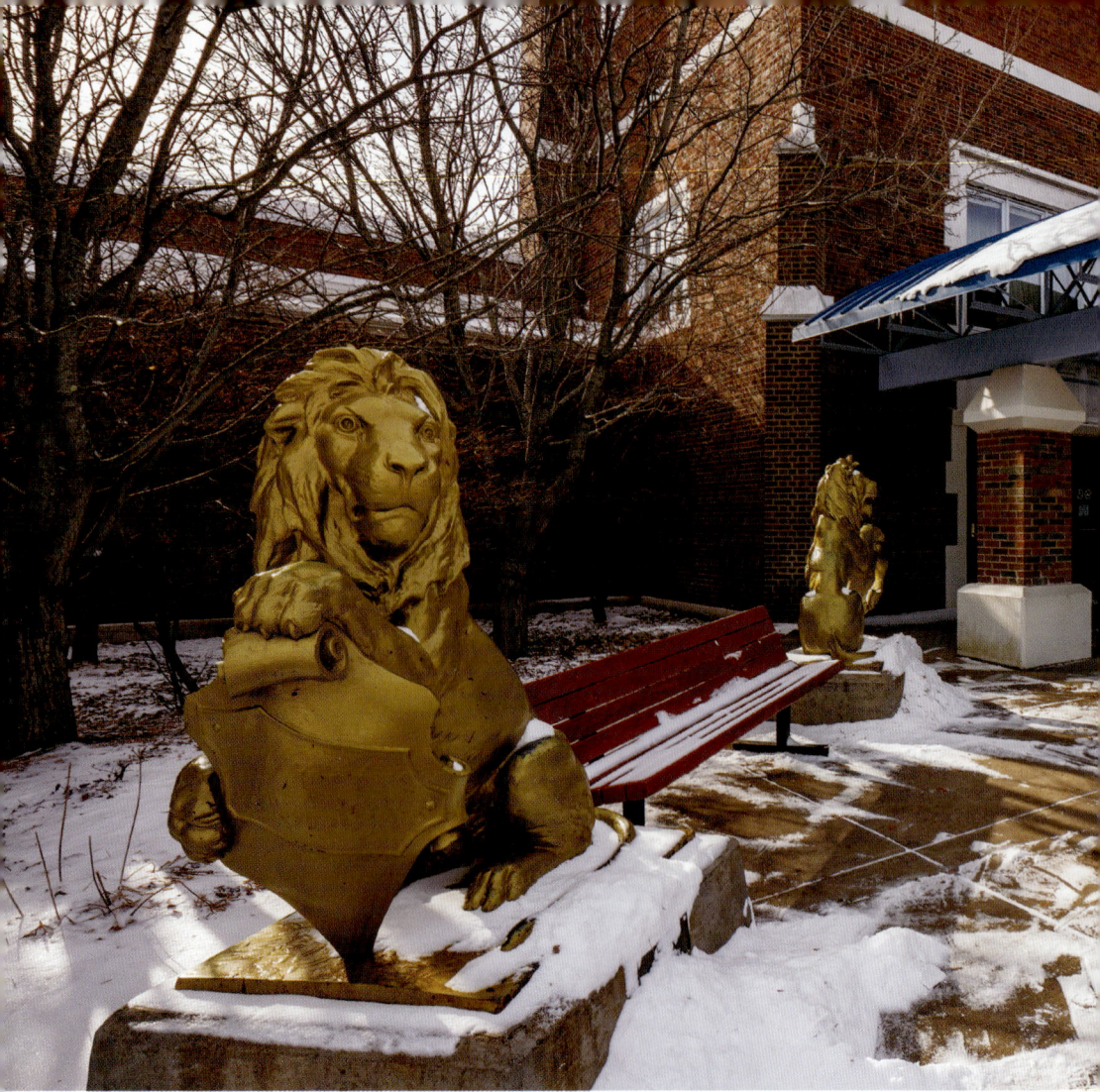

LAKE SUPERIOR ZOO

Established in 1923 when West Duluth businessman Bert Onsgard constructed a pen for "Billy," his pet deer, the Duluth Zoo's animal collection quickly grew to include exotic creatures from around the world, thanks to strong community support. Now accredited by the Association of Zoos and Aquariums and renamed "Lake Superior Zoo," its picturesque 19-acre site hosts animals from globally diverse habitats and is open year-round to visitors.

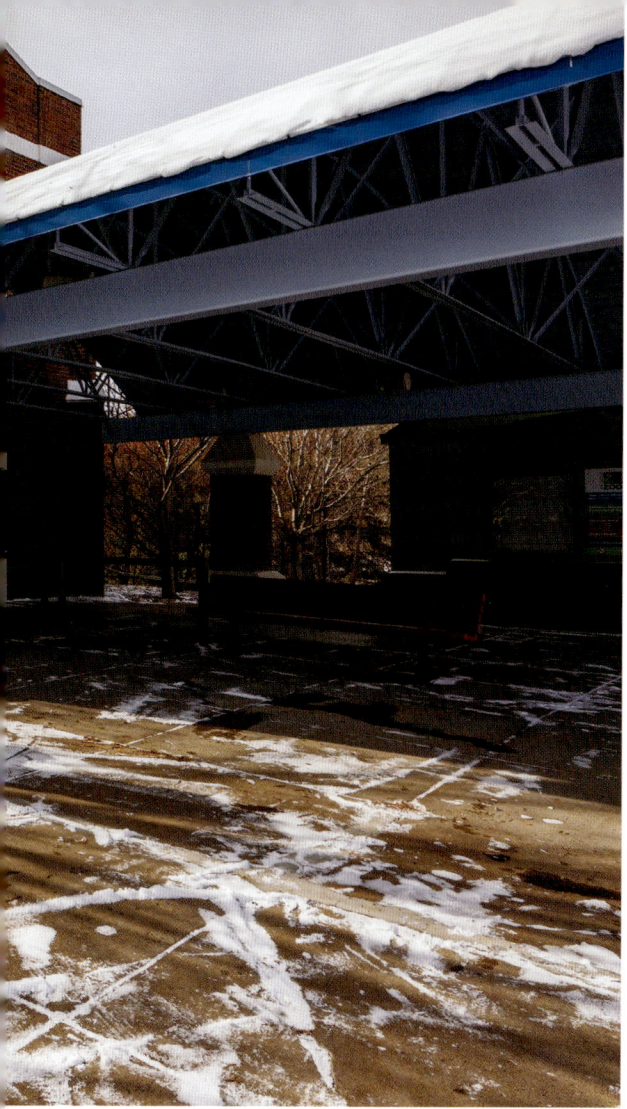

SKYLINE PARKWAY

Traversing the entire hillside of Duluth, from Becks Road in the southwest to Lester Park in the northeast, Skyline Parkway showcases bird's-eye views of the city, harbor, and Lake Superior, roughly 400–600 feet below. Paved for most of its 25-mile course, the scenic byway passes through woodlands, city parks, and neighborhoods. Numerous roadside pull-outs provide easy access to take in the stunning views.

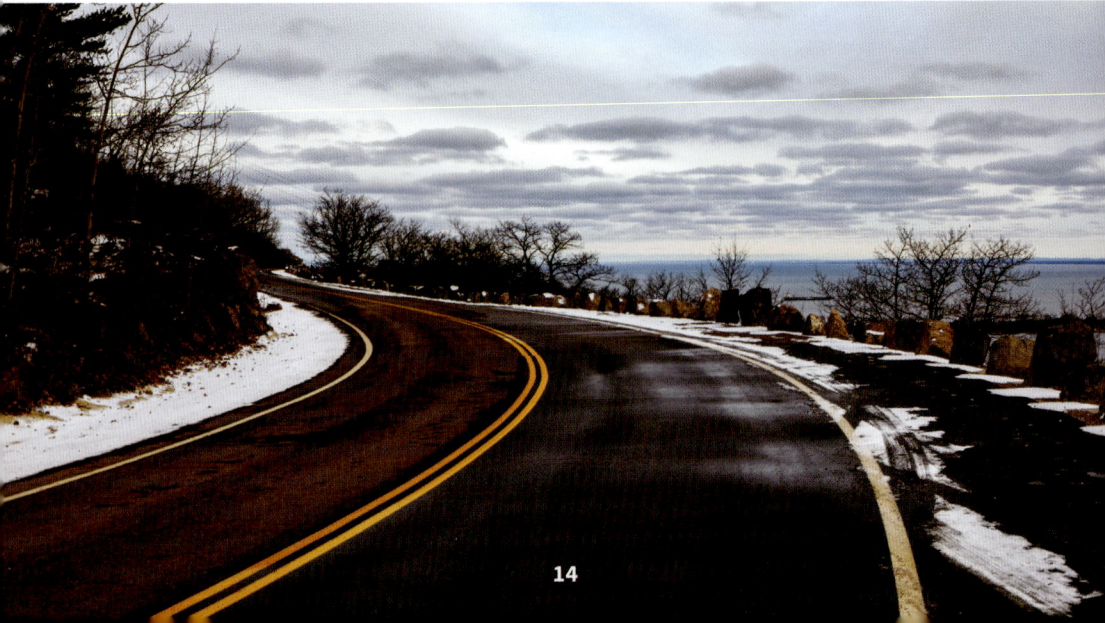

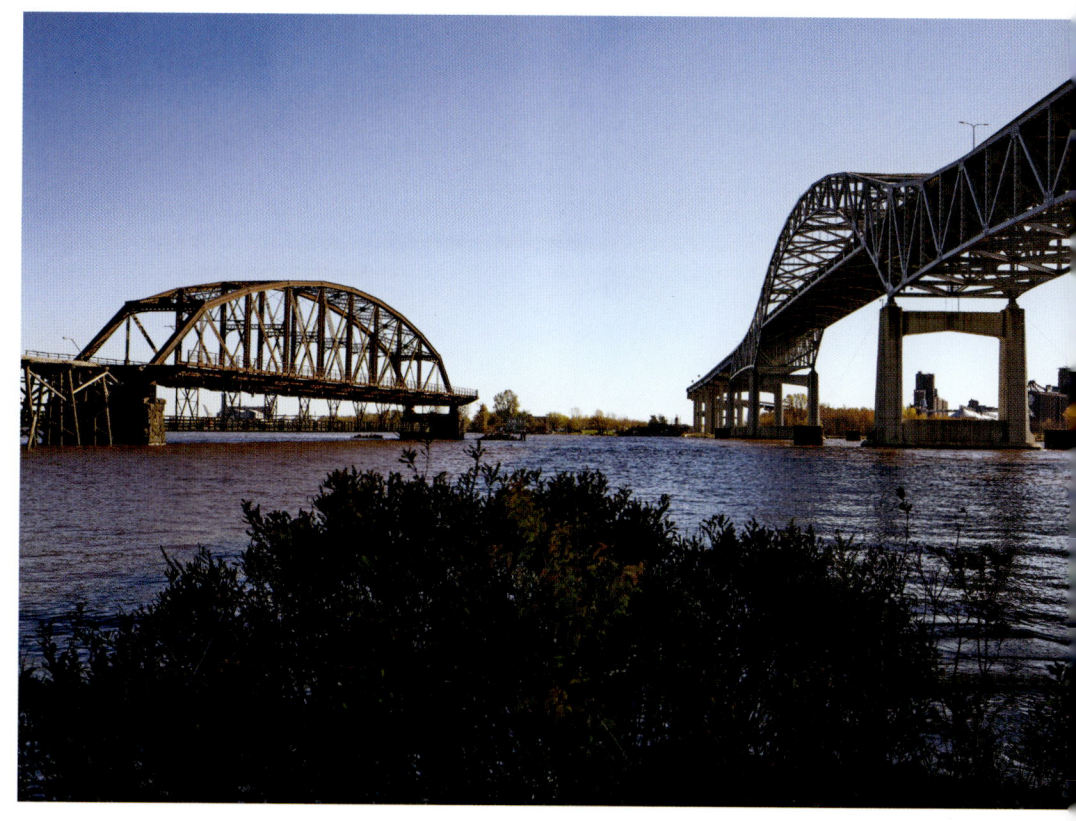

JOHN A. BLATNIK BRIDGE AND INTERSTATE FISHING PIER

As the northernmost bridge connecting Minnesota and Wisconsin, the Blatnik Bridge carries Interstate 535 and U.S. Highway 53 vehicle traffic over the St. Louis Bay between the twin ports of Duluth and Superior. Completed in 1961, it replaced the 1890s-era Interstate Bridge, which contained a large steel truss swing span that rotated to allow ships to pass. The current bridge was initially called the High Bridge because it was built to a clearance height of 120 feet, allowing ships to simply pass underneath. The bridge was renamed in 1971 in honor of U.S. Representative John Blatnik, who served Minnesota's Eighth District in Congress from 1947 until 1974 and championed the bridge's construction.

A surviving section of the Minnesota side of the old Interstate Bridge now serves as a fishing platform, visible from the Minnesota-bound lanes of the Blatnik Bridge.

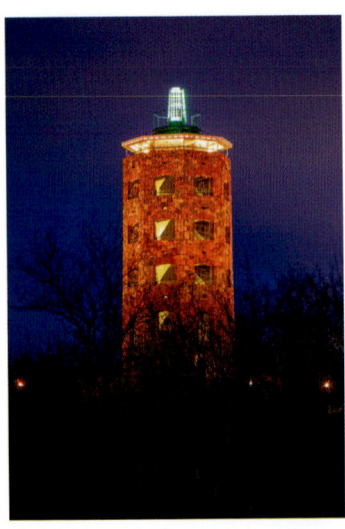

ENGER TOWER AND PARK

Standing more than 500 feet above Lake Superior, Enger Tower provides some of the finest aerial views of the Duluth Harbor and surrounding hillside. The five-story stone observation tower was built in 1939 to honor Norwegian immigrant and successful Duluth businessman Bert Enger, who donated land to the city upon which the structure now sits. The green beacon atop the tower can be seen for many miles at night.

The surrounding park includes a perennial garden; a small Japanese garden containing a peace bell from Duluth's sister city, Ohara, Japan; and a gazebo overlook. A 27-hole golf course lies just west of the main park.

A major restoration of the tower in 2011 brought upgrades, including new interior lighting and color-changing reflective exterior lighting.

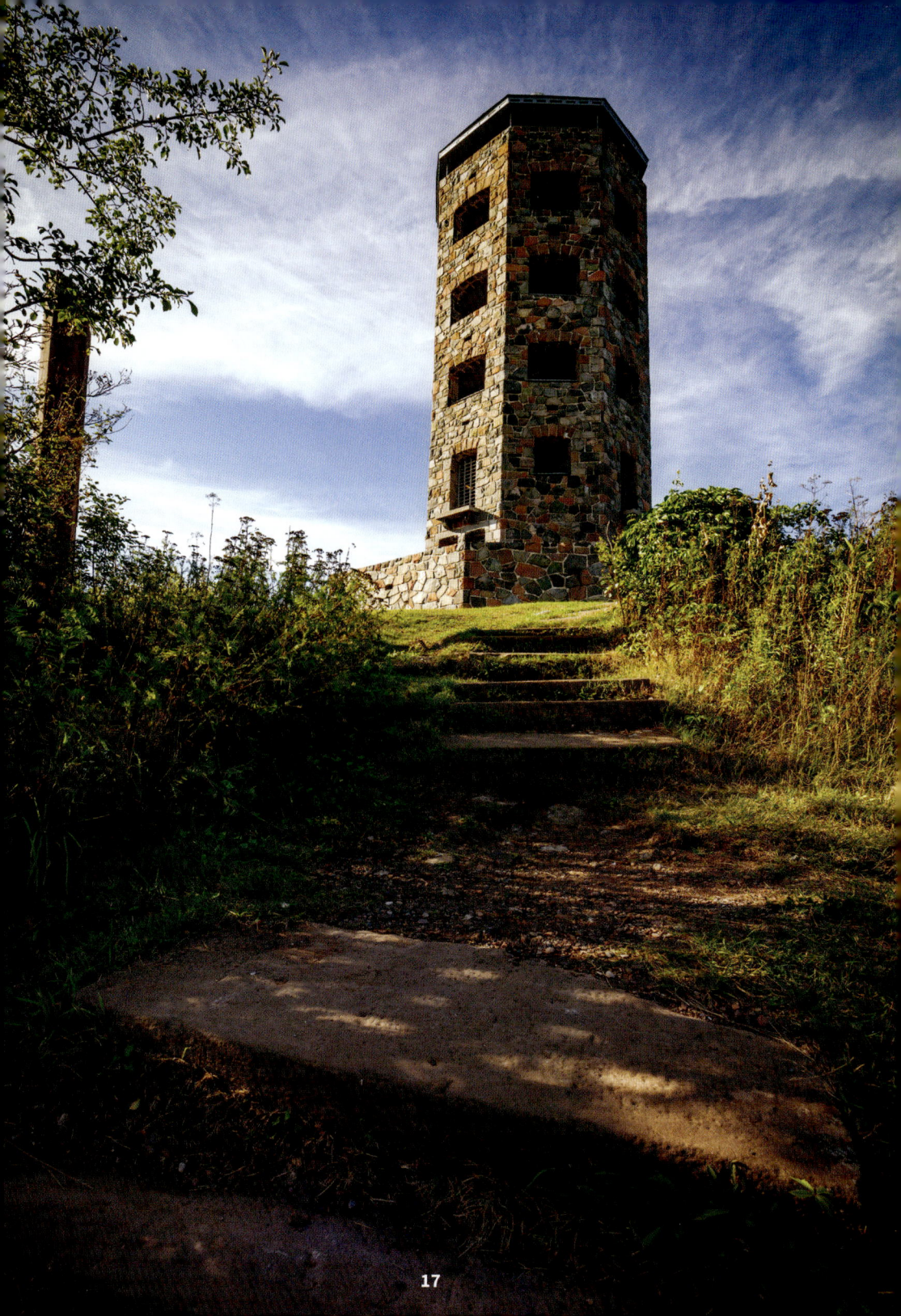

BAYFRONT FESTIVAL PARK

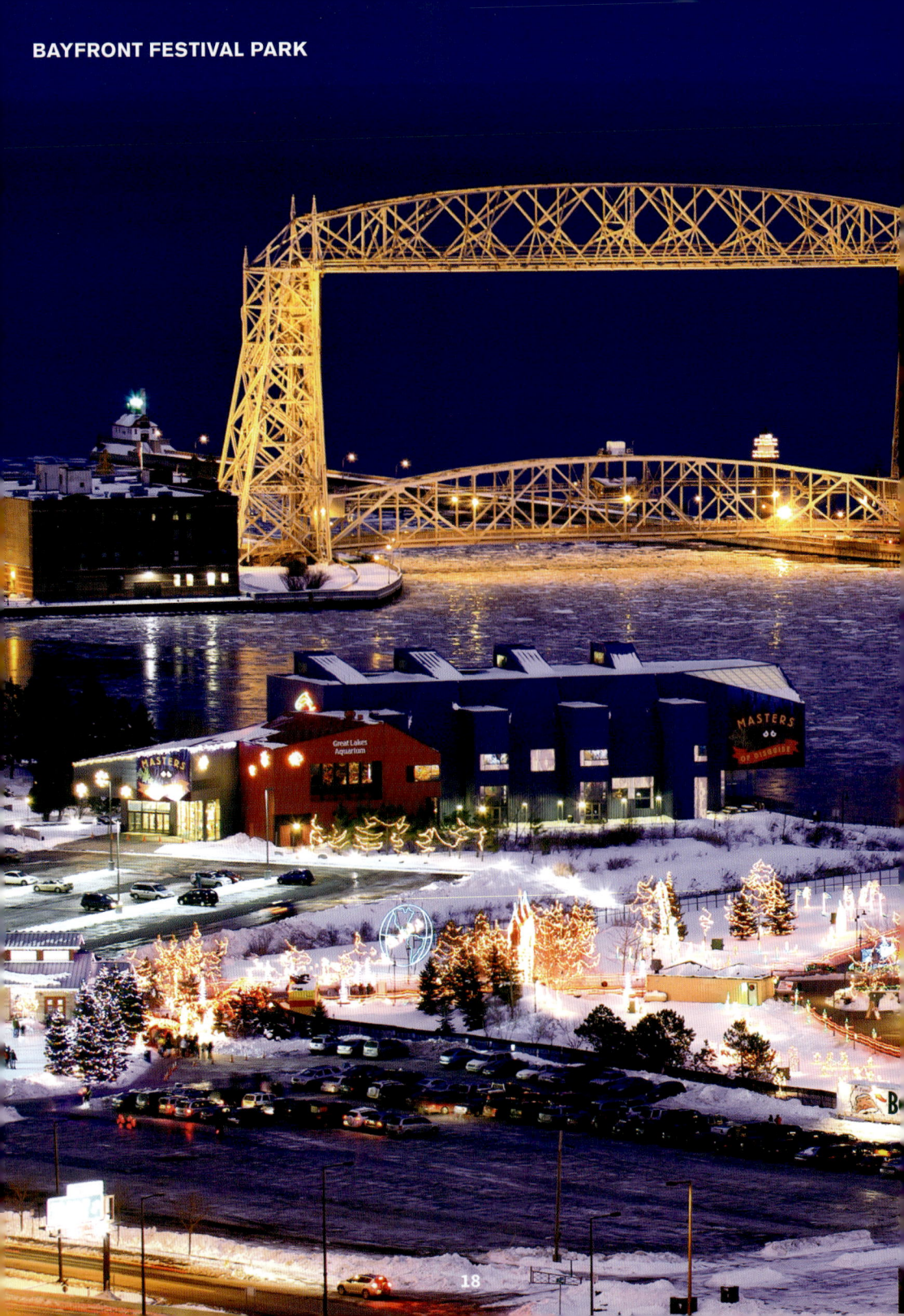

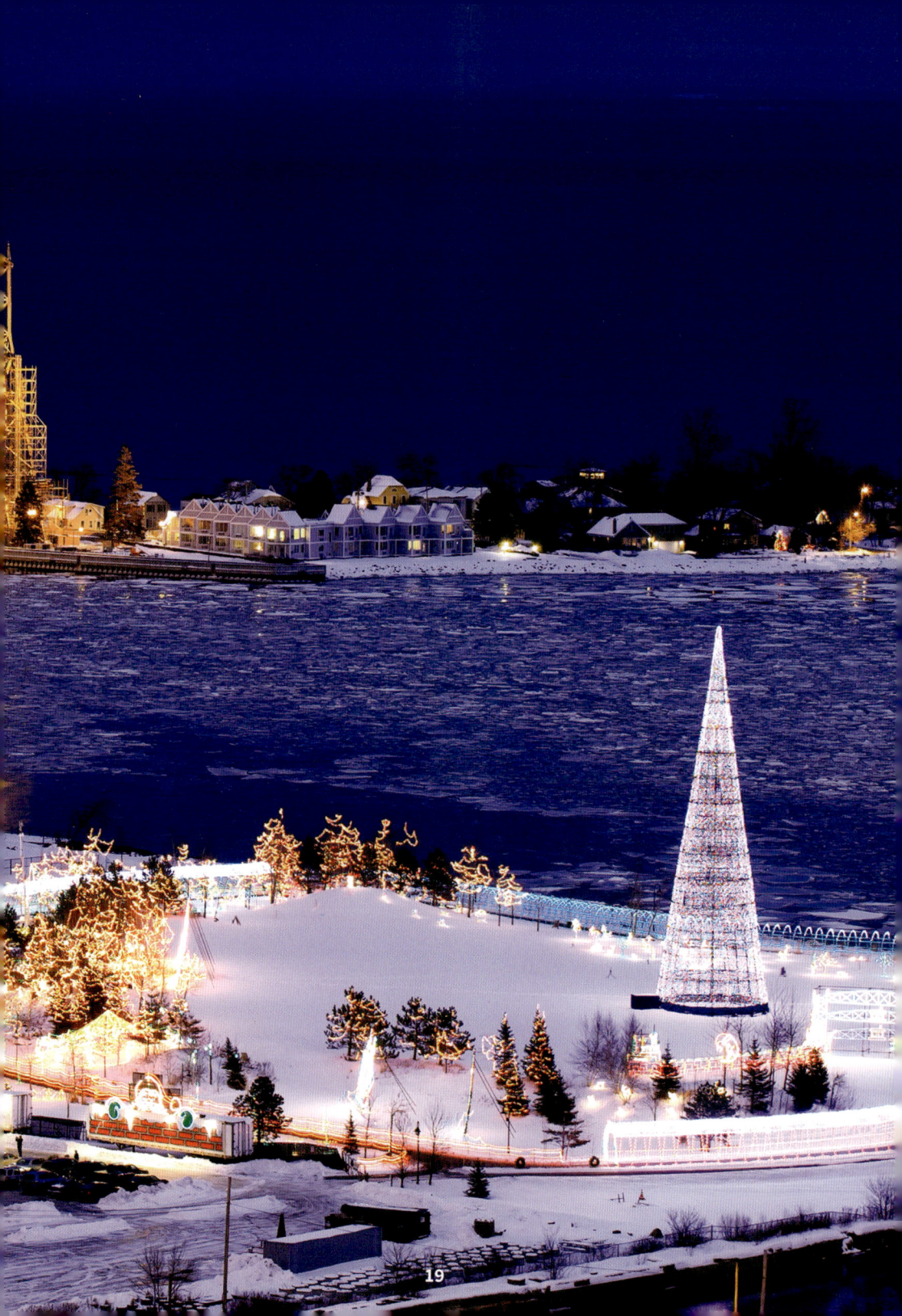

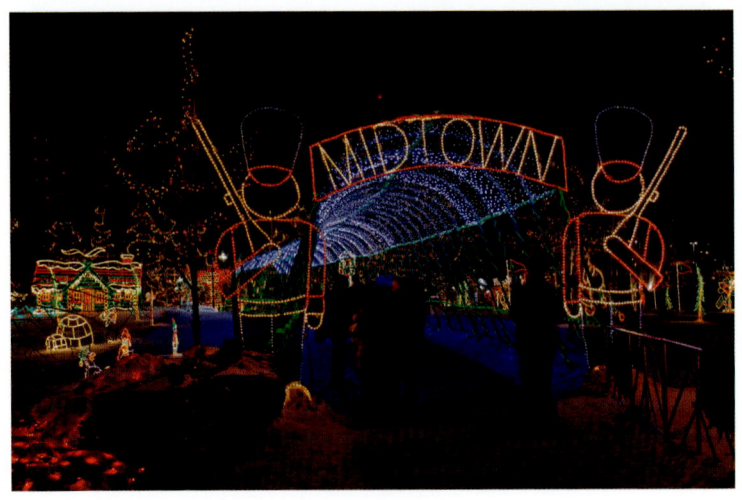

◄ BAYFRONT FESTIVAL PARK

Right on the waterfront with views of the Aerial Lift Bridge and occasionally passing ore boats, Bayfront Festival Park hosts a wide variety of outdoor public and private events throughout the year. The 10-acre park can accommodate up to 20,000 attendees for concerts and other large events. Popular events at the park, which officially reopened after renovations in 2001, include Duluth's Fourth Fest, Bayfront Blues Festival, Art in Bayfront Park, and Bentleyville Tour of Lights, believed to be the largest free walk-though holiday light display in the nation.

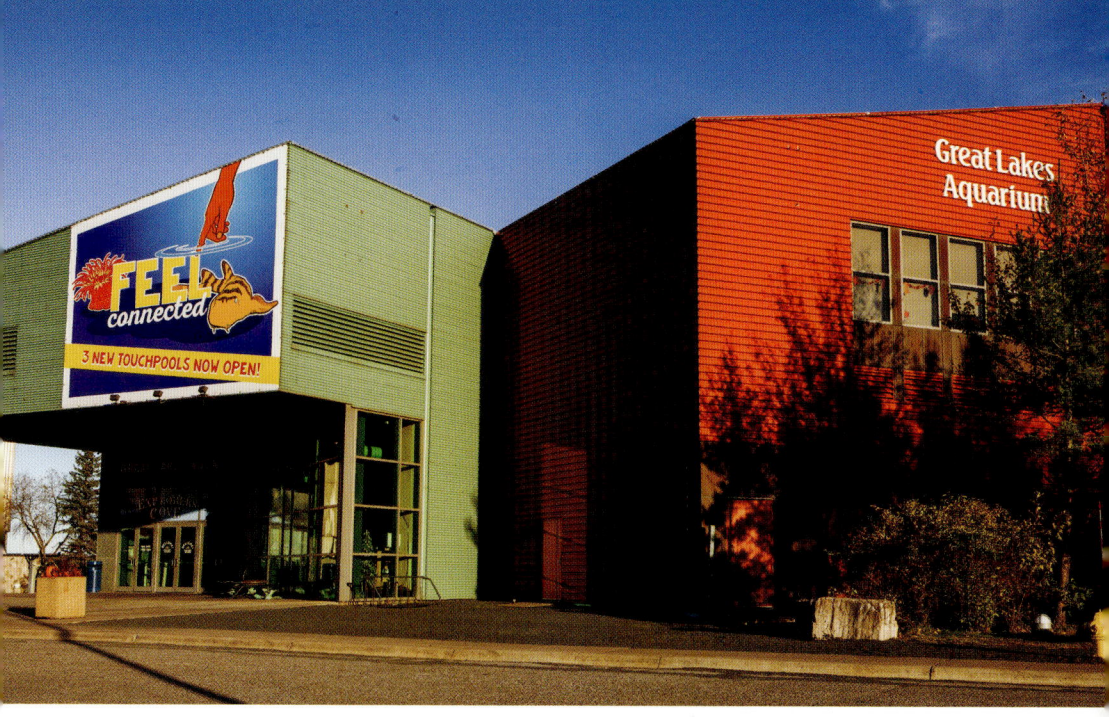

GREAT LAKES AQUARIUM

First opened in 2000, the 62,000-square-foot Great Lakes Aquarium, one of few of its kind in the country, showcases animals and habitats found within the Great Lakes basin and other freshwater ecosystems around the world. The aquarium is home to more than 200 species of fish, reptiles, birds, amphibians, and mammals. Its mission is to "inspire people to explore their connection with Lake Superior and the waters of the world."

THE DEPOT

Utilized today as the St. Louis County Heritage & Arts Center, the Duluth Depot once served seven rail lines and thousands of passengers. The elaborate structure, which includes distinctive conical towers and a steep roof, was designed by architects Peabody & Sterns of Boston and completed in 1892. Decommissioned in 1969 and slated for demolition shortly thereafter, the historic depot building was saved in response to public wishes. It reopened in 1973 and now houses the Duluth Art Institute, Lake Superior Railroad Museum, St. Louis County Historical Society, and four performing arts organizations.

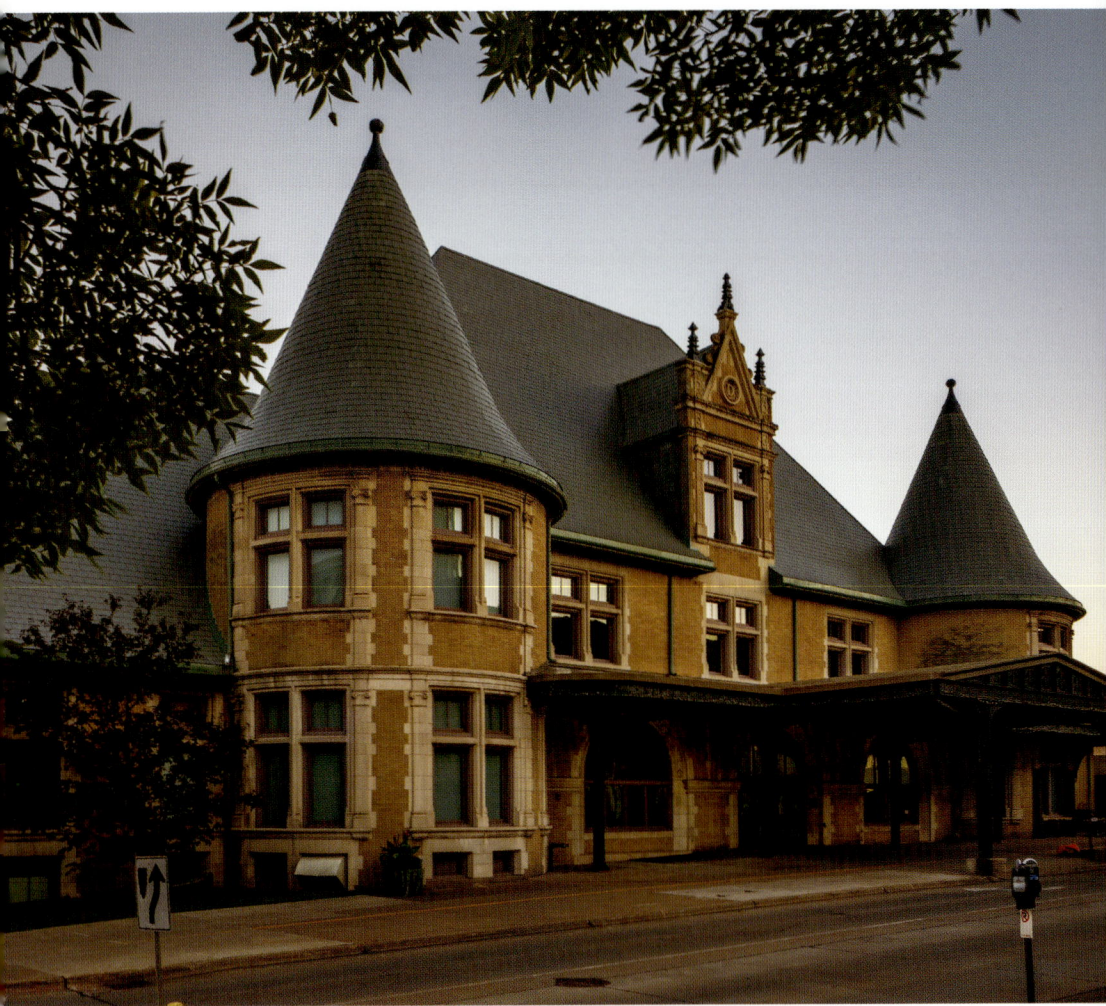

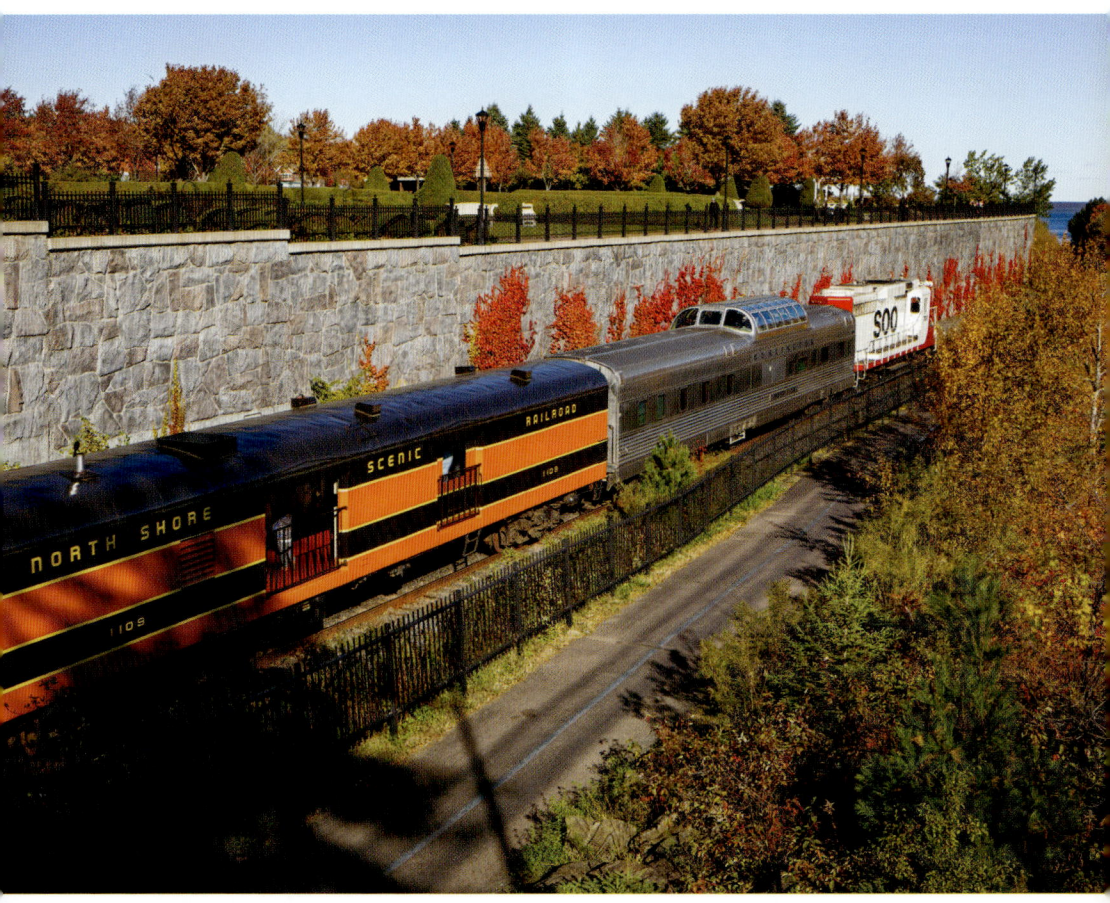

NORTH SHORE SCENIC RAILROAD

Operated by the Lake Superior Railroad Museum as a heritage railroad, the North Shore Scenic Railroad offers passenger excursions of varying lengths along the historic 26-mile Lakefront Line between Duluth and Two Harbors. The most popular excursion is the Duluth Zephyr, which runs daily in the summer between the Duluth Depot and the eastern end of Duluth and is about a 75-minute round-trip. A wide variety of specialty excursions are also offered, including seasonal, dinner, and steam-powered locomotive trips.

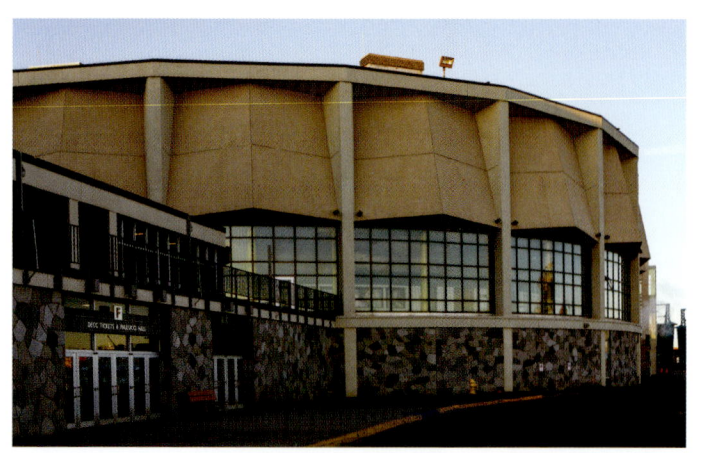

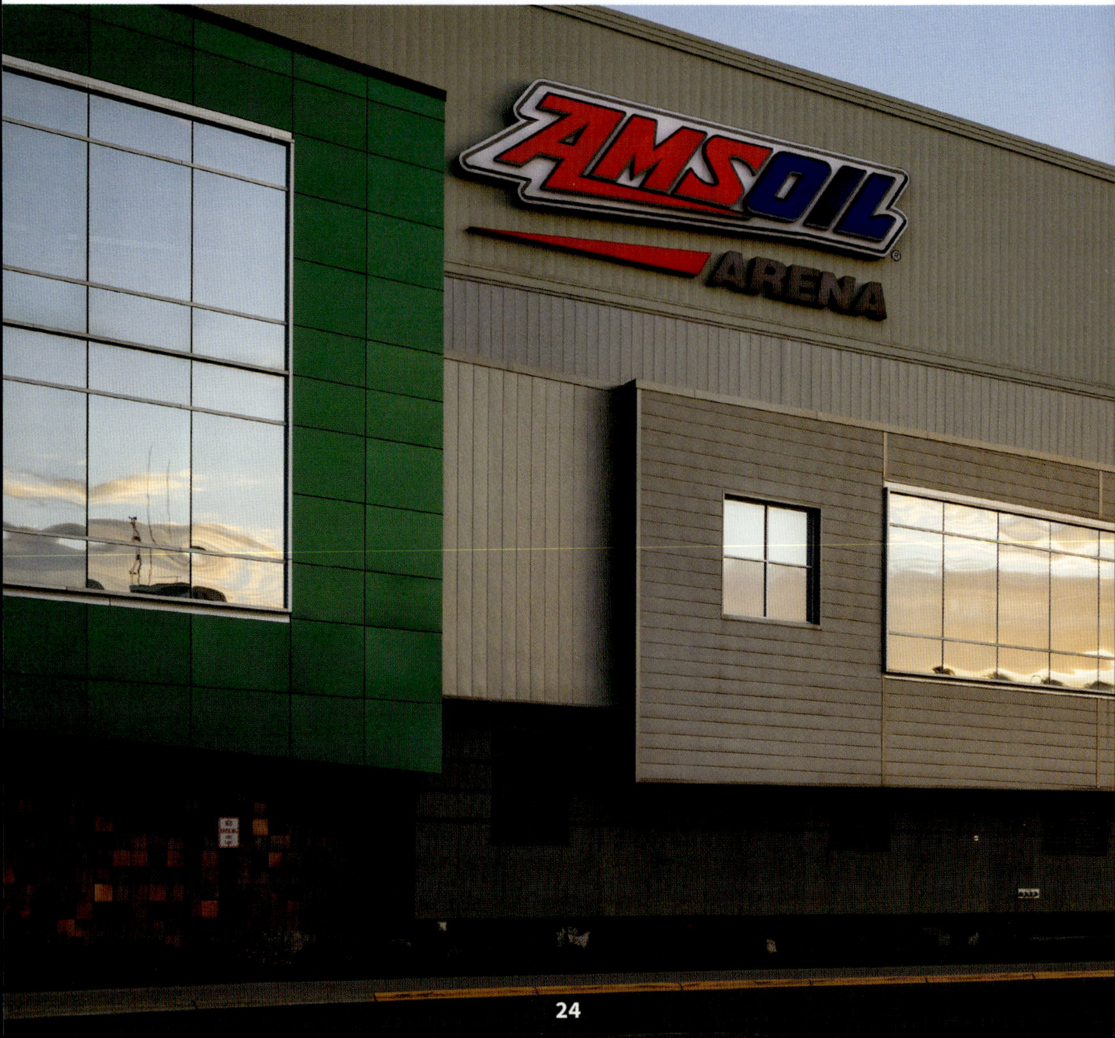

DULUTH ENTERTAINMENT CONVENTION CENTER/ AMSOIL ARENA

Originally built along Duluth's waterfront in 1966 as the Duluth Arena Auditorium, the Duluth Entertainment Convention Center (DECC) has expanded several times and is now a sprawling multipurpose facility, hosting sporting events, concerts, trade shows, business meetings, performing arts, and many other community events. Its most recent addition, AMSOIL Arena, was completed in 2010 and is home to UMD's Men's and Women's hockey teams. The Duluth Curling Club also calls the DECC home and maintains eight rinks there.

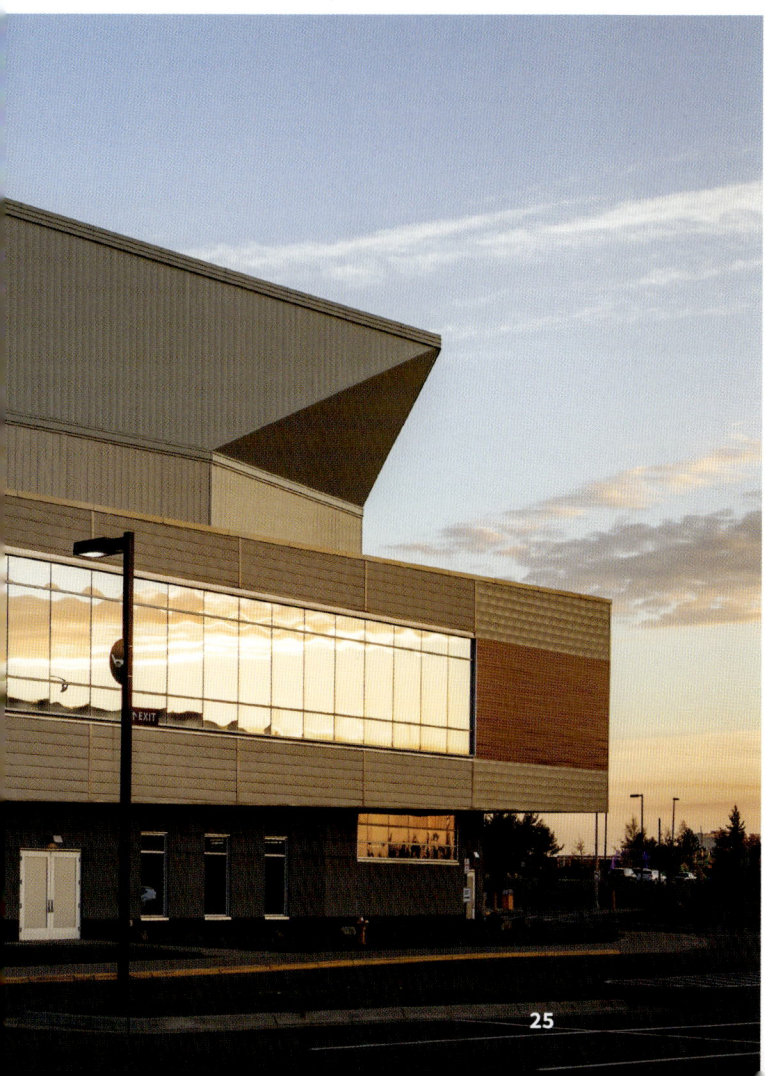

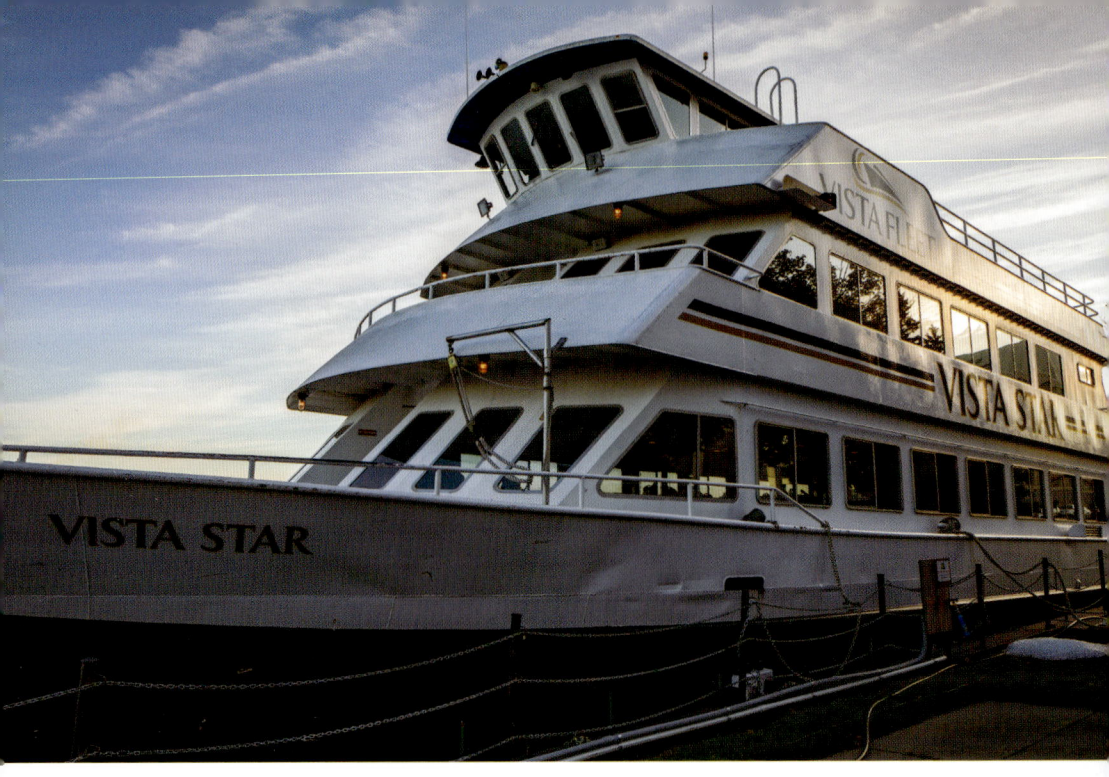

VISTA FLEET

The Vista Fleet has been cruising the Duluth-Superior Harbor for six decades, allowing passengers to get an up-close view of activity within the harbor while taking in the surrounding historic and scenic landmarks. The fleet's two vessels carry passengers on sightseeing tours of varying lengths and also offer private and special event cruises. Most tours even venture out onto Lake Superior, passing beneath the iconic Aerial Lift Bridge.

S.S. WILLIAM A. IRVIN

Named after William A. Irvin, president of U.S. Steel during much of the 1930s, the namesake ore boat was first launched in 1938 and served as the flagship of U.S. Steel's Great Lakes fleet until 1975. The ship was fully retired three years later. In 1986, the Duluth Entertainment and Convention Center purchased the vessel and converted it into a permanently docked floating museum ship available for tours. Each October, the *Irvin* is transformed into a haunted ship to celebrate Halloween and generate visitation beyond the peak summer season. In late 2018 and early 2019, repairs to the *Irvin's* hull and its home slip have led to the ship's temporary absence from the harbor. It is expected to return and reopen for tours by June 2019.

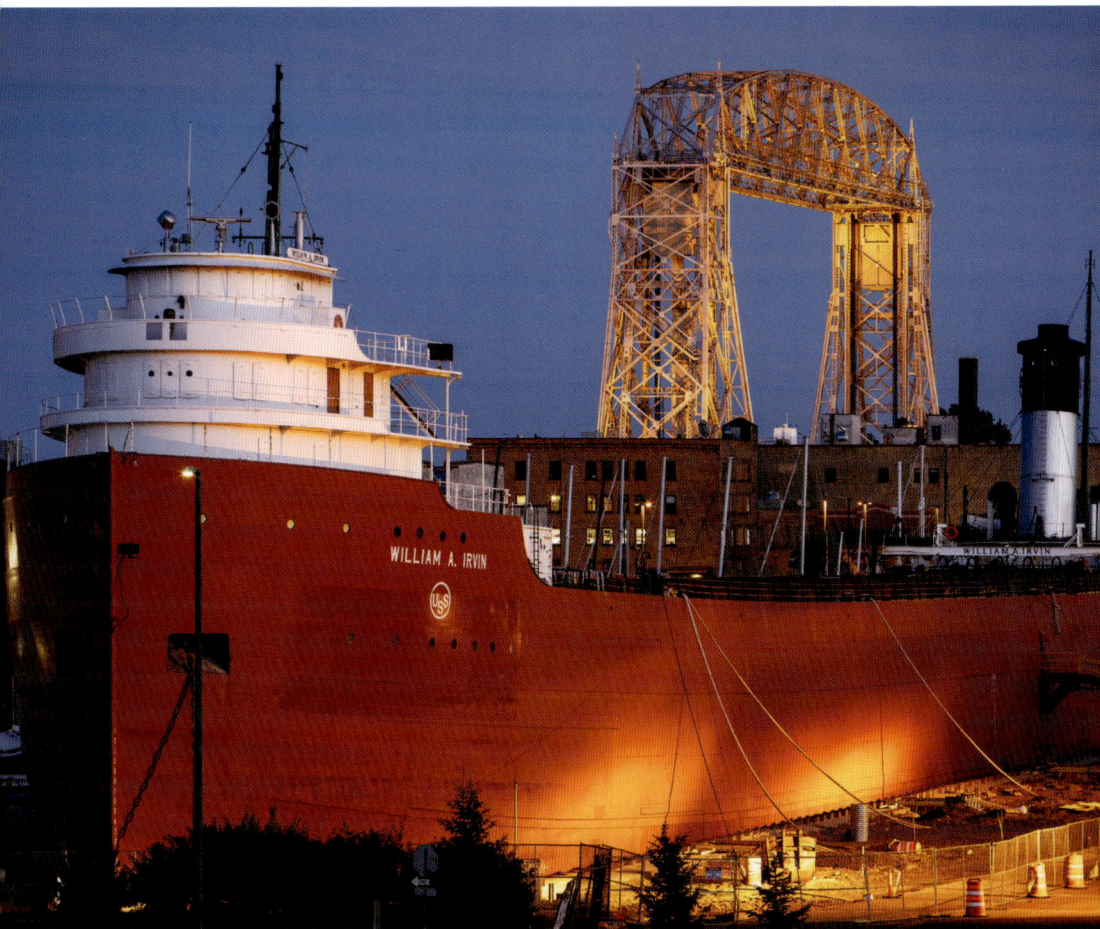

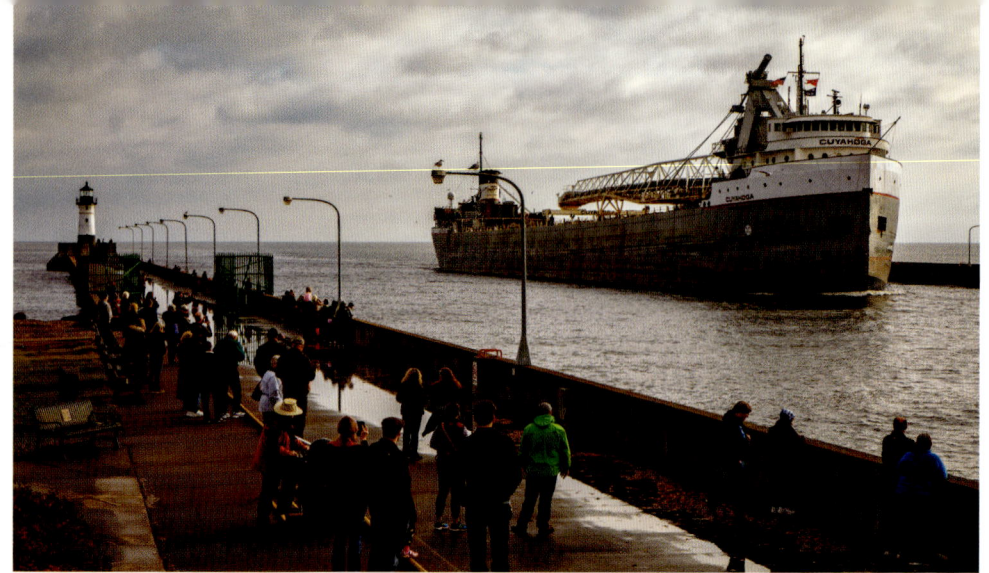

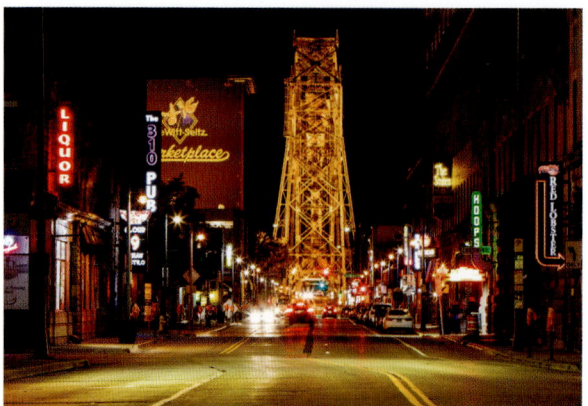

CANAL PARK

Once an area filled with aging warehouses and junkyards, the Canal Park district was re-envisioned in the 1980s as Duluth's tourist and recreational center. With large industry on the decline in the city, the redevelopment of this area helped establish tourism as a powerful economic force into the twenty-first century. Canal Park is now home to a number of hotels, restaurants, and specialty shops, in addition to attractions such as the famous Aerial Lift Bridge, lighthouse piers, 7.5-mile-long Lakewalk, and Duluth Entertainment Convention Center (DECC). The Lake Superior Maritime Visitor Center presents exhibits showcasing the history and operations of commercial shipping on the Great Lakes.

AERIAL LIFT BRIDGE

First constructed in 1905, Duluth's signature bridge began its life as an aerial transfer bridge. It utilized a gondola for ferrying passengers across the recently dug ship canal that separated mainland Duluth from the 7-mile-long sandbar known as Minnesota Point. Traffic across the bridge increased, and in 1929, the bridge was reconfigured into its modern-day appearance and function, with a lift span that travels up and down. The 390-foot span can be raised to its full height of 135 feet in about a minute, allowing large freighters access to the Duluth Harbor.

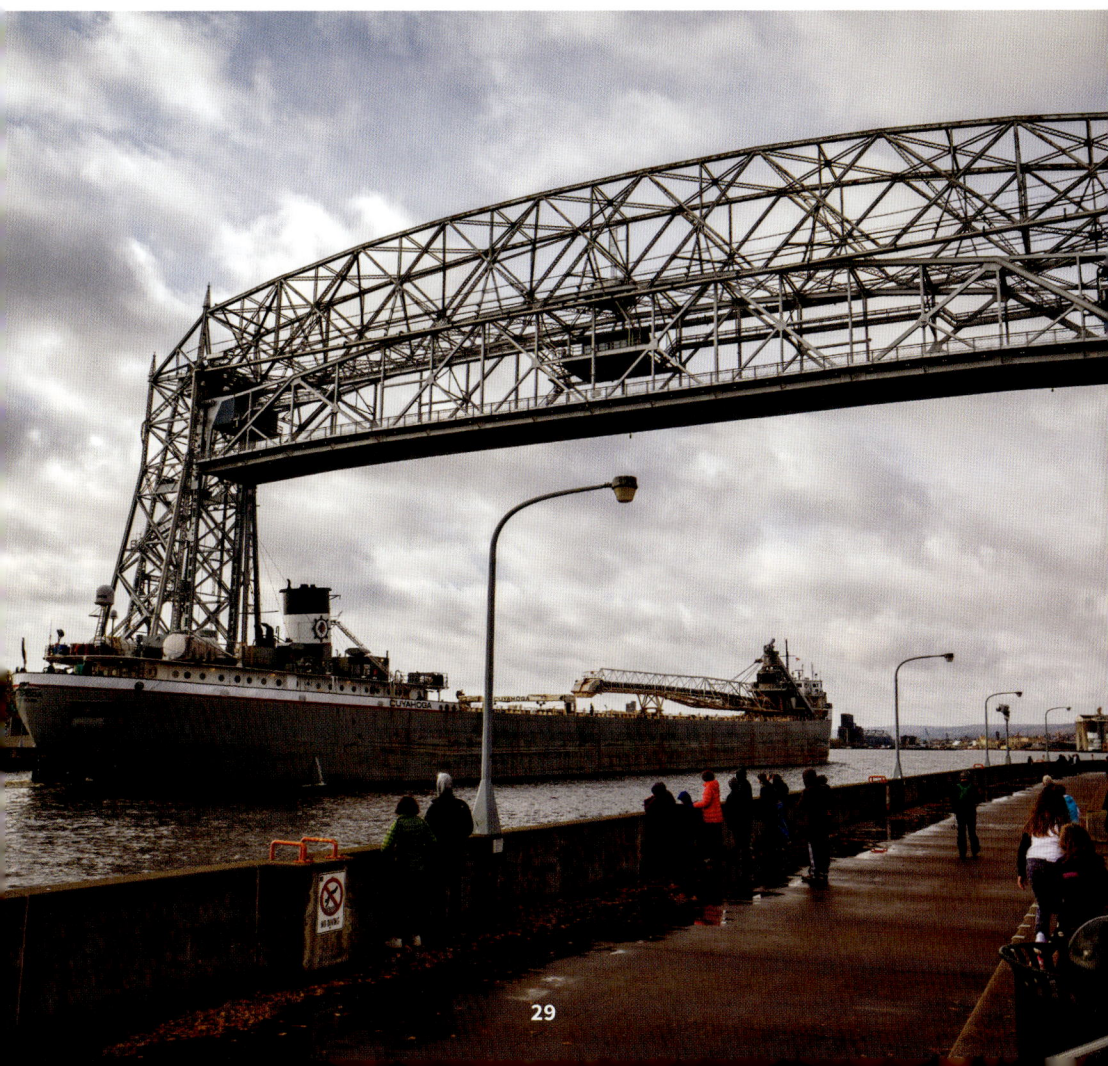

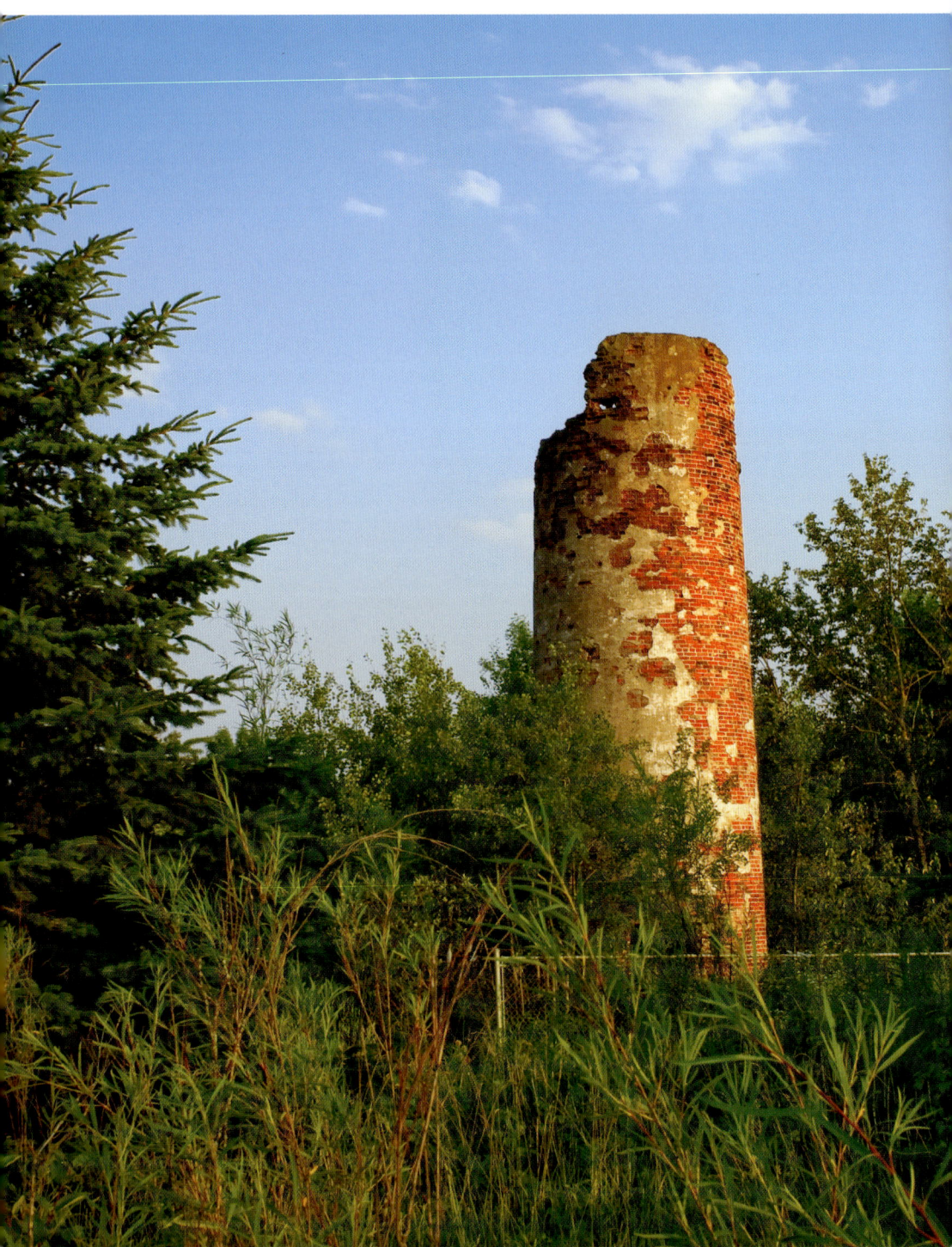

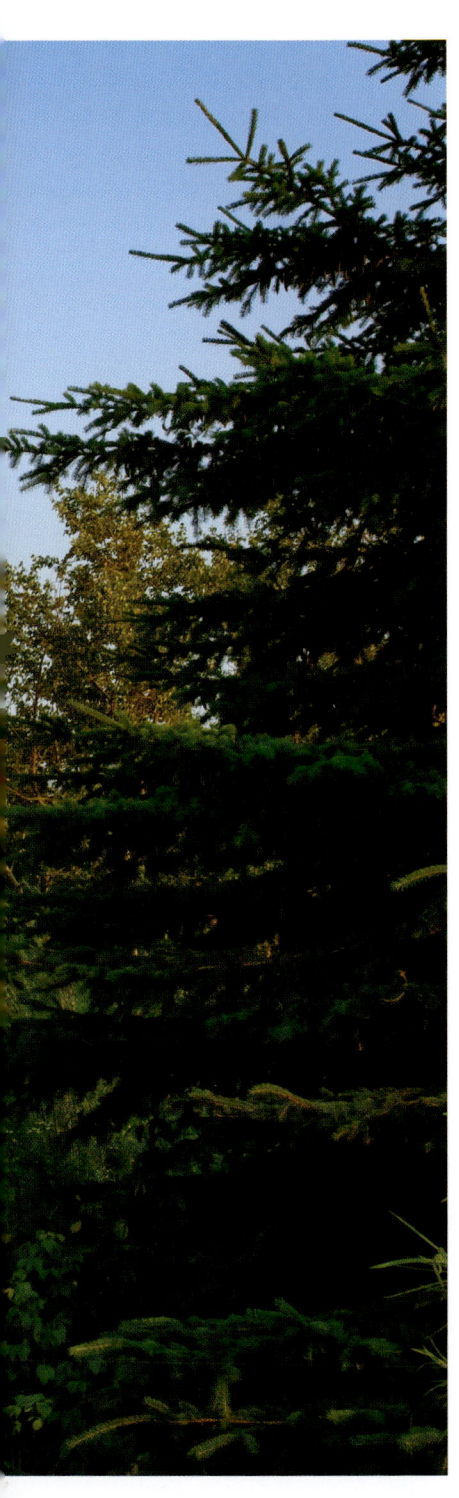

MINNESOTA POINT

Commonly known as Park Point to locals, Minnesota Point is a 7-mile-long sandspit extending southward from the Canal Park area of Duluth to the Superior, Wisconsin, harbor entry. When combined with the 3-mile-long Wisconsin Point, it is considered the world's largest freshwater sandbar, separating Lake Superior from Superior Bay. Minnesota Point is renowned in the area for its miles of sandy lakeside public beaches. The point is also home to a small airport, several parks and trails, and the ruins of Minnesota's first lighthouse, built in 1858. The Park Point community hosts two long-standing and well-attended annual events on the point: the Park Point Rummage Sale and the Park Point Art Fair, each held on separate weekends in June.

MINNESOTA POINT

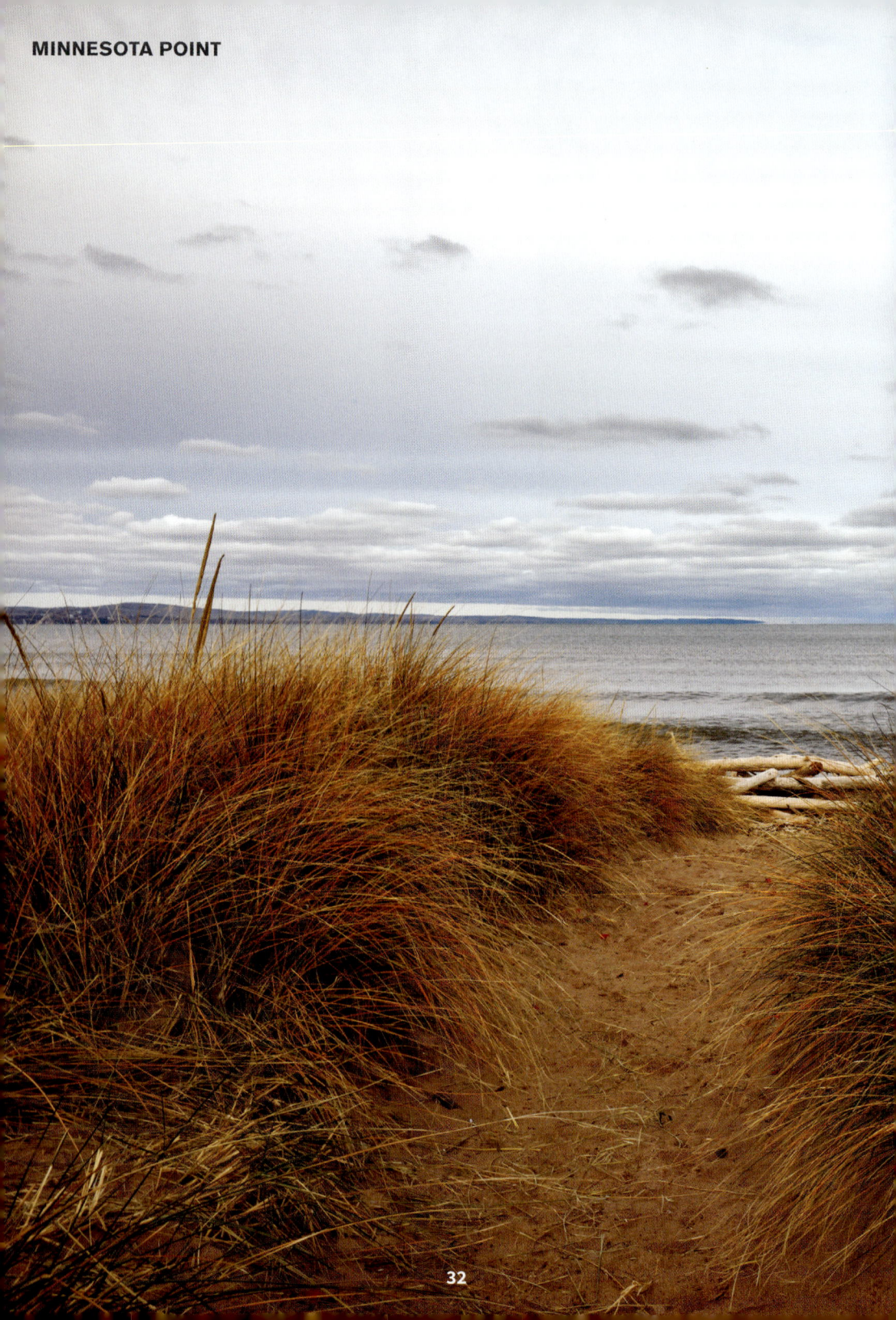

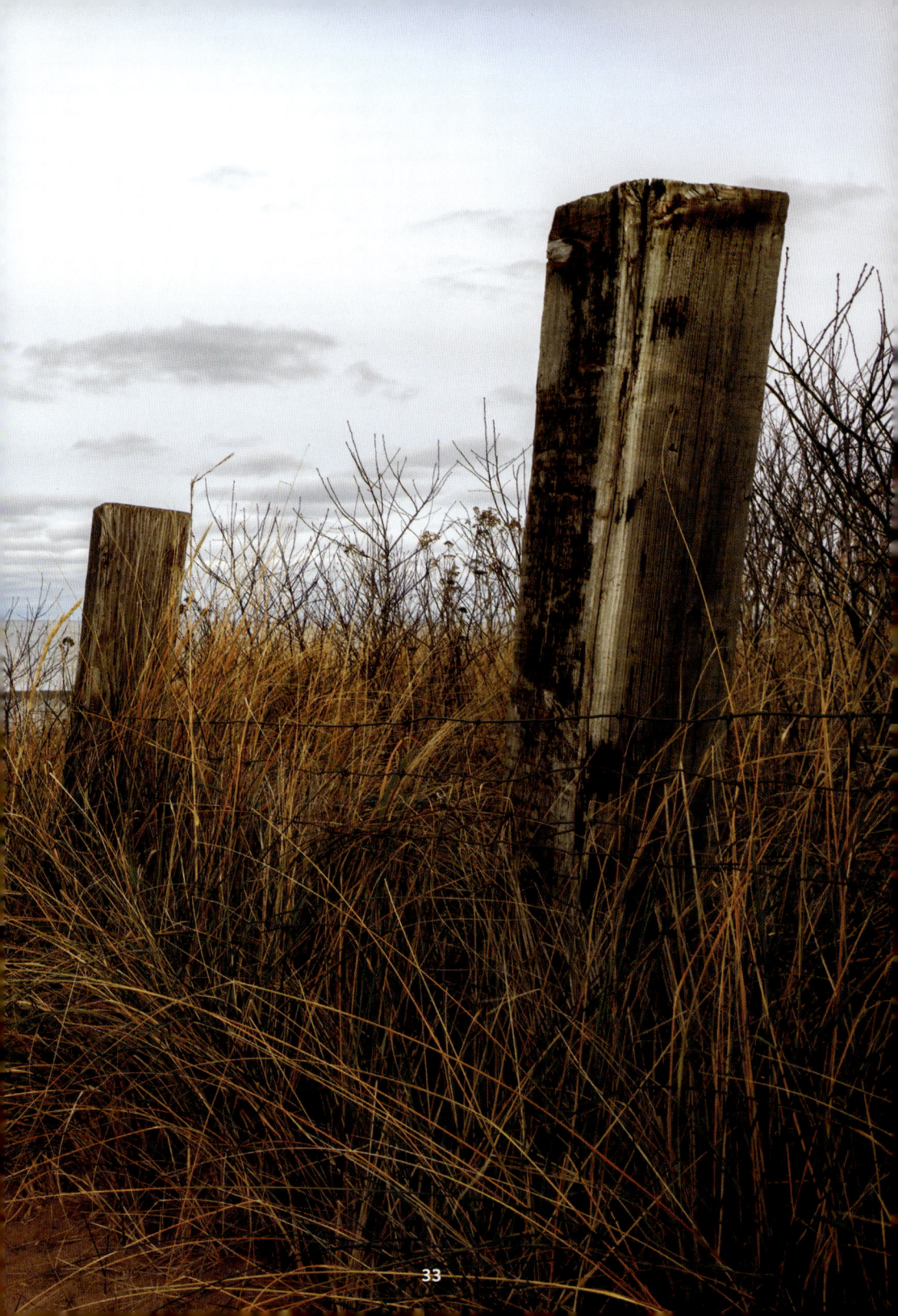

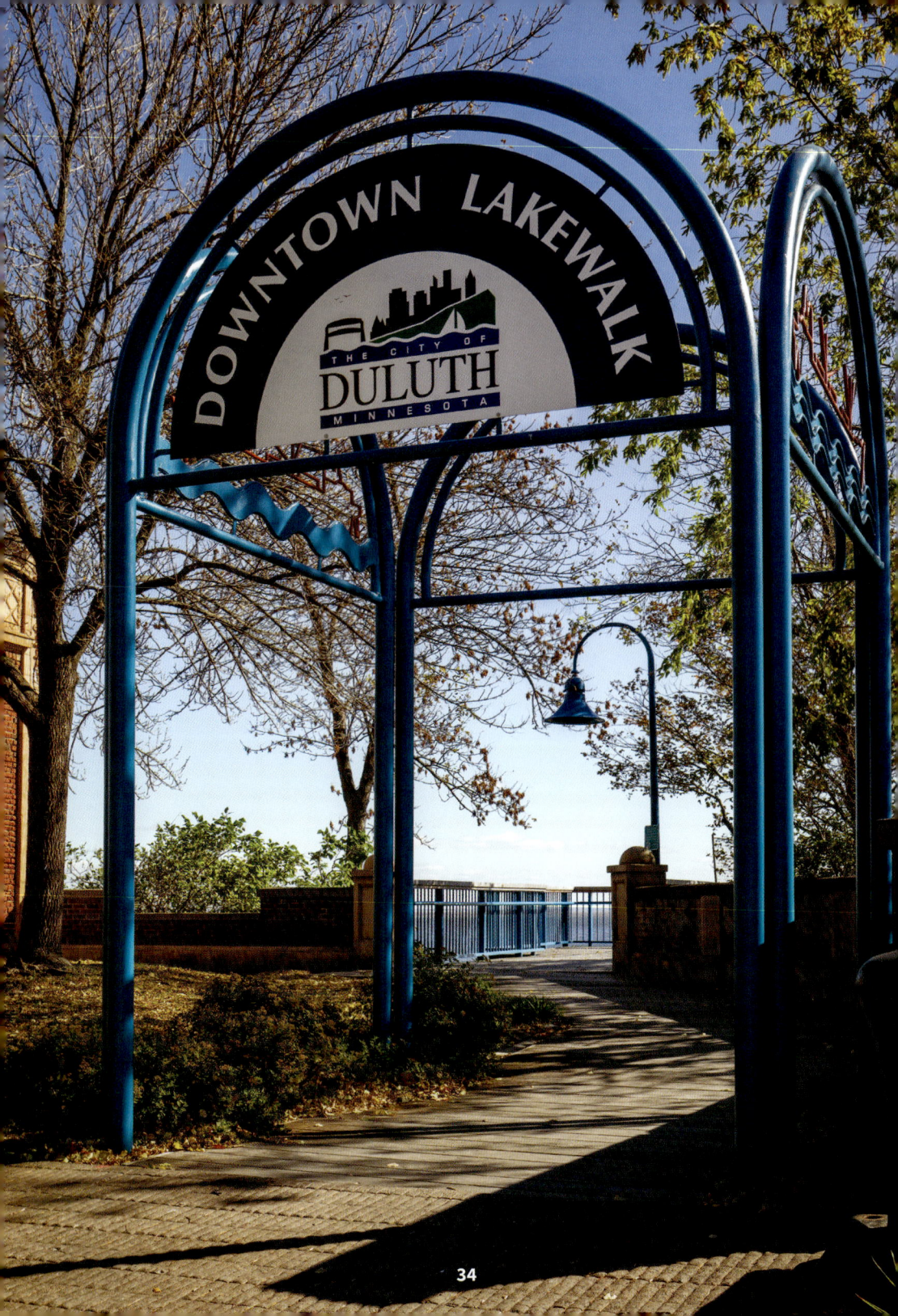

THE LAKEWALK

Extending 7.5 miles from Bayfront Festival Park to Brighton Beach (aka Kitchi Gammi Park), The Lakewalk connects many of Duluth's waterfront parks and attractions via boardwalks and paved trails for use by pedestrians, runners, cyclists, and skaters. It grew out of the city's vision to make its waterfront more accessible, beginning as a short half-mile path in 1986. The most popular segment runs immediately adjacent to Lake Superior from Canal Park to Leif Erikson Park on London Road. The northern half veers away from the lake somewhat and traverses the neighborhoods of Lakeside and Lester Park.

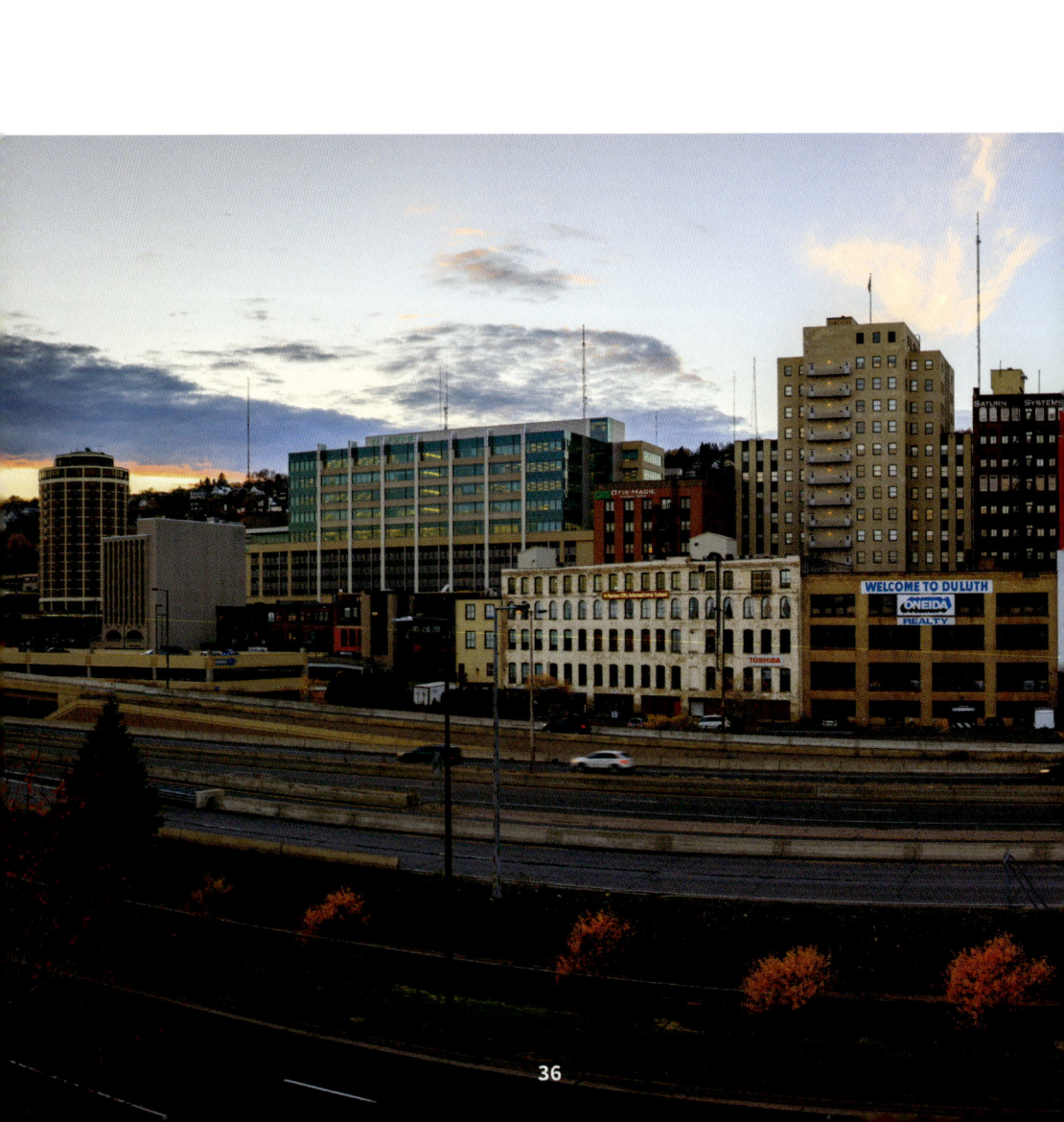

DOWNTOWN DULUTH

With Superior Street at its heart, Downtown Duluth is an active economic center and home to numerous locally owned businesses, government and financial offices, medical facilities, and cultural attractions. Many buildings were constructed in the late nineteenth and early twentieth centuries, when Duluth was economically at its peak, and are listed on the National Register of Historic Places.

Due to the city's northern climate, an extensive network of skywalks was built to provide climate-controlled connections between buildings, including the Duluth Entertainment and Convention Center (DECC) south of Interstate 35.

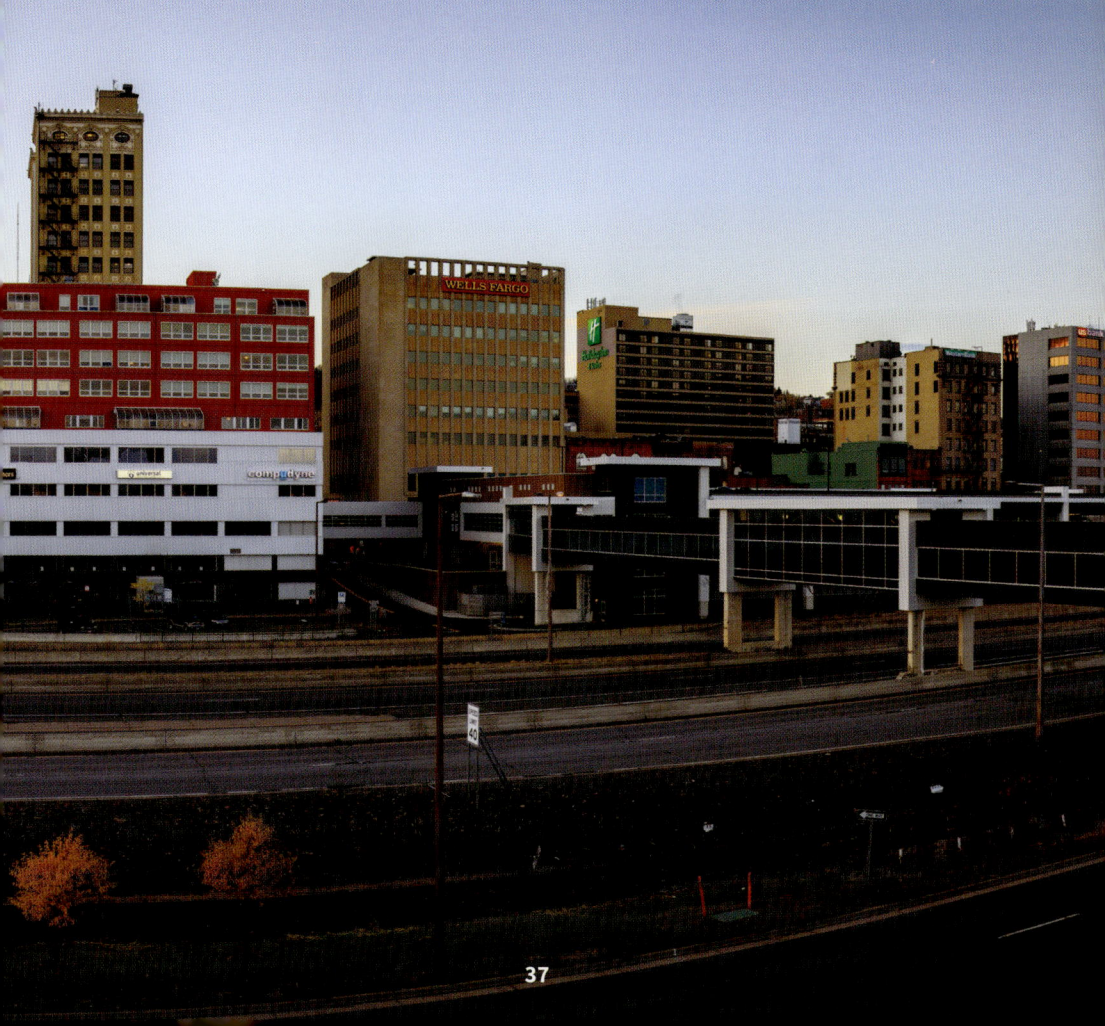

HISTORIC OLD CENTRAL HIGH SCHOOL

Built in 1892 from local sandstone and at a cost of $460,000, Old Central High School served students until 1971, when a new Central High School (now closed) was constructed on the hilltop overlooking Duluth. Old Central's stunning Richardsonian Romanesque architecture, modeled after the Allegheny County Courthouse in Pittsburgh, Pennsylvania, provides evidence of Duluth's great economic status at the turn of the twentieth century. The building includes a 230-foot clock tower with chimes patterned after London's Big Ben, wide hallways, massive stairways, and large chandeliers. The Duluth Public School District currently owns the building and houses district offices and an alternative learning center within.

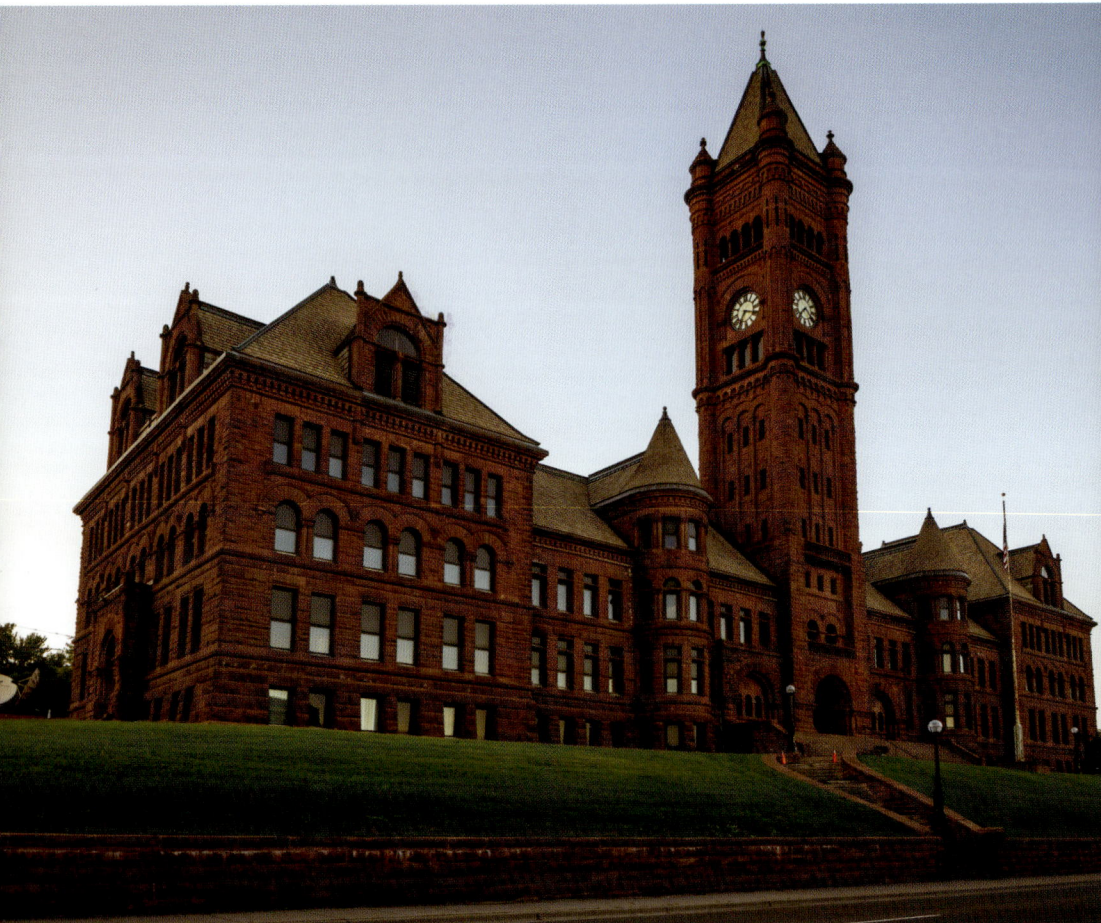

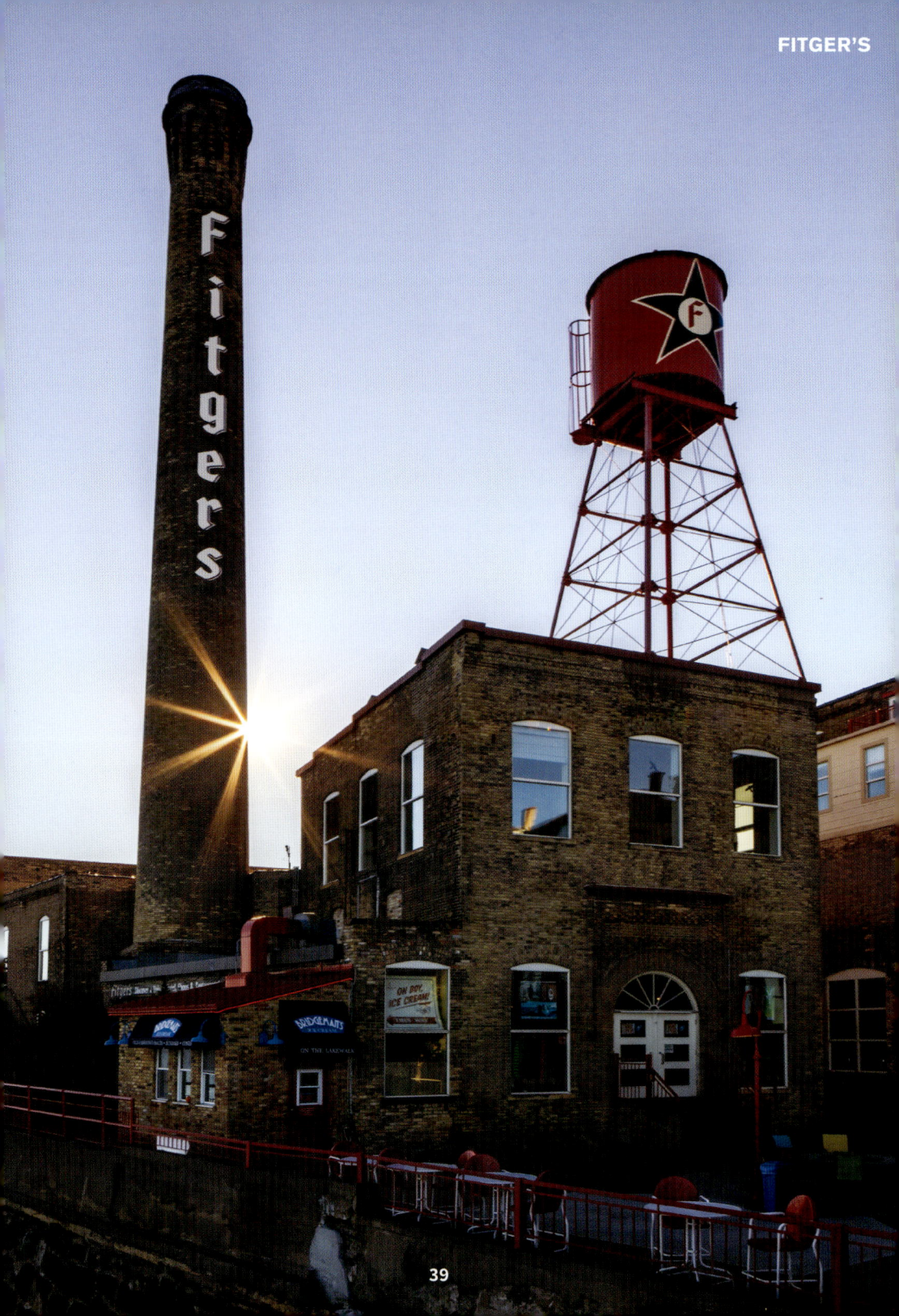

◄ FITGER'S

Established in its present location as Fink's Lake Superior Brewery in 1881 and later renamed after its brewmaster and co-owner August Fitger, Fitger's Brewery produced beer until its closure in 1972. While many breweries were shuttered during the Prohibition era of the 1920s and early '30s, Fitger's found success in selling soda and candy bars. After the brewery's closure, the Fitger's building was repurposed and reopened in 1984 with a hotel, three restaurants, and several specialty shops. Beer is once again brewed on-site at Fitger's Brewhouse and distributed locally.

LEIF ERIKSON PARK

With a long history dating back to 1905, Leif Erikson Park is one of Duluth's most visited parks, with the Lakewalk passing through its boundaries. For many years, the park displayed a 42-foot replica Viking ship of the same name that was built in Norway in 1926 and sailed across the Atlantic and through the Great Lakes to Duluth. Norwegian immigrant and Duluth businessman Bert Enger purchased the ship soon after the voyage and donated it to the city. As of this writing, the ship is undergoing restoration off-site with plans for its return. The park also boasts a life-sized statue of Leif Erikson and an amphitheater stage.

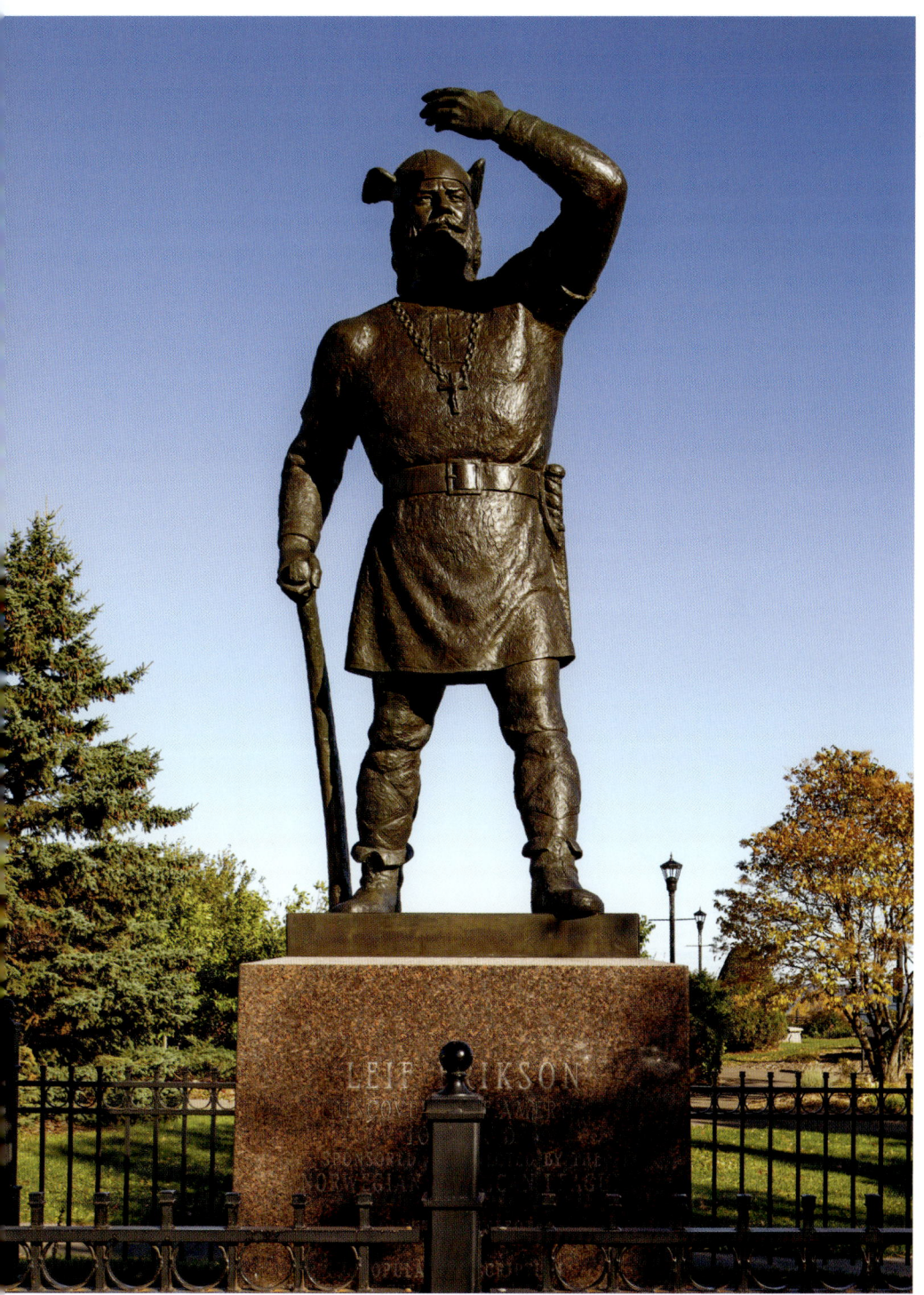

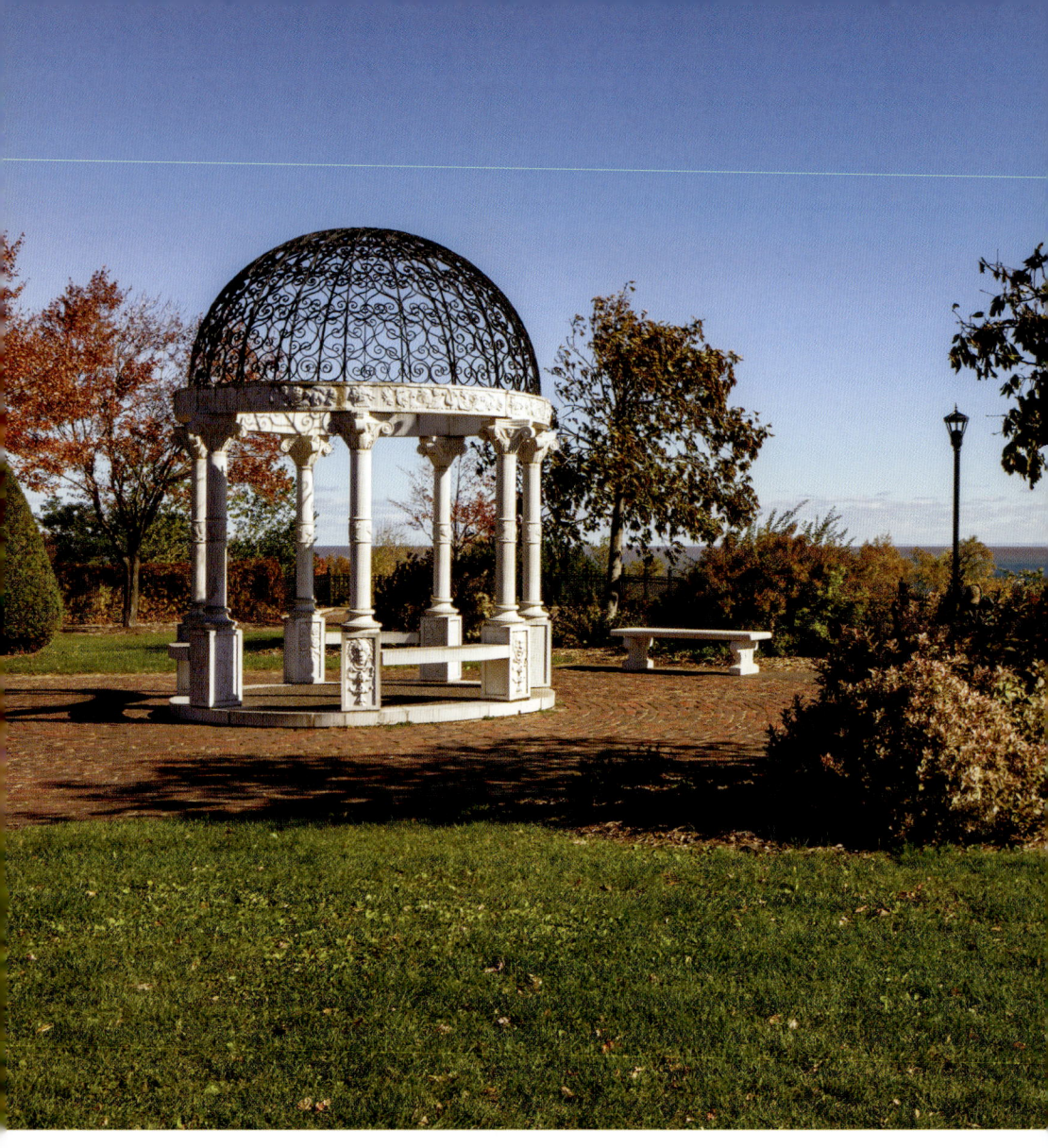

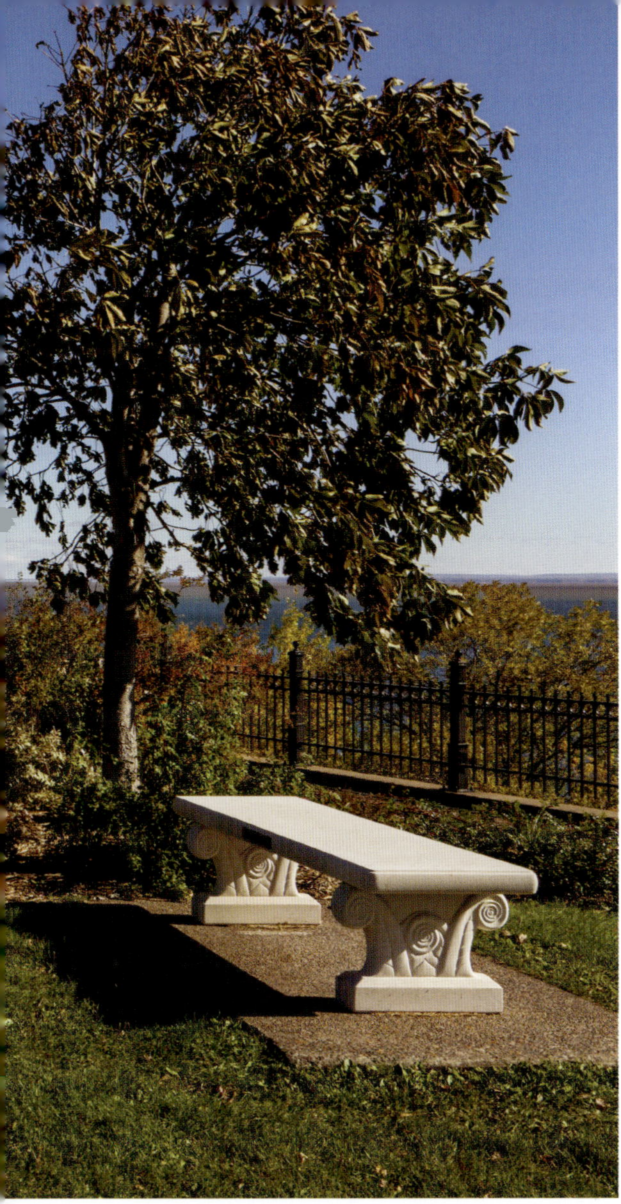

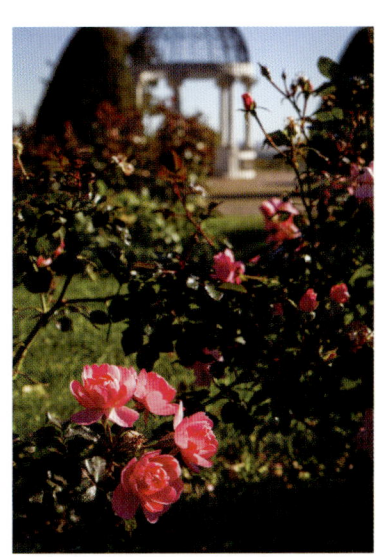

DULUTH ROSE GARDEN

Located within Leif Erikson Park and overlooking Lake Superior, the 4.5-acre Duluth Rose Garden showcases more than 3,000 rose bushes, perennials, trees, shrubs, and herbs. The garden actually grows in soil above the northernmost Interstate 35 freeway tunnel. The location is a popular venue for outdoor weddings, with its marble gazebo and stone fountain.

GLENSHEEN HISTORIC ESTATE

Perched on a 12-acre tract of Lake Superior waterfront, this elaborate mansion was constructed between 1905 and 1908 as the family home of lawyer and capitalist Chester Congdon. It cost $854,000 to build, which included a 27,000-square-foot main home, magnificent gardens, bridges, and several other buildings. Glensheen is famous, not only for its stunning early twentieth-century architecture and craftmanship, but also for the murders of Elisabeth Congdon (Chester's daughter) and her nurse, Velma Pietila, in the mansion on June 27, 1977. The estate is owned by the University of Minnesota Duluth and is available for tours year-round.

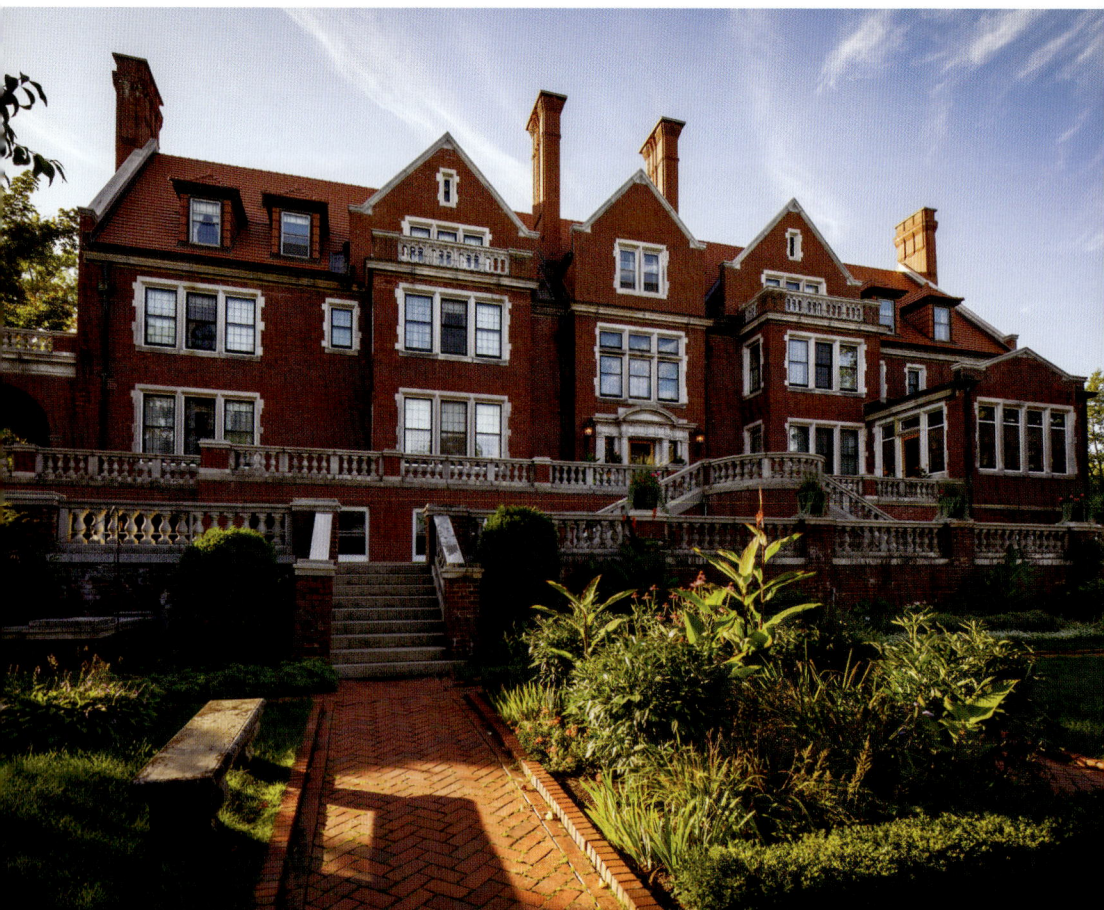

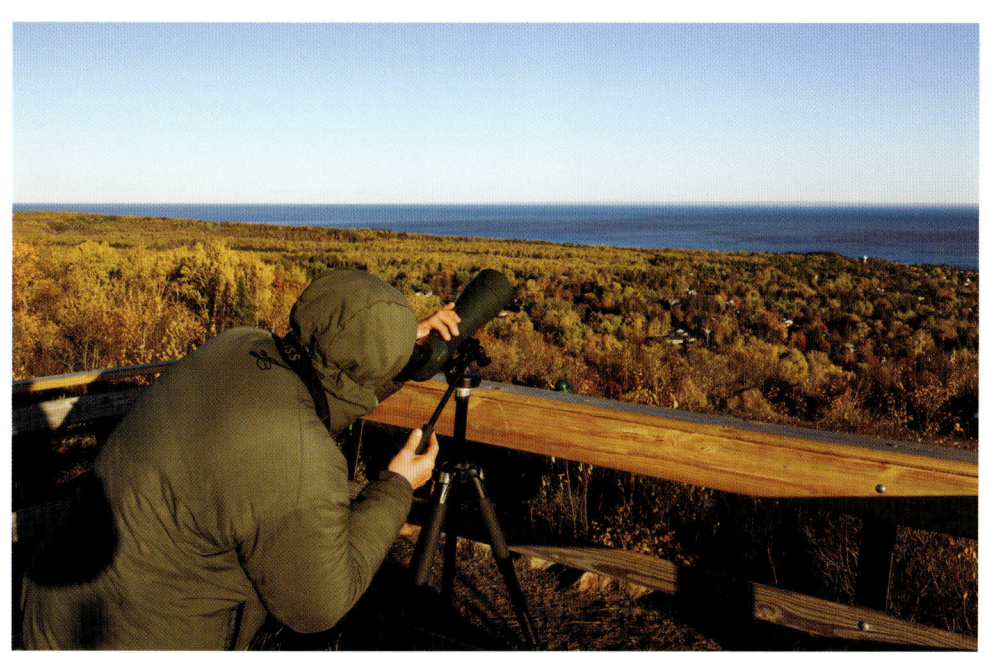

HAWK RIDGE NATURE RESERVE

Situated on 235 acres of undeveloped land along Skyline Parkway in northeastern Duluth, Hawk Ridge attracts bird-watchers from around the world, especially during the annual raptor migrations in the fall. Most raptors hesitate to cross large bodies of water and therefore travel southwest along the lakeshore. High concentrations of birds, sometimes in the thousands, can be seen migrating past the area on autumn days with northwest winds. Established in 1972, Hawk Ridge is owned by the City of Duluth and managed by the non-profit Hawk Ridge Bird Observatory.

LESTER PARK

Bordered between Amity Creek and Lester River near the eastern limits of Duluth, Lester Park offers more than 9 miles of hiking and mountain biking trails as well as several waterfalls along the two streams. Occidental Boulevard, just west of Amity Creek, serves as the starting point of Seven Bridges Road, which crosses the creek seven times over stone bridges before intersecting with Duluth's Skyline Parkway.

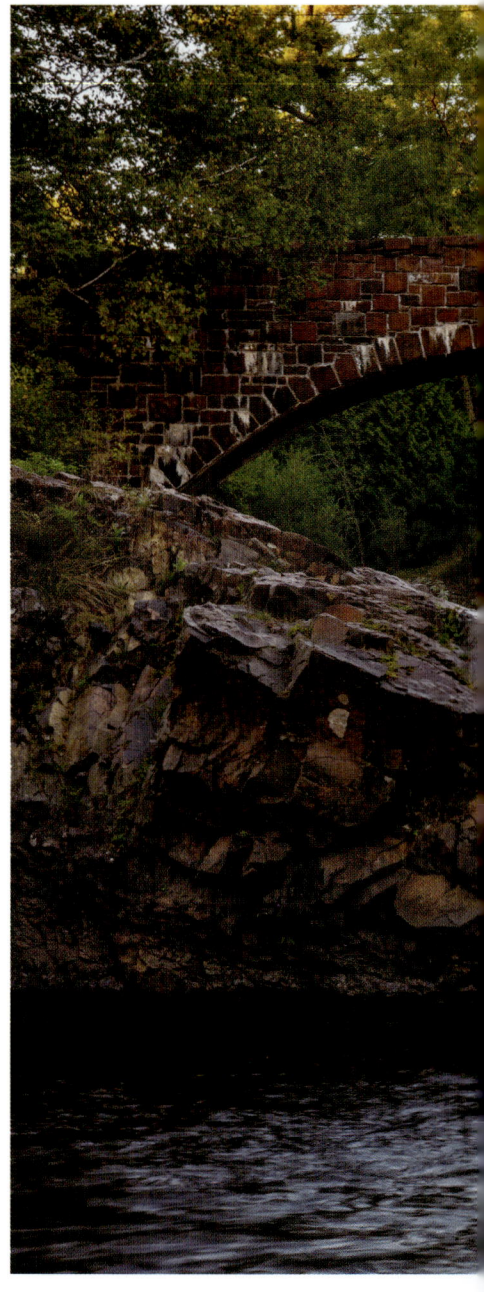

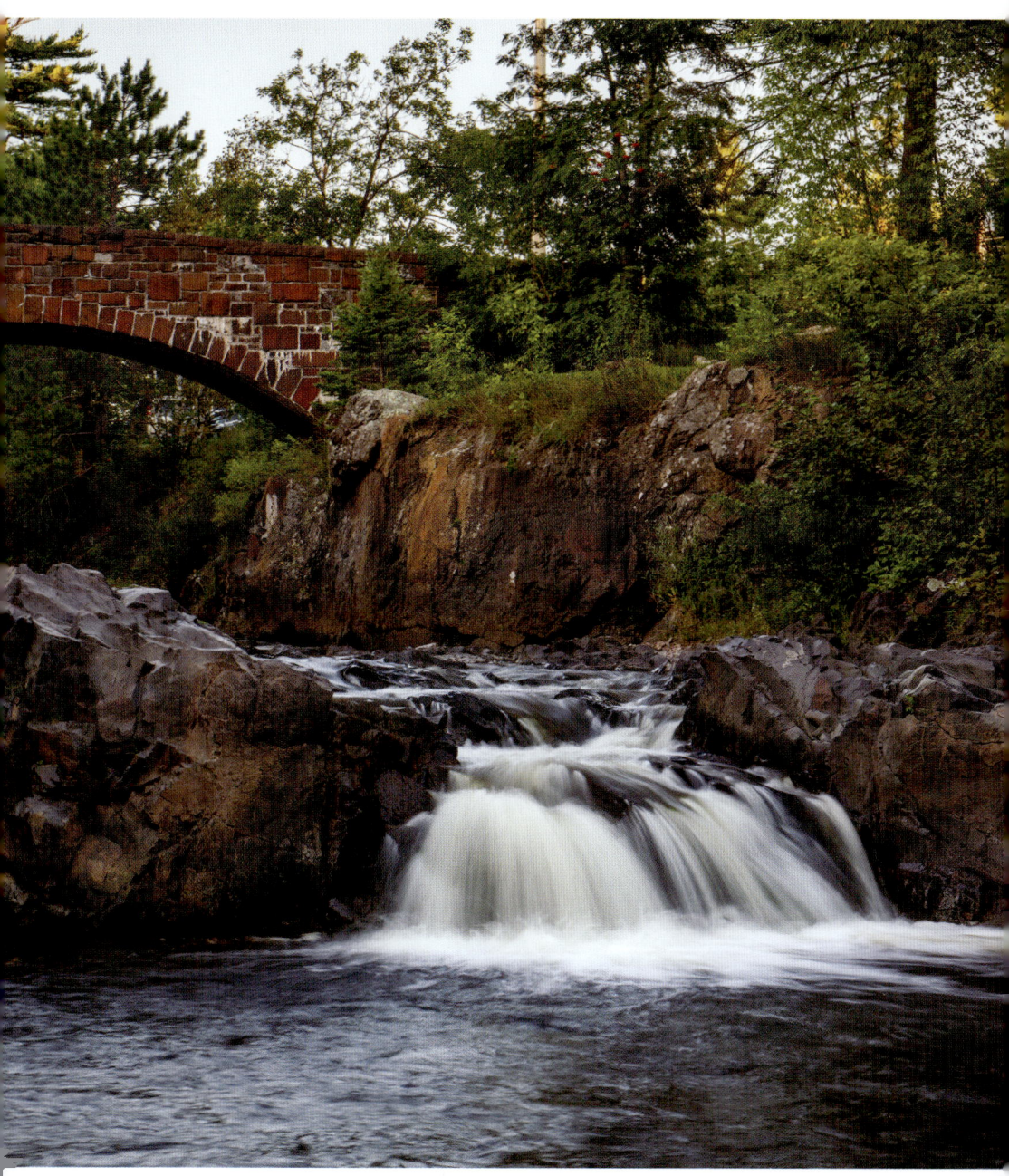

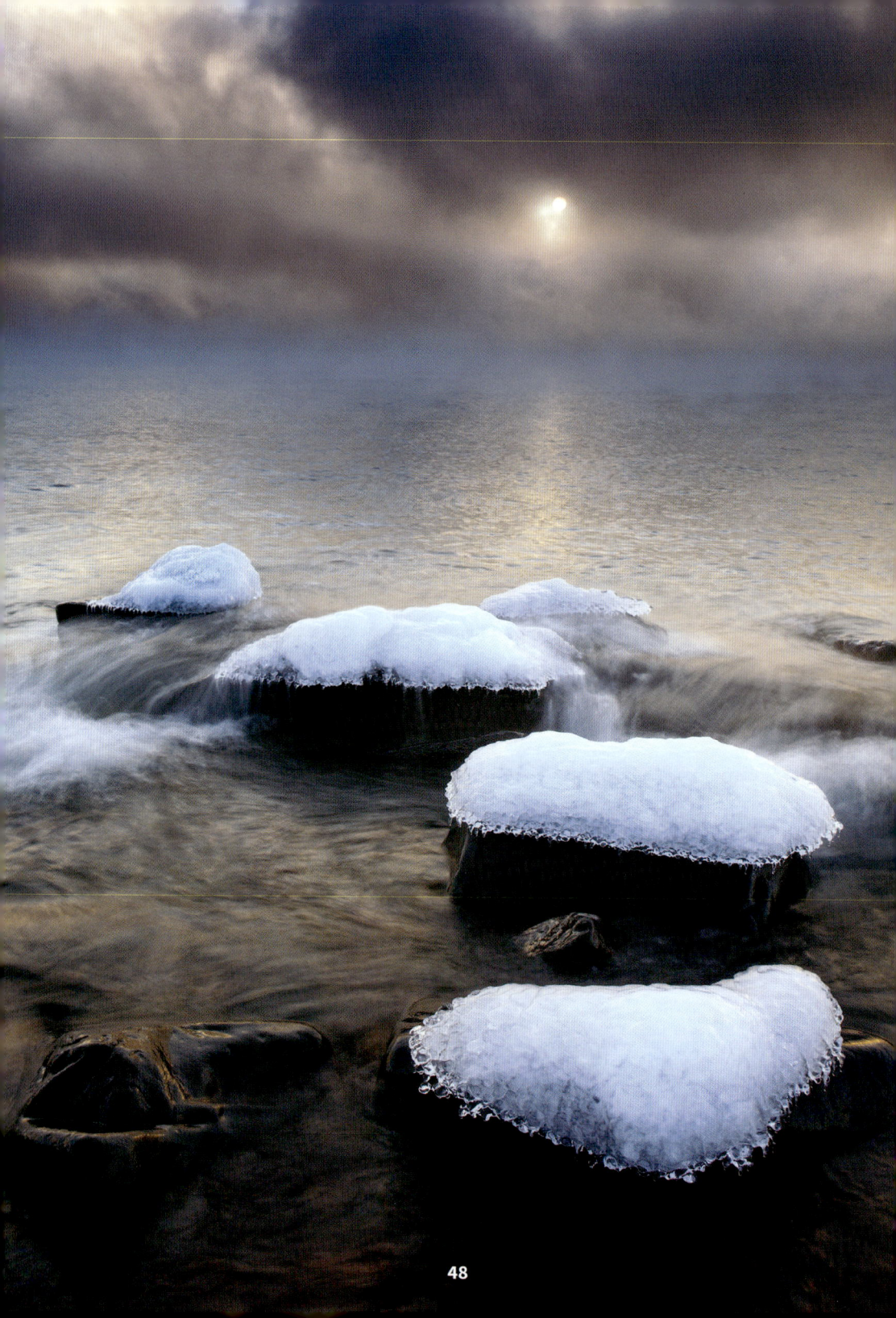

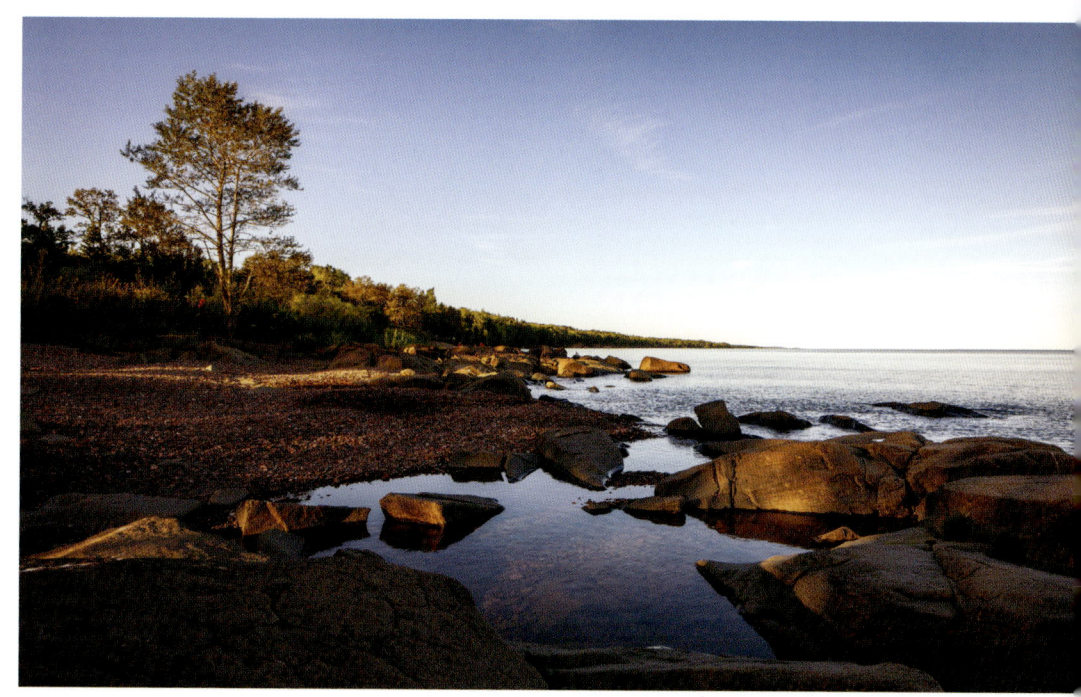

KITCHI GAMMI PARK (BRIGHTON BEACH)

As the easternmost of Duluth's city parks that travelers encounter on their journeys up the North Shore, Kitchi Gammi Park was originally developed as a campground for motorists way back in 1922. Today, it attracts both locals and tourists for its picnic areas, rocky beach, and unobstructed views of Lake Superior. The park is a local favorite for observing winter-induced phenomena caused by the lake, including sea smoke during subzero temperatures and ice shards, pieces of surface ice that are pushed ashore by easterly winds.

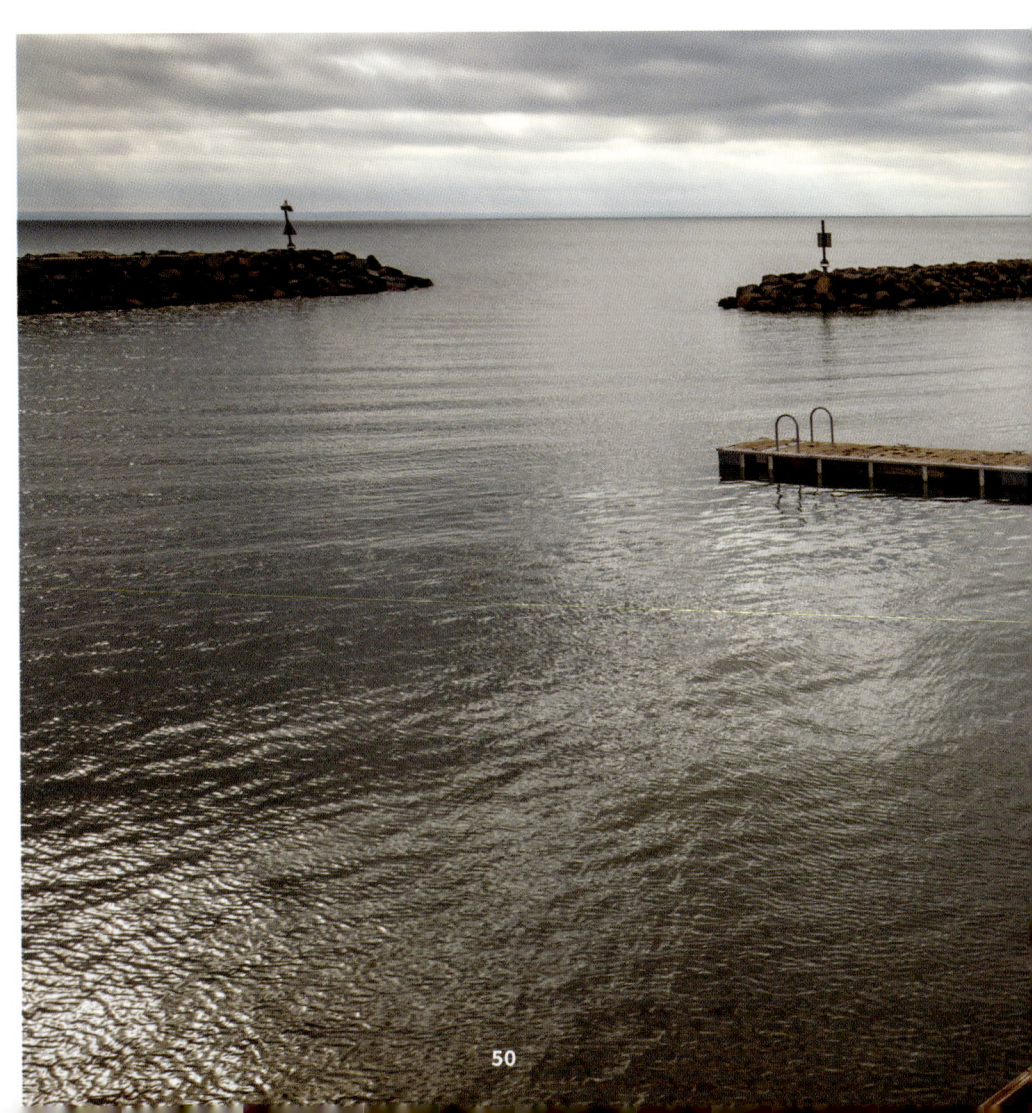

MCQUADE SMALL CRAFT HARBOR

With four public boat ramps, McQuade Small Craft Harbor was built in 2008 to provide safe harbor and a launching point for small boats on Lake Superior. A modern facility administered by the Minnesota DNR, the harbor area also provides a large paved parking lot, public restrooms, a fishing platform, and accessible walkways with benches to enjoy the lake views.

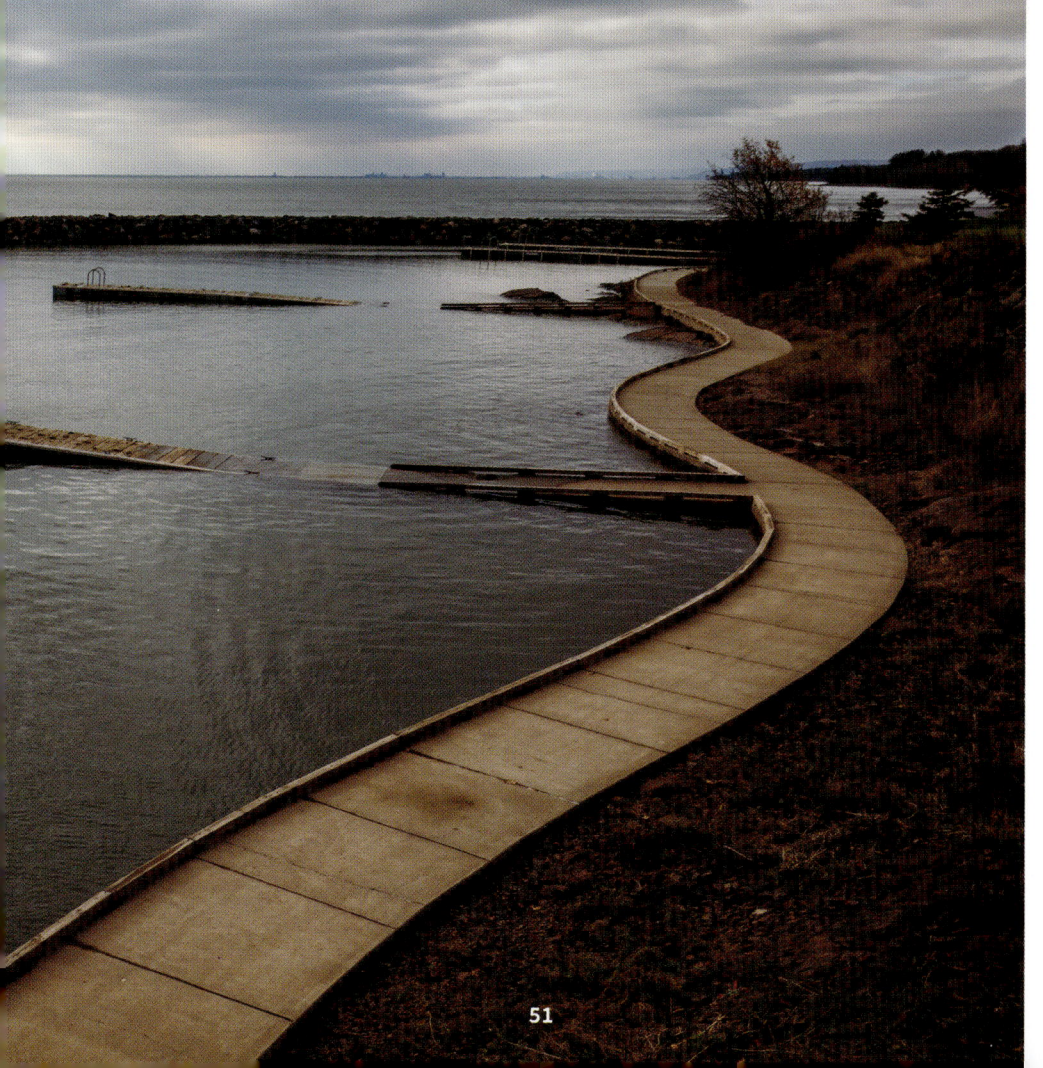

STONEY POINT

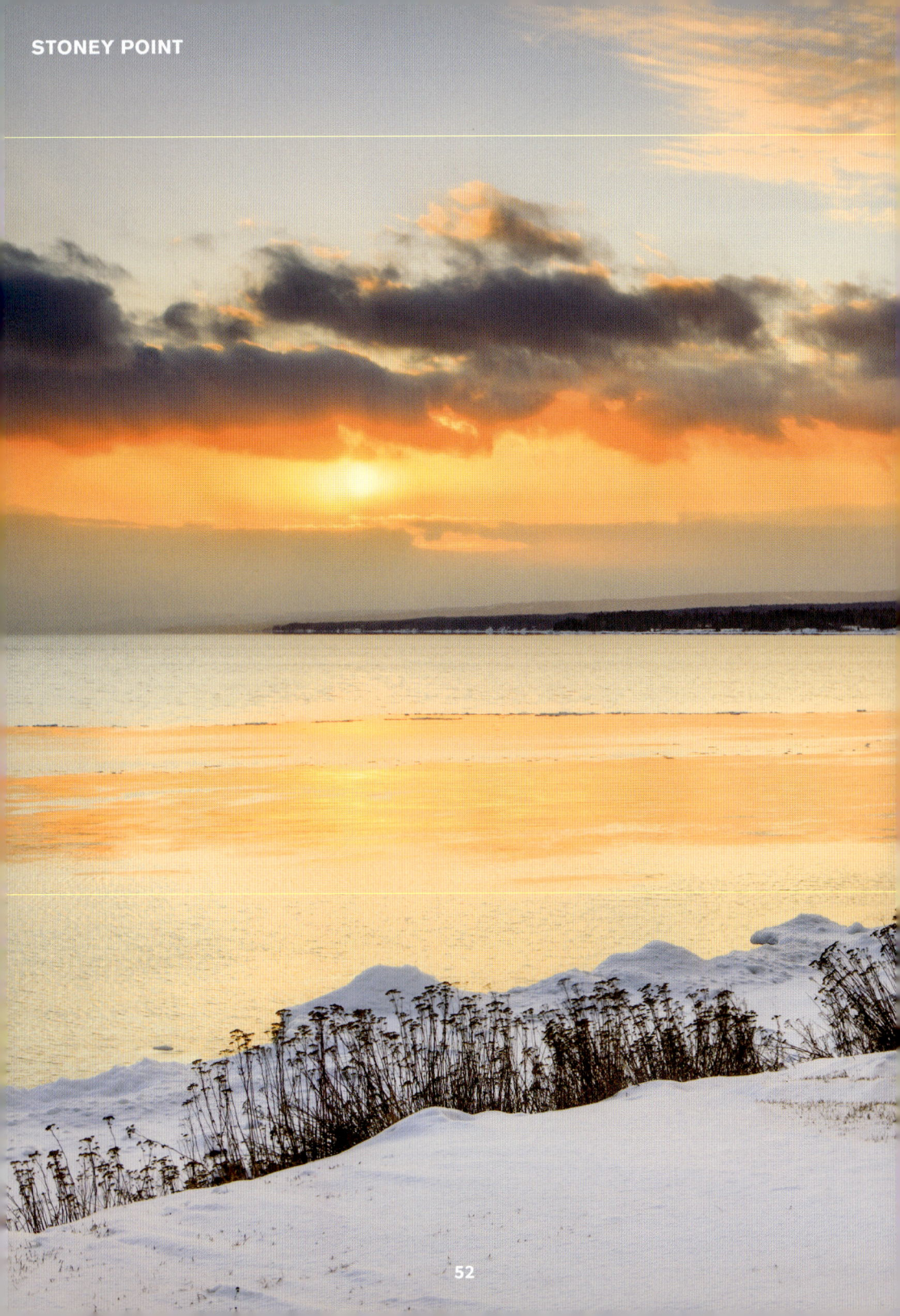

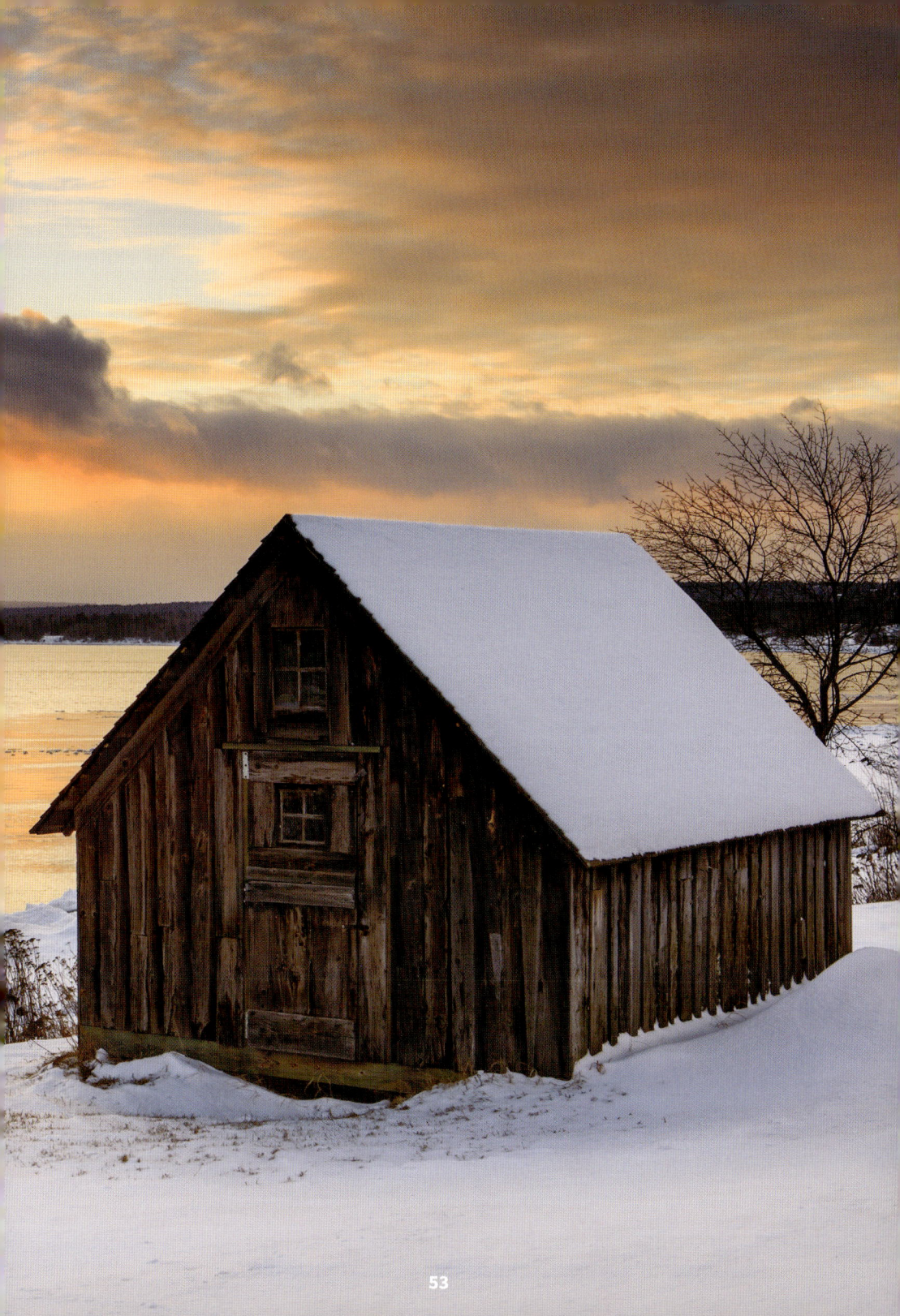

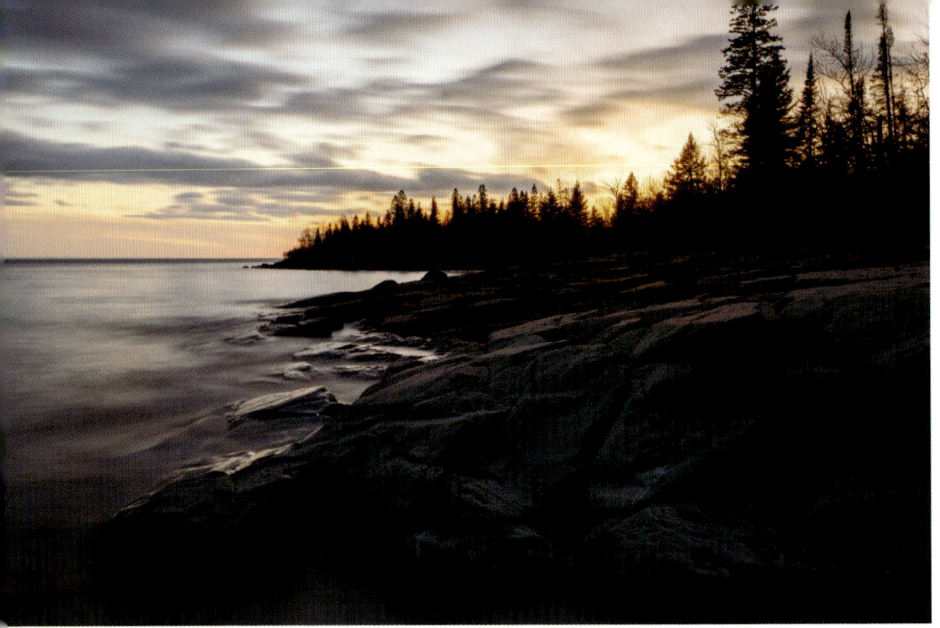

◀ STONEY POINT

Roughly halfway between Duluth and Two Harbors, Stoney Point offers excellent wave-watching opportunities thanks to its exposed shoreline. These waves are also enjoyed by local surfers, who can be seen riding the surf in all seasons (in wetsuits, of course!), even though the surface temperature of Lake Superior is usually well below 50 degrees Fahrenheit. On the south side of the point sits an old fishing cabin, a relic of the days of small-scale fishing operations on the big lake.

PIERRE THE VOYAGEUR

Once a fixture in front of a museum and gift shop near the Voyageur Motel in Two Harbors, Pierre the Voyageur now greets visitors approaching Two Harbors from the south along Highway 61. The 20-foot-tall mesh and fiberglass statue was purchased by the Earthwood Inn and moved to its current location in 2011.

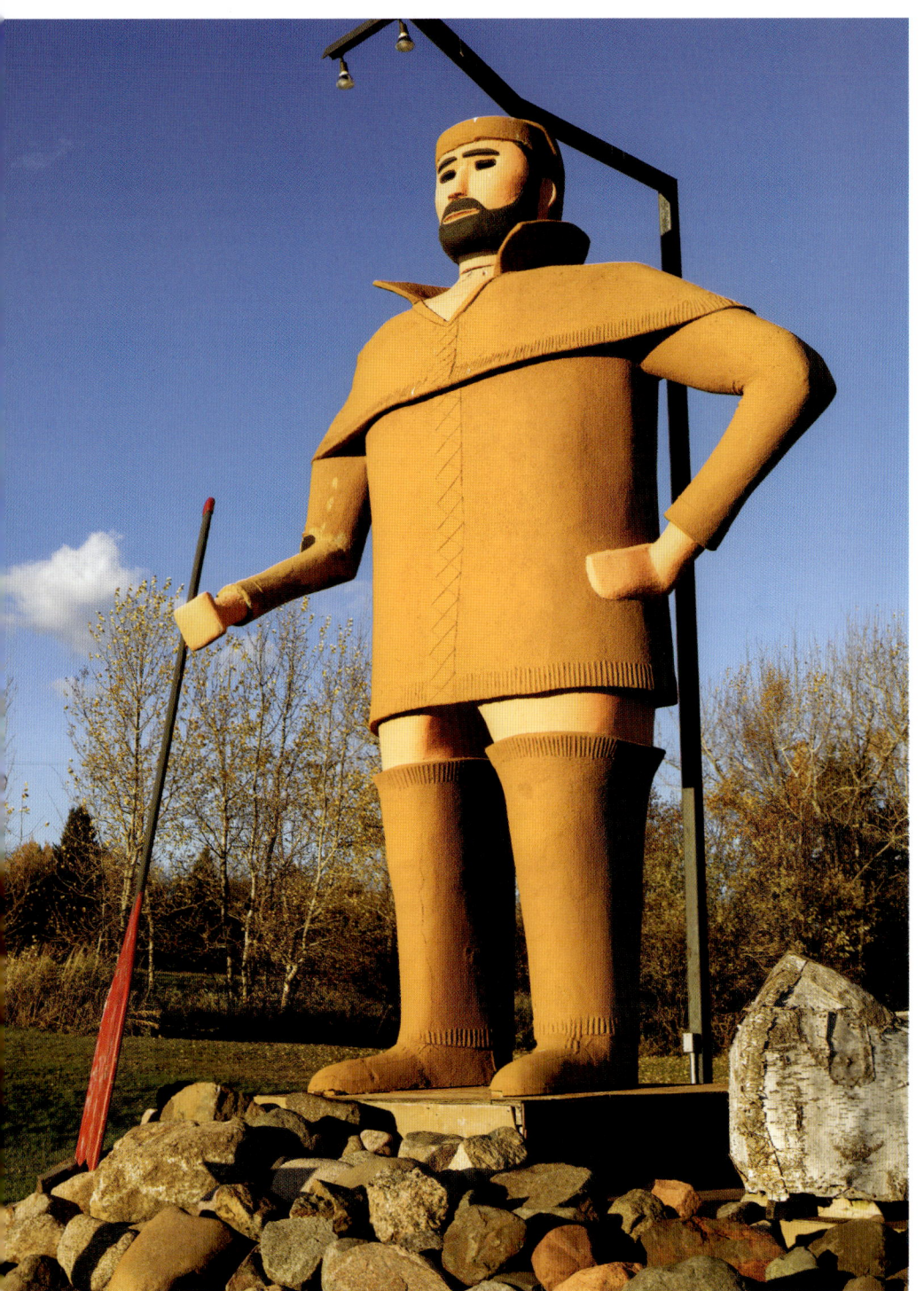

TWO HARBORS ORE DOCKS

Home of the first ore shipment from Minnesota's Iron Range in 1884, six docks were in operation at this site during the height of Minnesota's iron ore industry in the mid-twentieth century. Today, three docks remain standing with two of them still operating and shipping about 12 million tons of taconite annually.

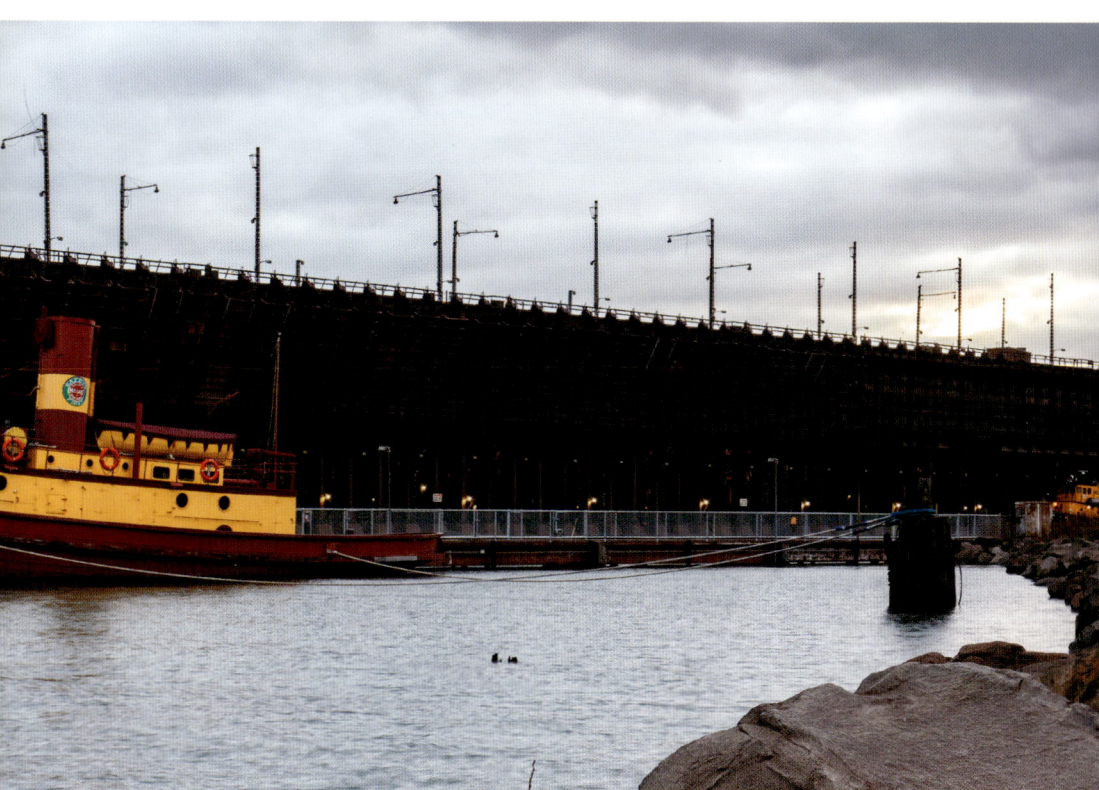

EDNA G TUGBOAT

Preserved as a floating museum ship, the *Edna G* was the last steam-powered tugboat that operated on the Great Lakes. Built in 1896 for the Duluth and Iron Range Railroad, it served the Two Harbors shipping industry until its retirement in 1981. The only time it was away from Two Harbors was a brief stint on the east coast of the United States during World War I. The boat has become an icon of the community and appears in various logos and banners.

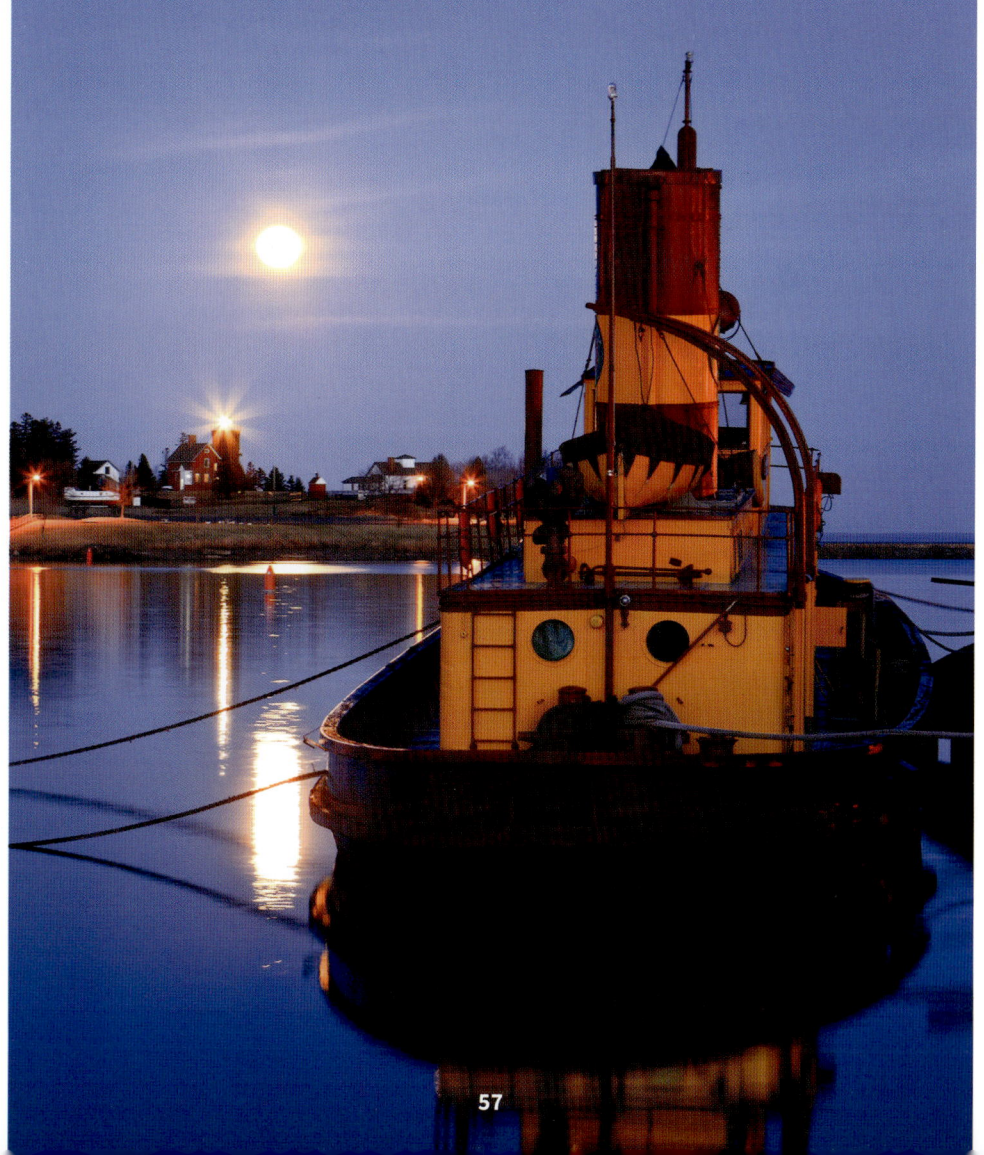

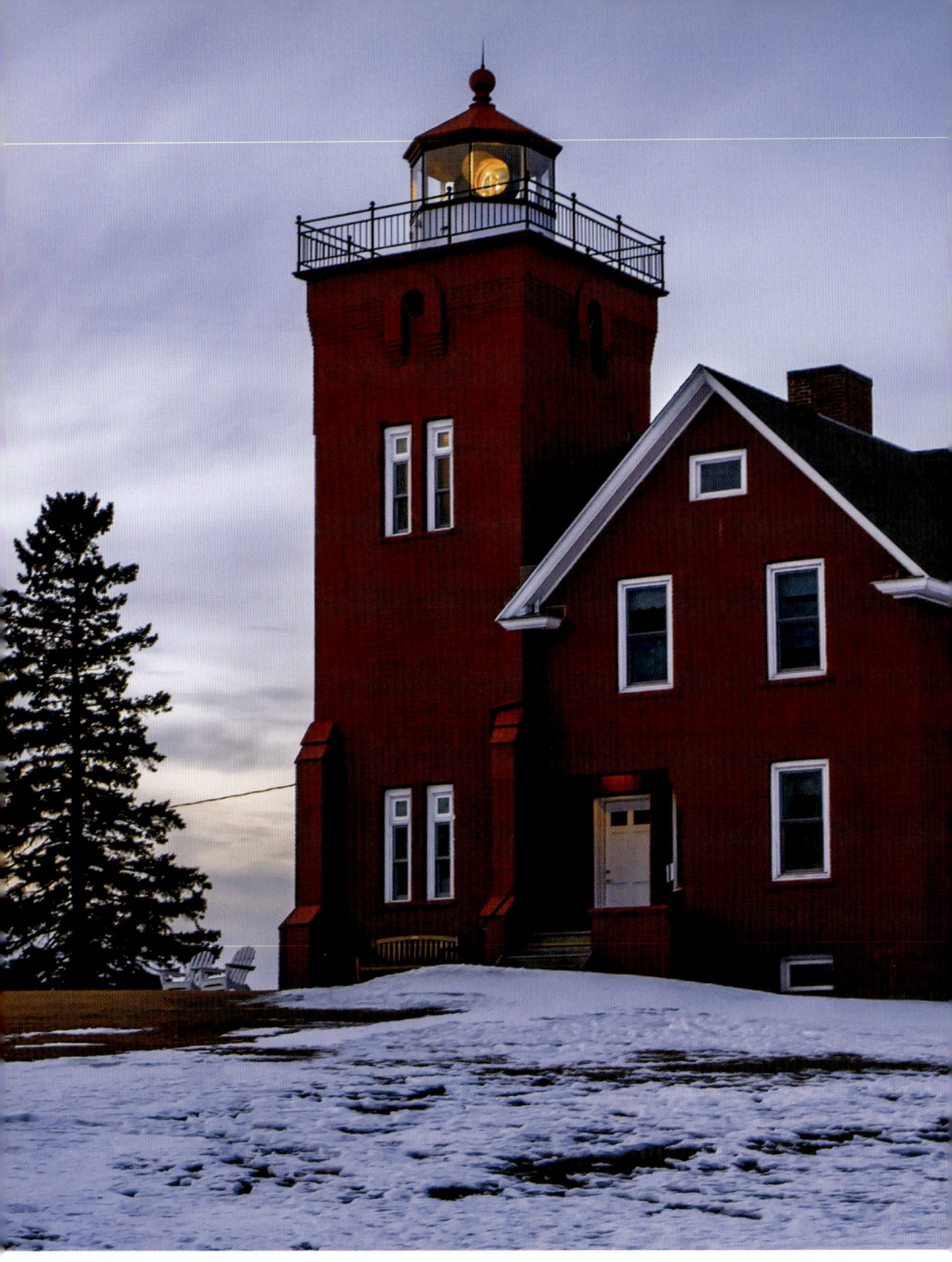

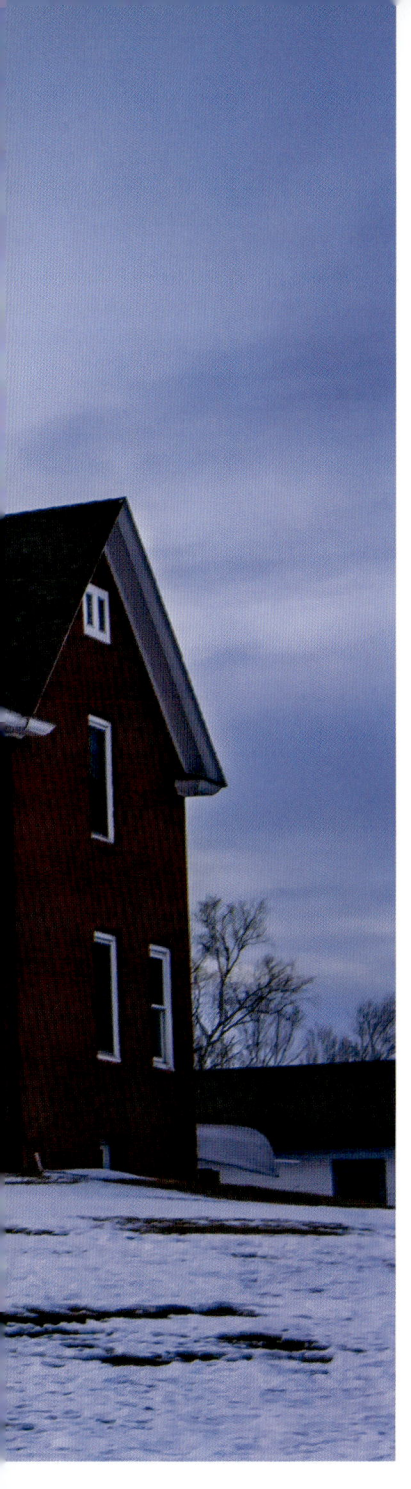

TWO HARBORS LIGHTHOUSE MUSEUM

First lit in 1892, the Two Harbors Light Station is the oldest still-operating lighthouse in Minnesota. In addition to its service as an aid to navigation, the attached head keeper's dwelling has operated as a bed & breakfast since 1999, making it the only lighthouse on the North Shore in which visitors can spend the night. The Lake County Historical Society owns and operates the light station and provides tours throughout the summer season.

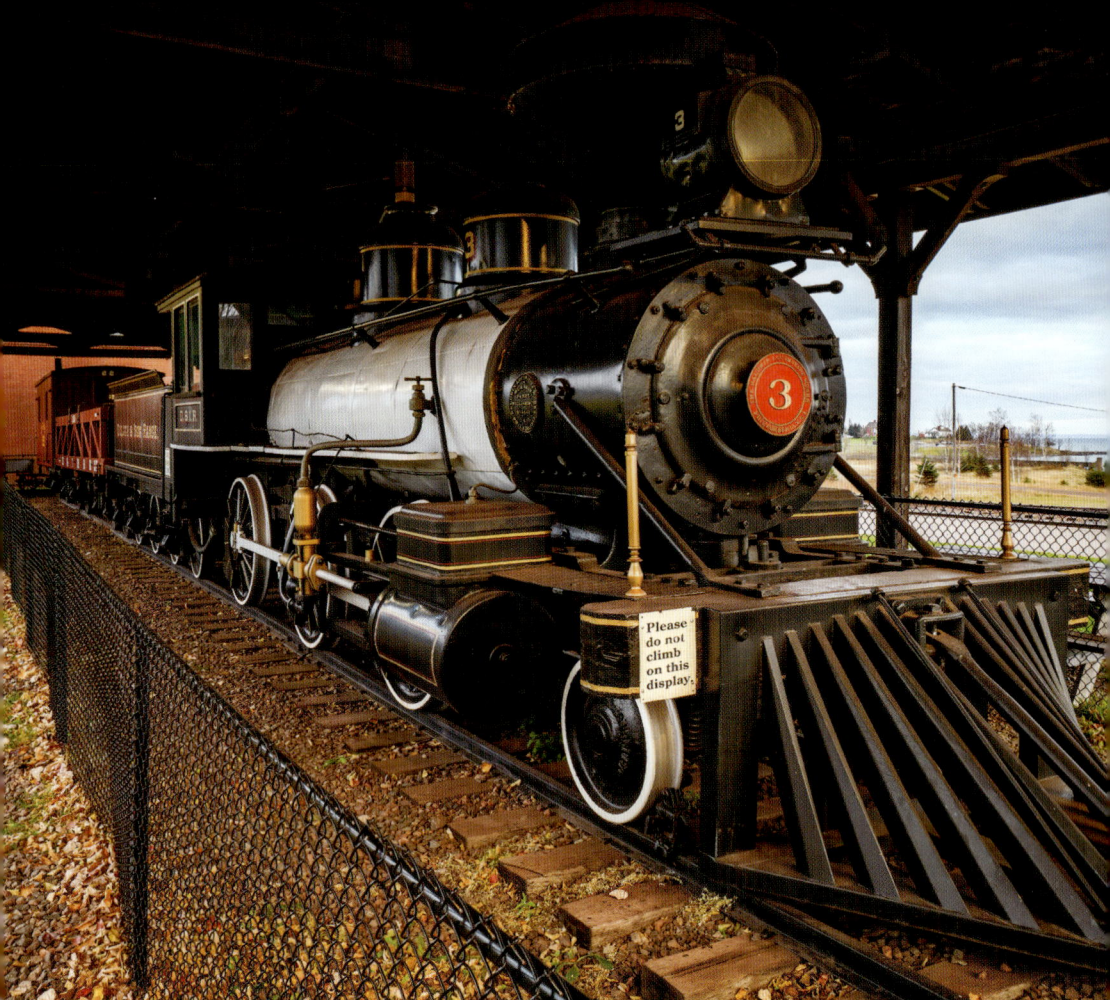

DULUTH AND IRON RANGE RAILROAD DEPOT MUSEUM

Erected in 1907 as the corporate headquarters for the Duluth and Iron Range Railroad, this location oversaw the very first shipment of iron ore from Minnesota and served an essential role in Minnesota's iron ore industry. The depot discontinued operations in 1961, and the Lake County Historical Society now operates a museum within the site. Outside the museum, two locomotives are permanently displayed: 3 Spot, the first locomotive purchased (in 1883) by the Duluth & Iron Range Railroad, and Yellowstone Mallet #229, built in 1943 as one of the largest locomotives ever made and among the last of the steam-powered age.

3M BIRTHPLACE MUSEUM

Maker of such useful everyday items as Scotch Tape and Post-it Notes, the Minnesota-based Fortune 500 company 3M began operations in this modest Two Harbors office building in 1902. The building is now a museum that presents the account of 3M's rise to success as a multinational conglomerate, and it also shares the story of a major mistake that almost sank the company in its infancy. The founders invested heavily in mining corundum, valuable as an abrasive, on the north shore of Lake Superior. The "corundum" they had extracted was later found to be anorthosite, which was commercially useless. The company soon relocated to Duluth, and then to St. Paul, and found success in industrial sandpaper and—yes—Scotch Tape.

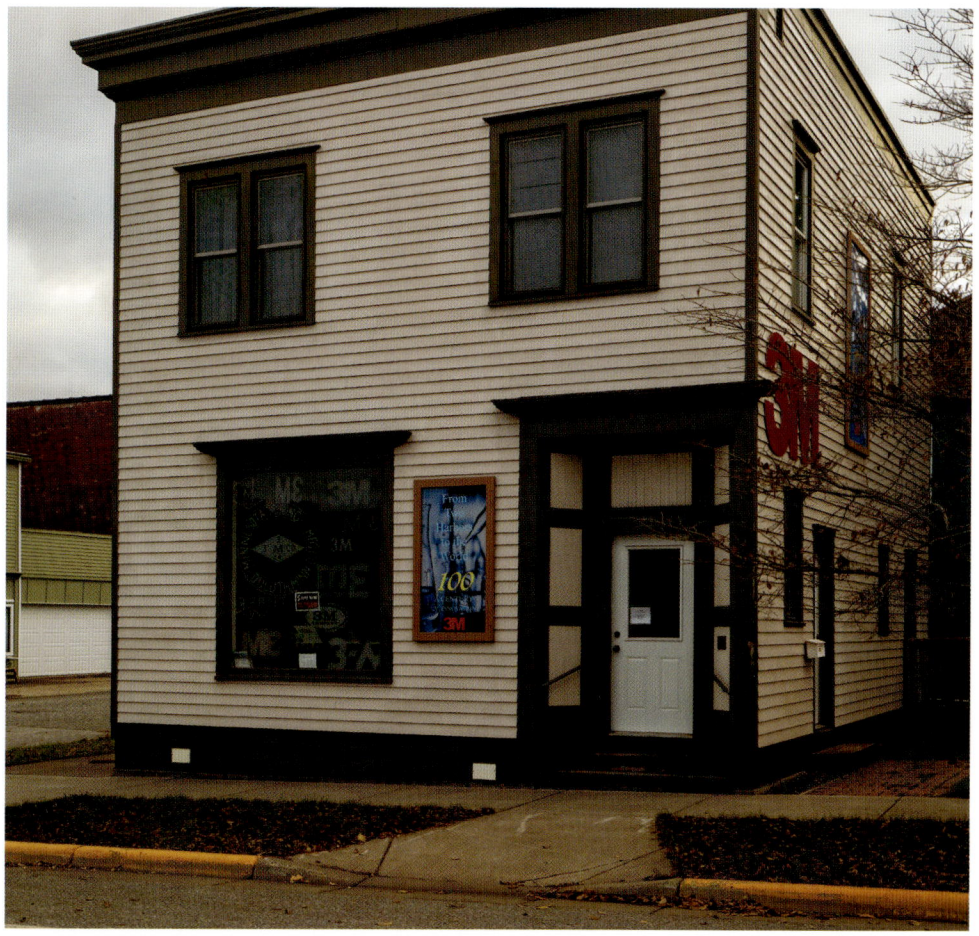

HIGHWAY 61 TUNNELS

Before the mid-1990s, motorists driving north on Highway 61 from Two Harbors had to navigate a narrow, winding roadway hugging the edge of two prominent North Shore headlands: Silver Creek Cliff and Lafayette Bluff. However, occasional rockfalls and the threat of the roadbed collapsing into Lake Superior, among other safety concerns, prompted construction of Highway 61's only two tunnels, each named after the headland it passes through. A portion of the Gitchi-Gami multi-use paved trail follows the original highway alignment around Silver Creek Cliff.

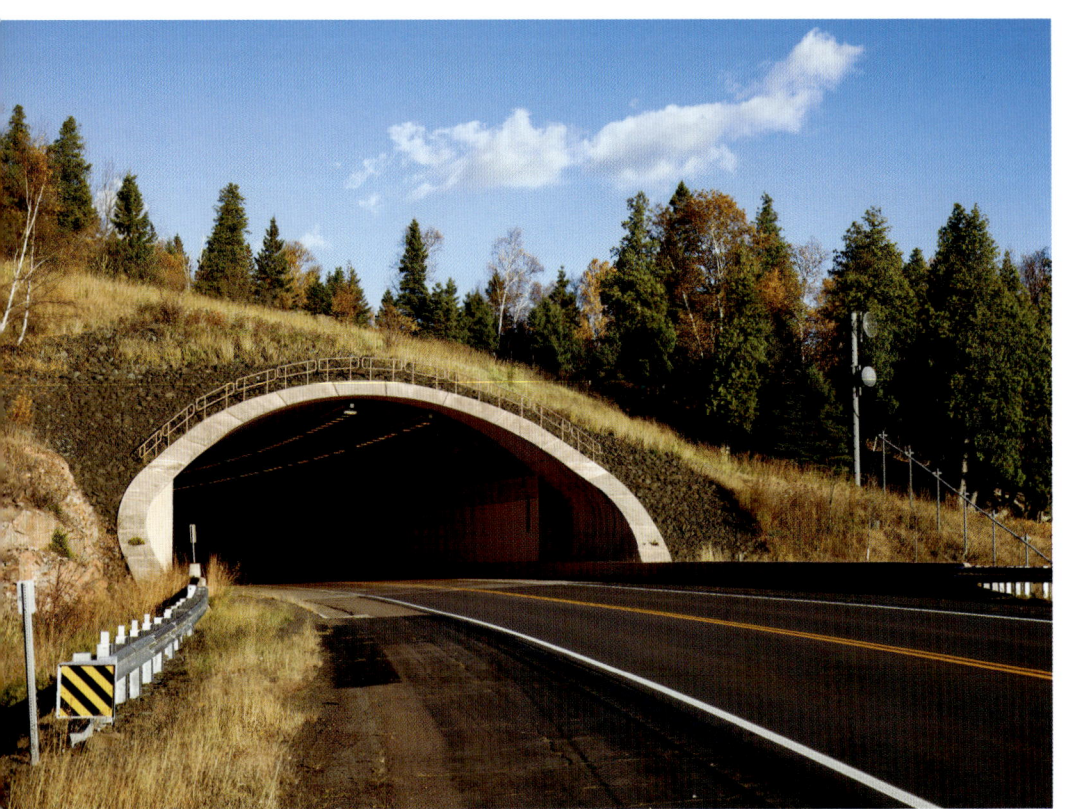

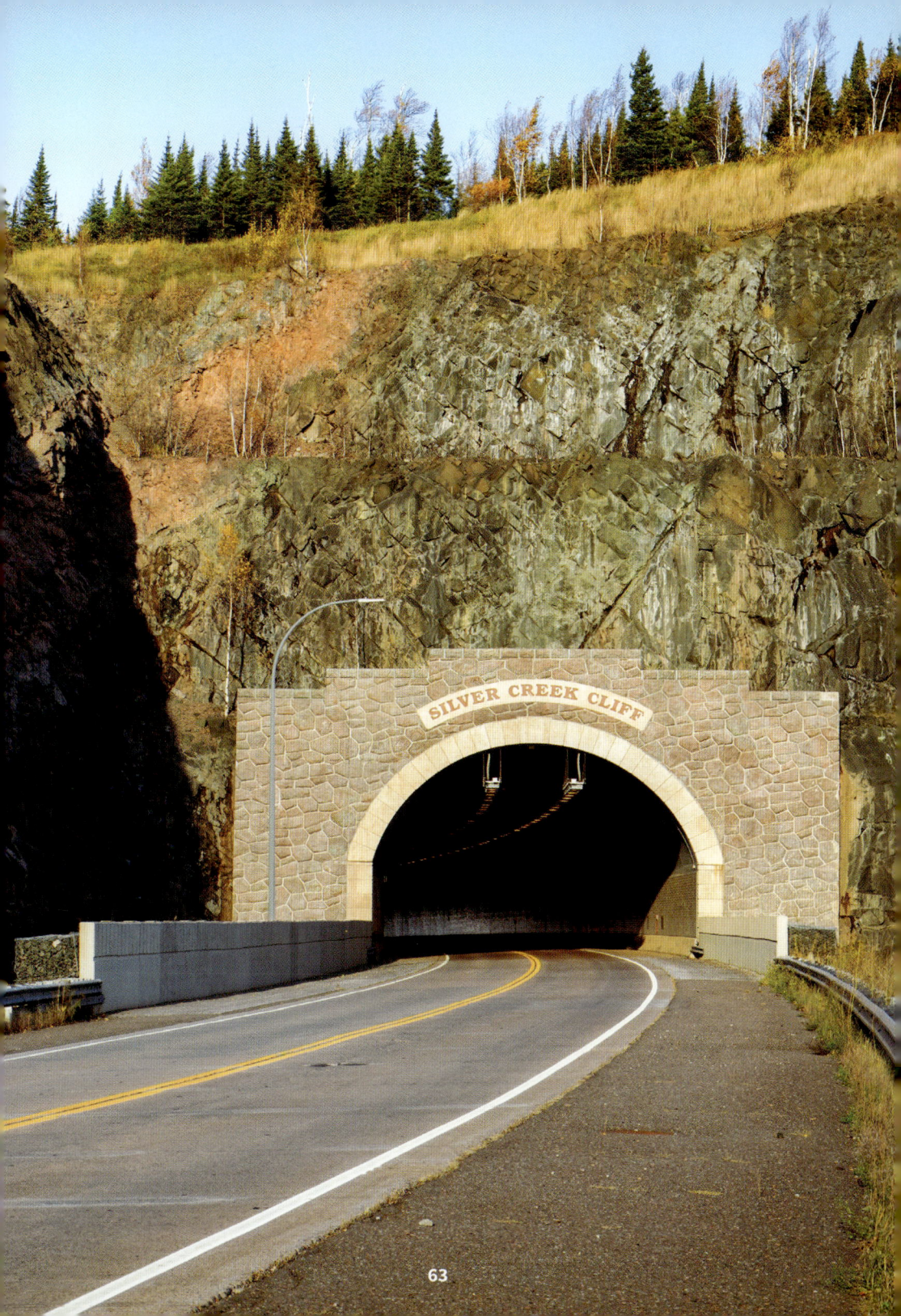

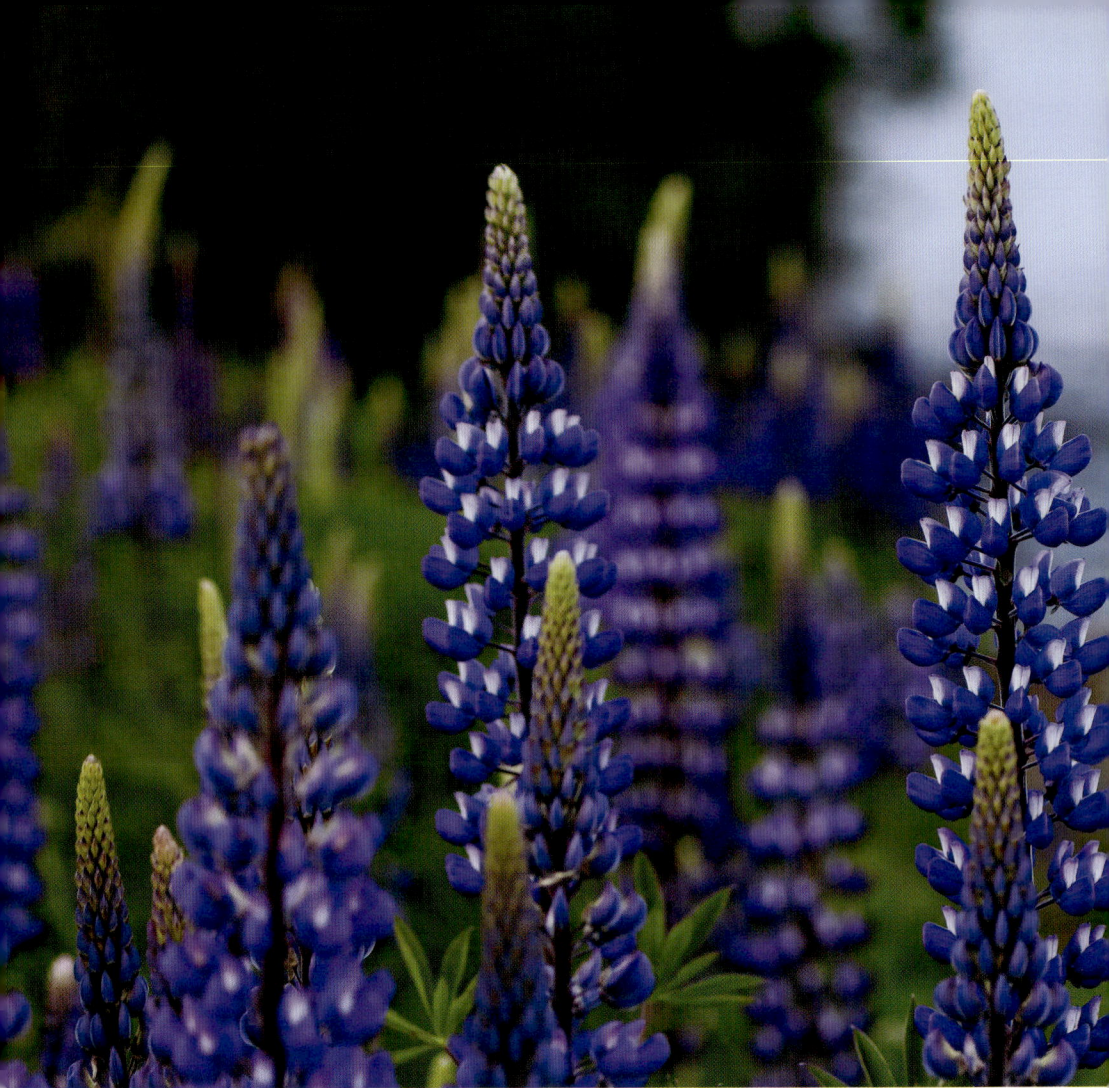

LUPINES

In bloom between mid-June and early July, lupines are a must-see attraction for any North Shore traveler. Typically growing along Highway 61 and other roadsides, their blossomed spikes form majestic carpets of purple-blue with occasional mix-ins of white and pink varieties. Areas with the highest concentration of lupines include Highway 61 near Gooseberry Falls State Park and along the Caribou Trail near Lutsen. As beautiful as they are, most lupines growing along the North Shore are non-native plants and have become invasive after being introduced by local gardeners.

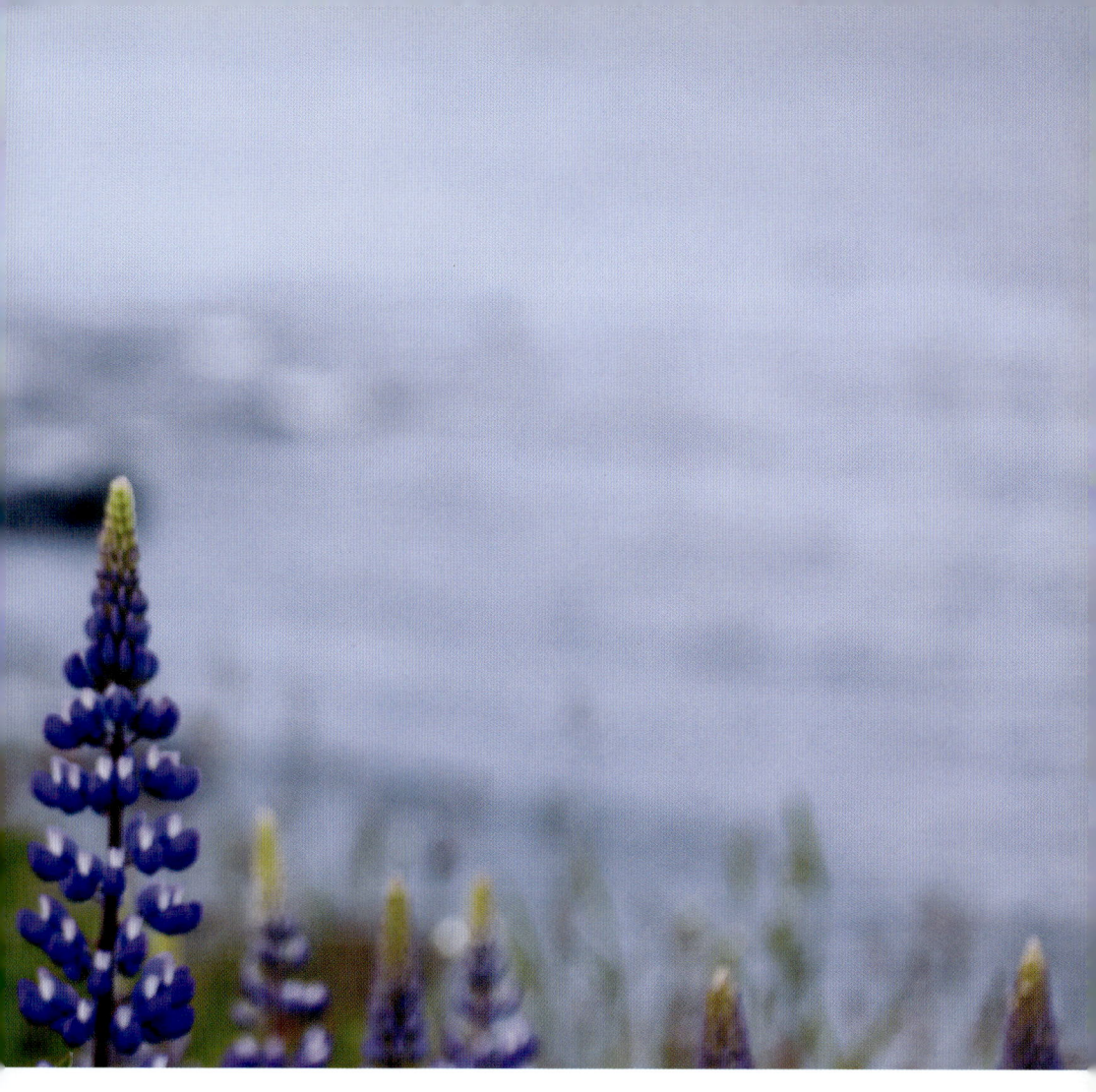

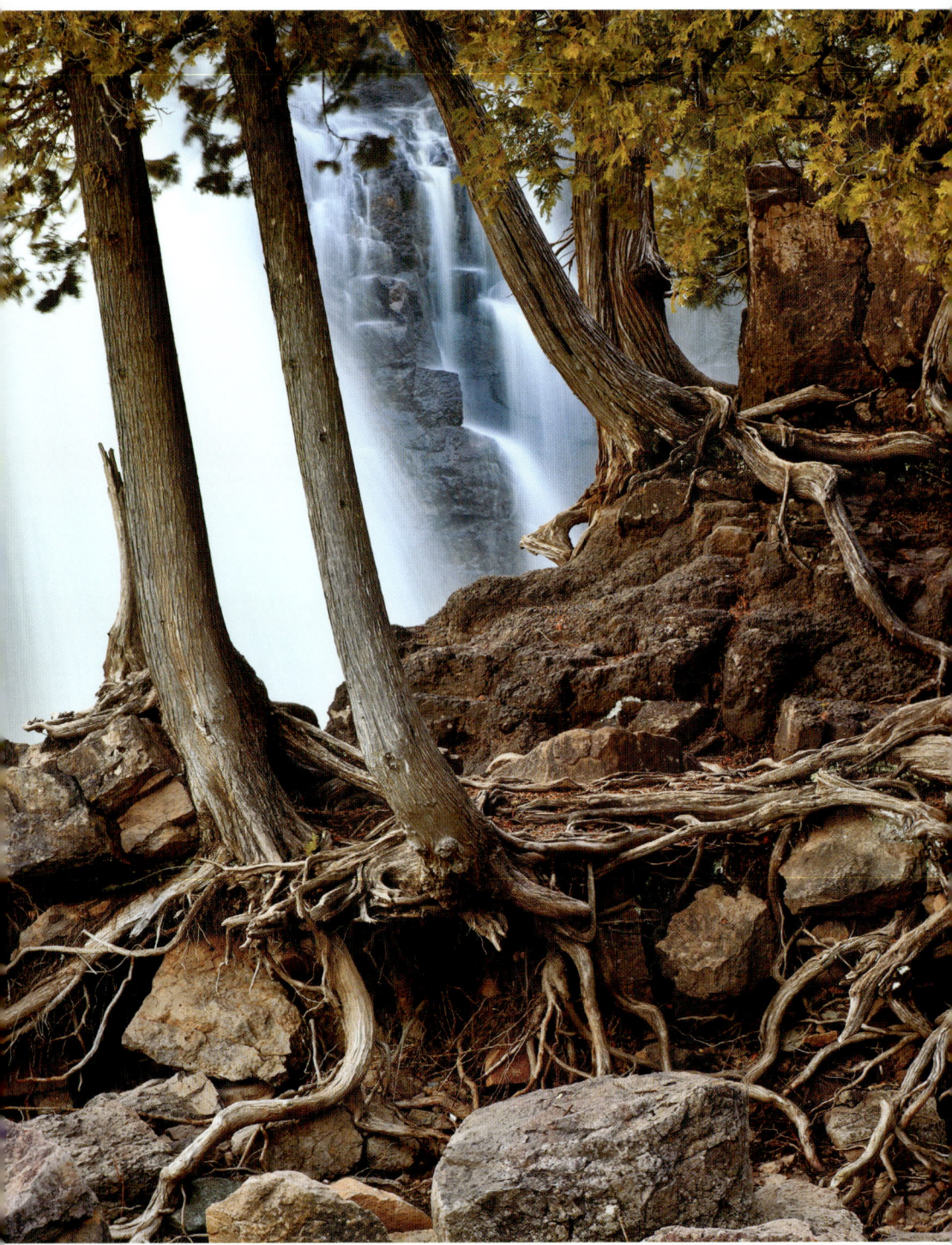

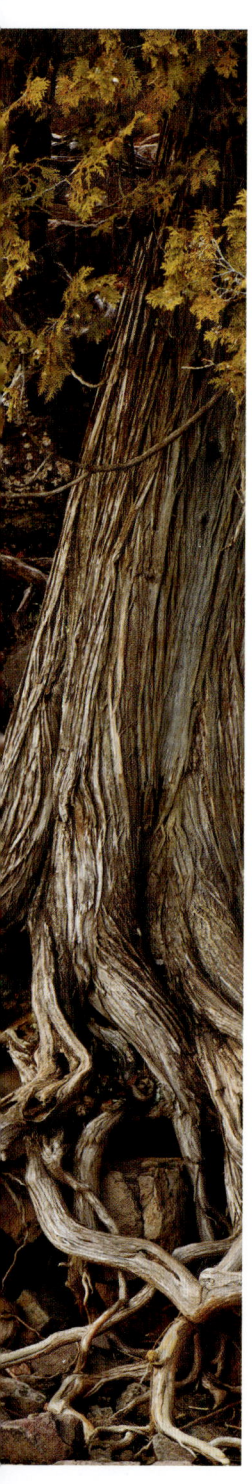

GOOSEBERRY FALLS STATE PARK

Serving as the gateway to the North Shore state parks, Gooseberry Falls is one of the most visited state parks in Minnesota. Established in 1933 to preserve public access to the scenic beauty of the area, the park includes five waterfalls on the Gooseberry River as well as rocky Lake Superior shoreline formed by ancient basalt lava flows. The Civilian Conservation Corps (CCC) had a major presence here between 1934 and 1941, constructing a campground and many of the park's trails and well-preserved stone and log buildings.

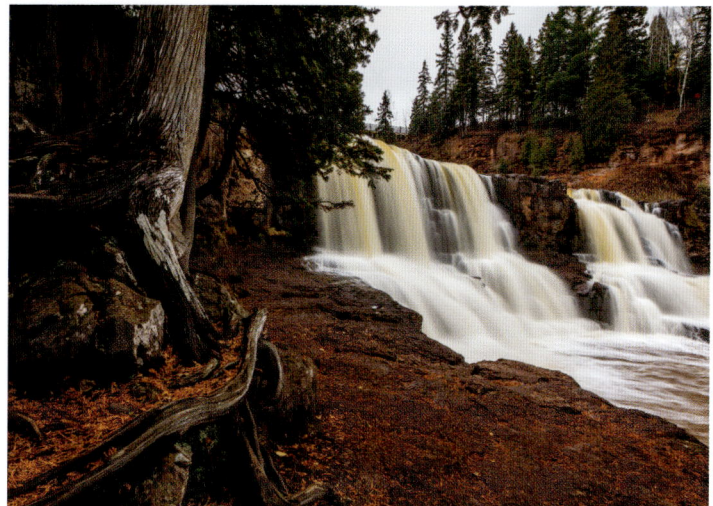

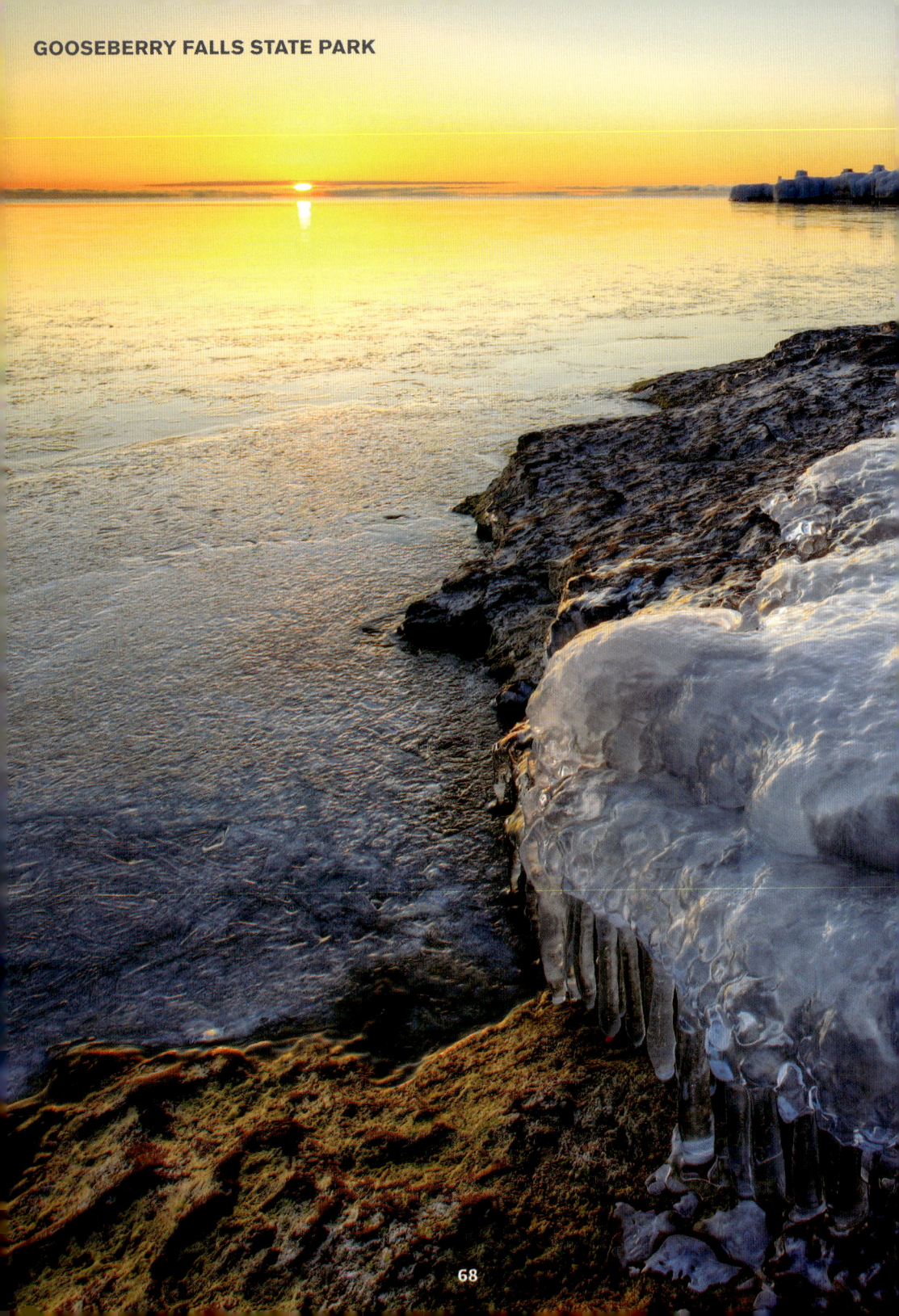
GOOSEBERRY FALLS STATE PARK

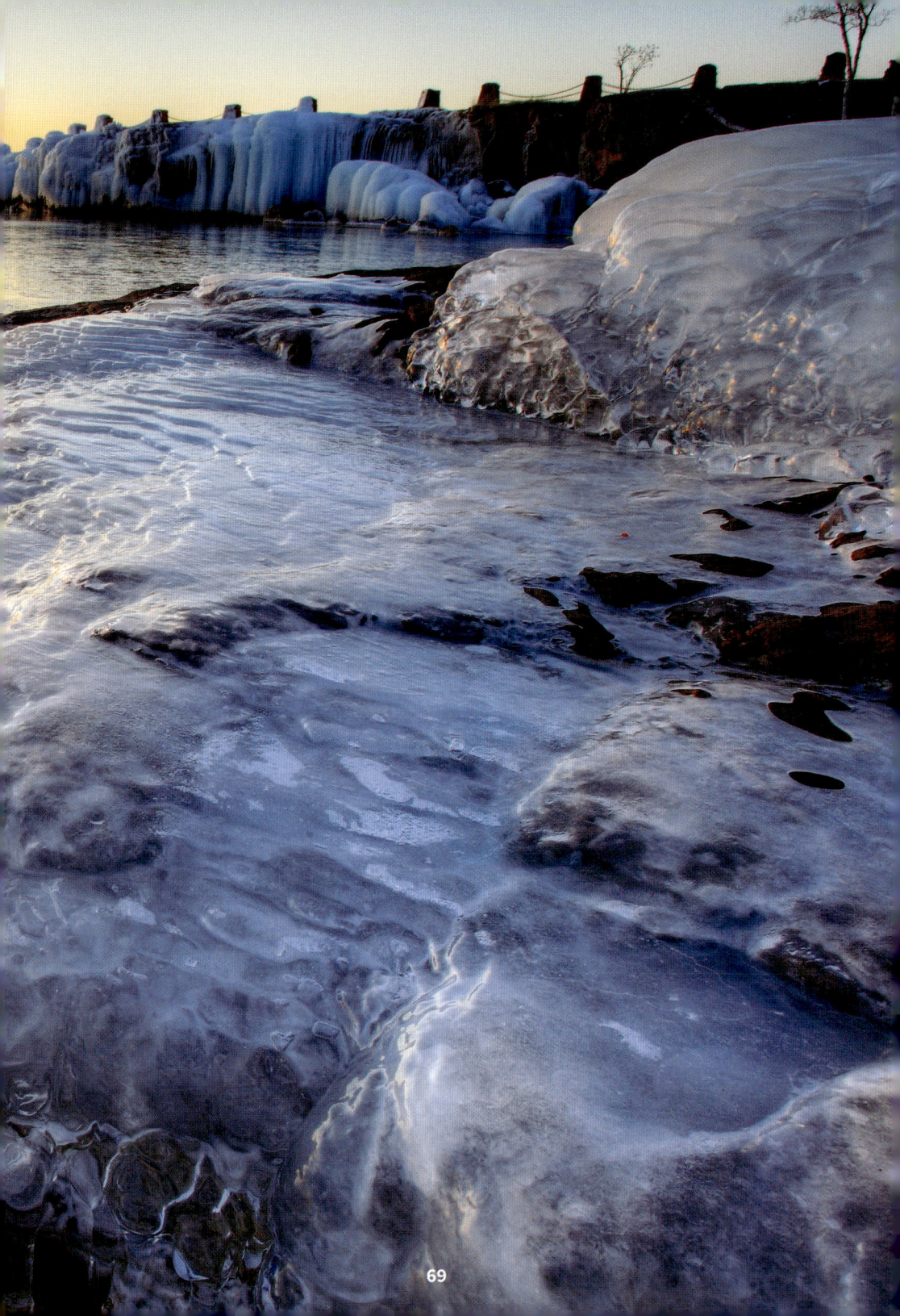

IONA'S BEACH SCIENTIFIC AND NATURAL AREA

Once the location of the bustling Twin Points Resort, owner Iona Lind bequeathed the land she loved and worked on for nearly 50 years to the public to enjoy. The most notable feature of the property is the 900-foot-long Lake Superior beach, filled with salmon-colored stones. The stones are formed from erosion of the 30-foot-high pink rhyolite cliff to the north and are smoothed by the action of the lake and washed ashore. Due to the unique characteristics of the stones, when waves wash against the beach, a distinctive "tinkling" sound can be heard.

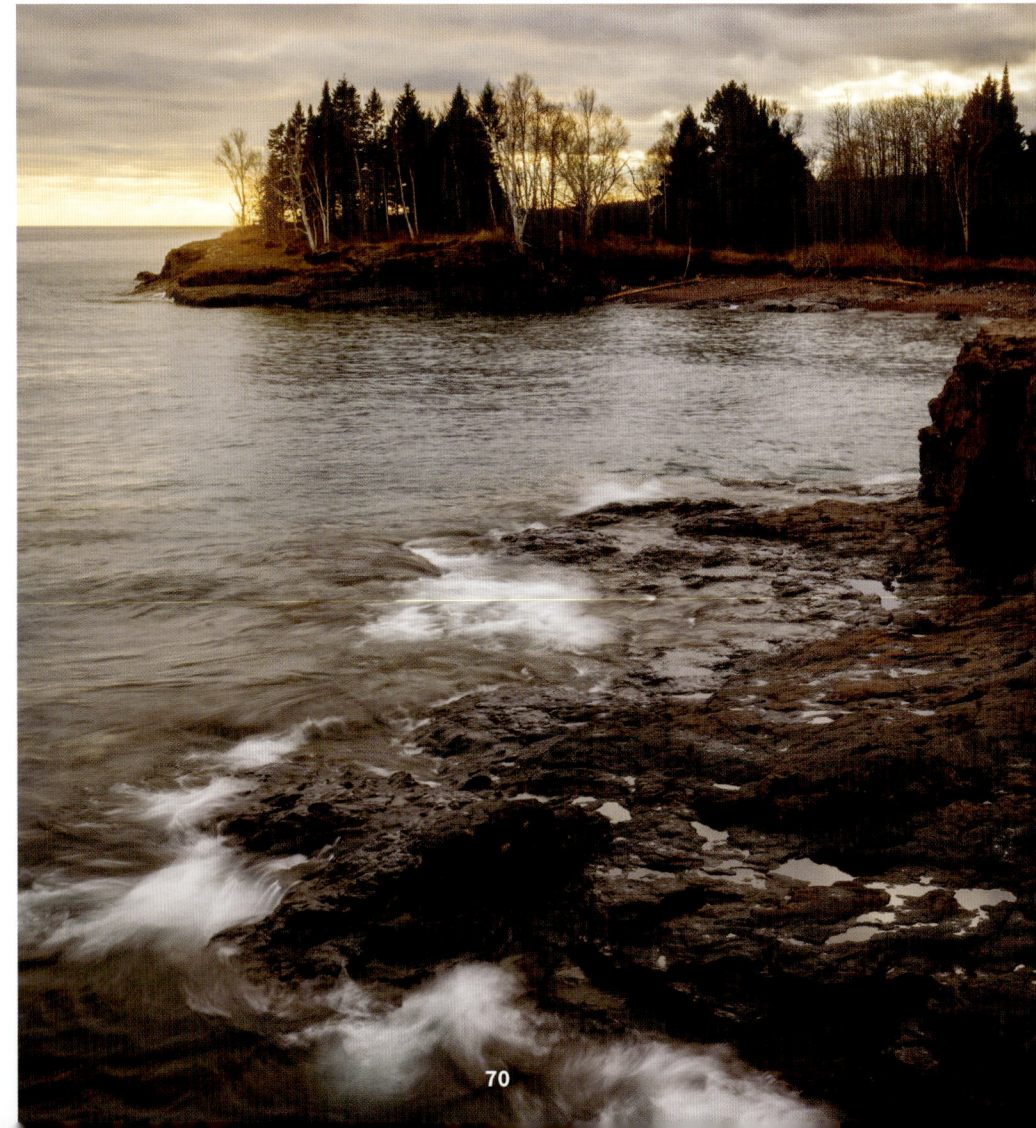

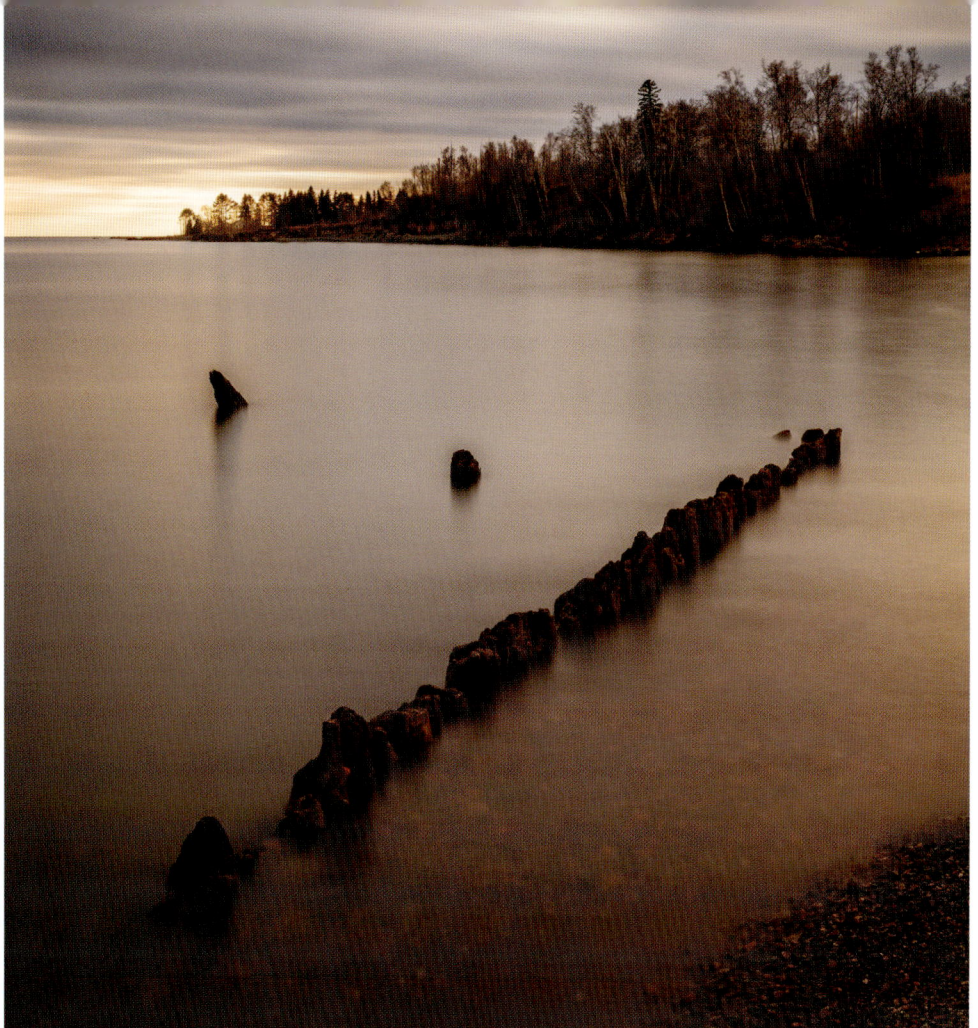

SPLIT ROCK RIVER

The mouth of the Split Rock River was the site of a small logging town around the turn of the twentieth century. The town, called Splitrock, included a railroad, a coal dock, a store, and even a post office. The wooden pilings from a wharf and train trestle near the river's mouth are all that remain today. The wayside rest on the north side of Highway 61 also provides access to the Split Rock River Loop Trail, a popular section of the Superior Hiking Trail that includes several waterfalls and views of Lake Superior.

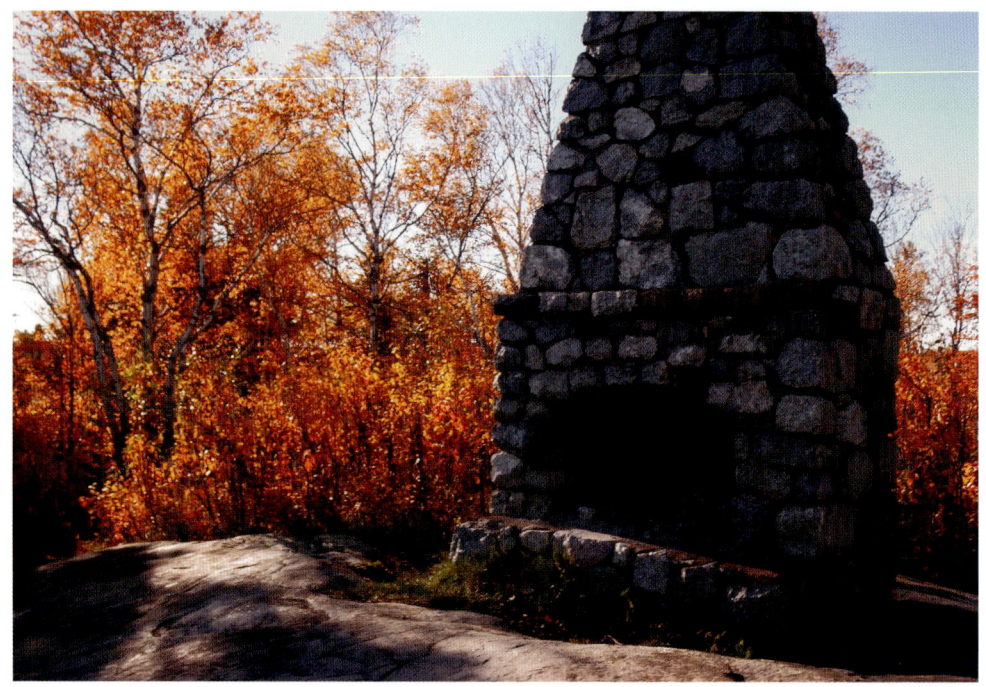

DAY HILL

A moderately difficult 1.5-mile round-trip trail within Split Rock Lighthouse State Park takes hikers to a summit more than 200 feet above Lake Superior, providing a bird's-eye view of the mile-distant Split Rock Lighthouse and surrounding lakeshore. A mysterious stone fireplace stands at the top of the anorthosite hill, believed to have been built by its namesake, Duluth businessman Frank Day. Exactly why it was built remains a mystery.

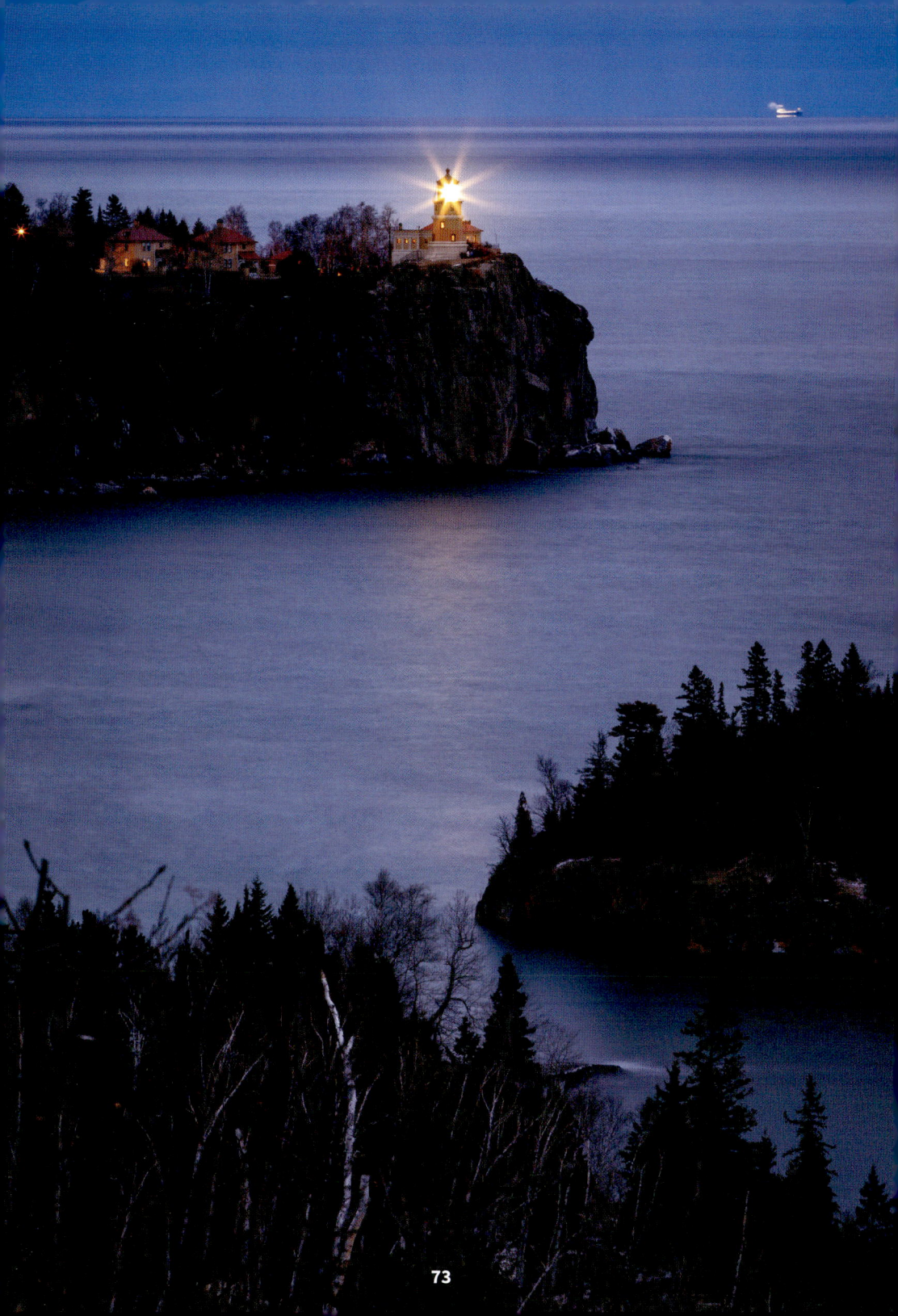

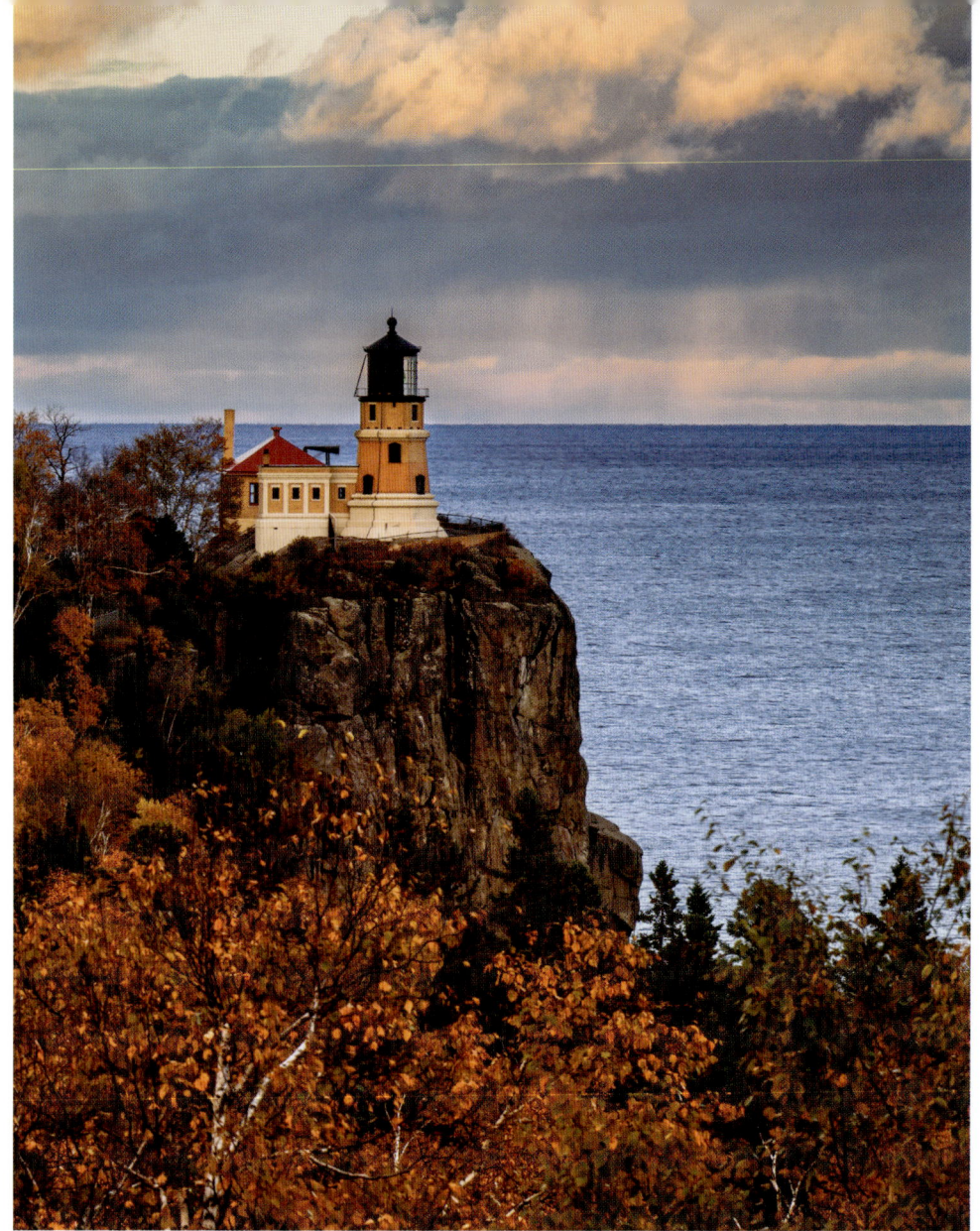

SPLIT ROCK LIGHTHOUSE WAYSIDE REST OVERLOOK

Built in 1948 as a small highway pull-out for viewing Split Rock Lighthouse in the distance, this wayside rest now enjoys greater separation from Highway 61 and a restored stone-and-concrete viewing area. The overlook has long been a popular spot for taking photos or enjoying a quick peek of the lighthouse while passing through.

PEBBLE BEACH

A great place to take in unobstructed views of Split Rock Lighthouse, Lake Superior, and Ellingsen Island, Pebble Beach was home to a small commercial fishing village, known as Little Two Harbors, from 1910 into the 1940s. A few foundations from the former townsite still exist near the southeast corner of the beach. Just southwest of Pebble Beach lies Split Rock Lighthouse State Park's campground, one of only two cart-in campgrounds on the North Shore.

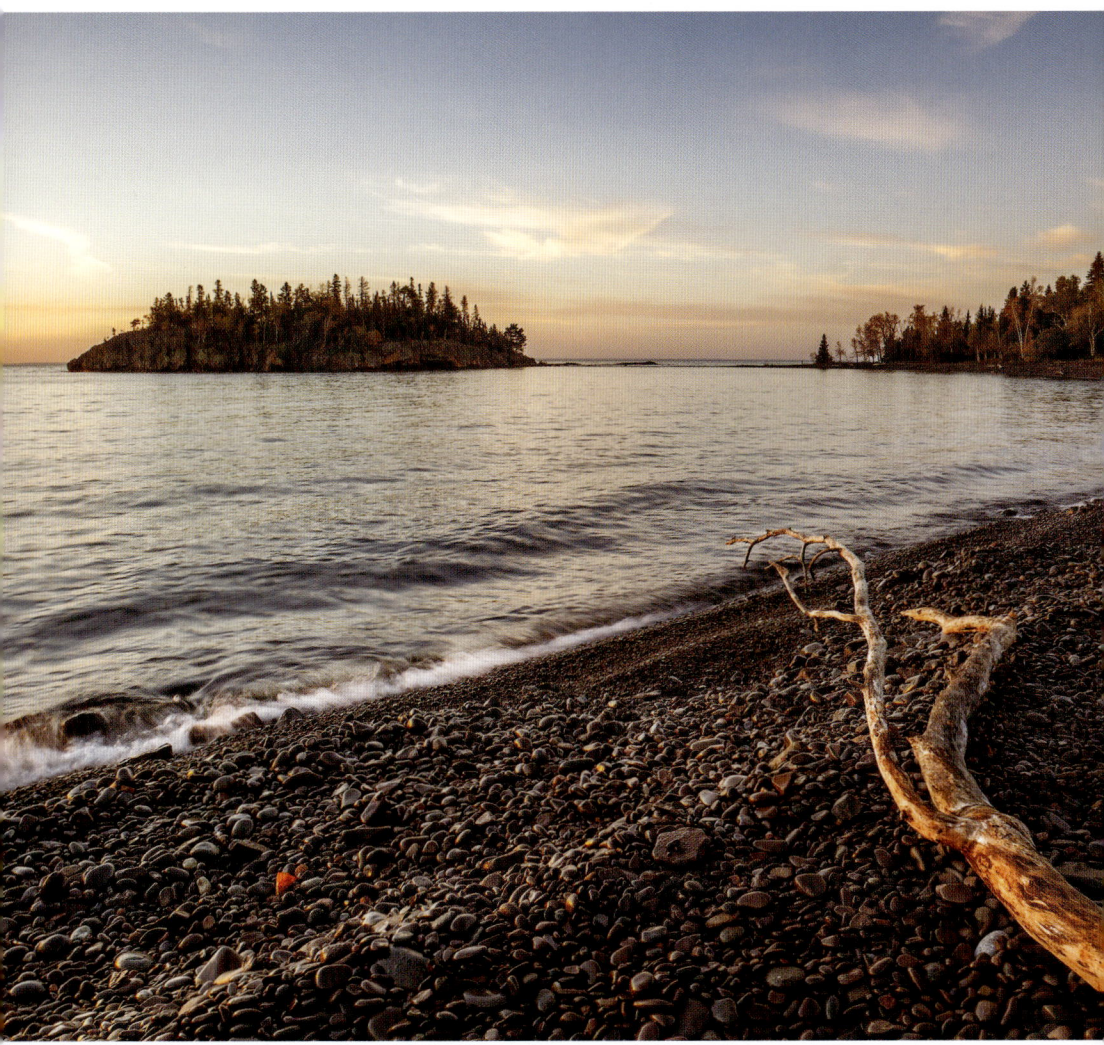

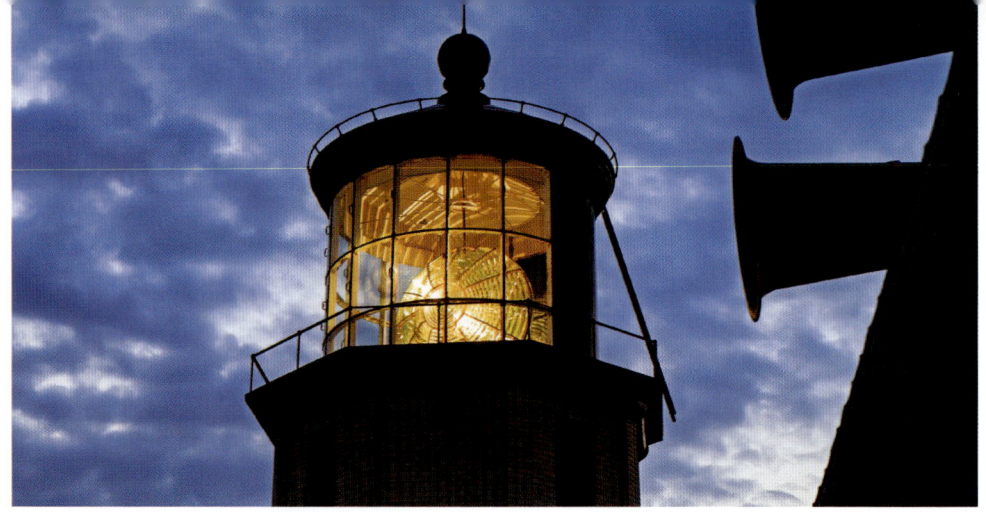

SPLIT ROCK LIGHTHOUSE

Constructed in 1910 atop a then-remote 130-foot cliff, Split Rock Lighthouse stood watch over a particularly treacherous section of Lake Superior's waters until its decommission in 1969, when modern navigation rendered it obsolete. The lighthouse was conceived in response to the infamous 1905 *Mataafa* Storm that destroyed numerous vessels on Lake Superior and killed 36 seamen. Since 1976, the Minnesota Historical Society has operated the lighthouse and surrounding structures as a state historic site, offering guided tours and other interpretive programs. Due to its clifftop location and surrounding scenery, it is one of the most photographed of all lighthouses on the Great Lakes.

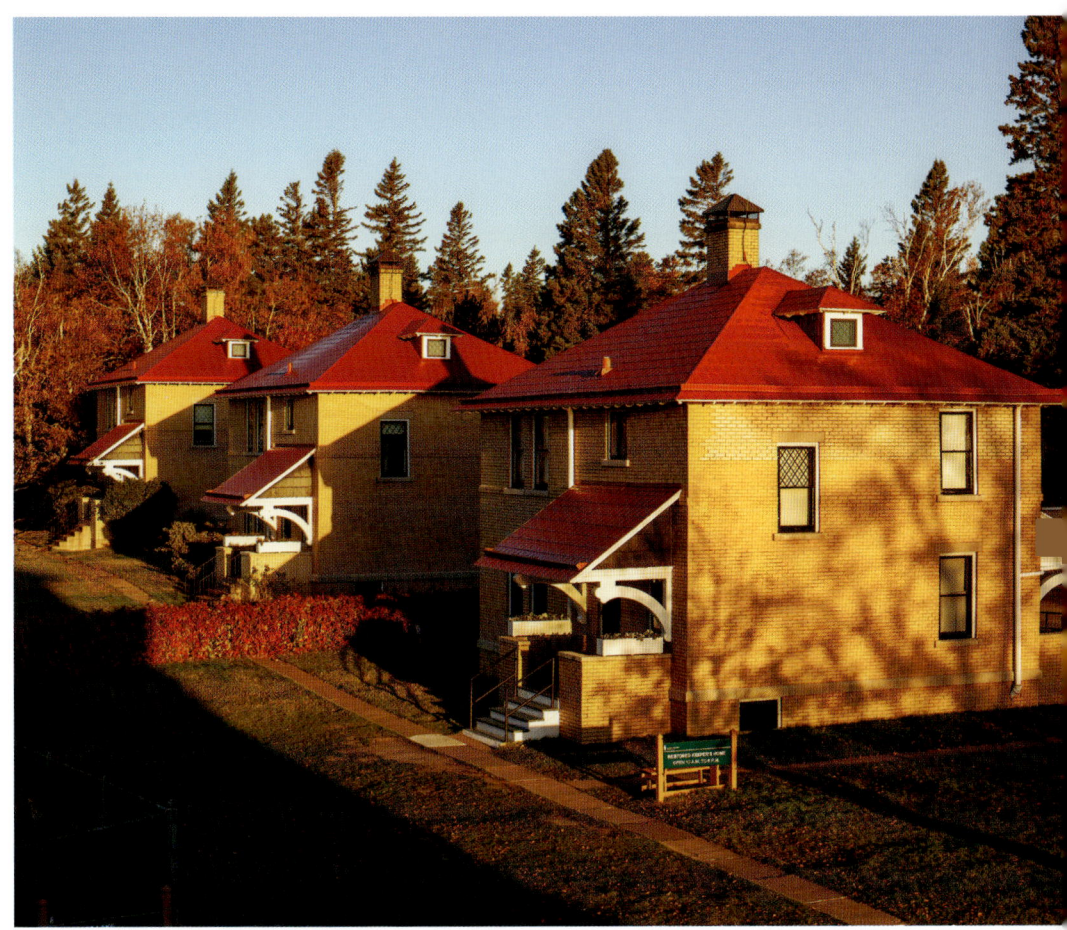

LIGHTHOUSE KEEPERS' HOMES

The three dwellings at Split Rock Lighthouse served as summer homes for the head and assistant keepers during the early years of operation and as year-round abodes for keepers when tourists began frequenting the site. One of the homes has been restored to its 1920s appearance and is open for guided tours. The other two currently serve as private residences, one of which is occupied by the lighthouse's historic site manager, who could be considered a modern-day "keeper."

BEAVER BAY

Established in 1856, Beaver Bay is the North Shore's oldest permanent settlement. Originally settled by German immigrants, the city is bordered on the east by the Beaver River, which empties into a Lake Superior bay that shares its name. Today, the community is home to several gift stores, restaurants, and lodging.

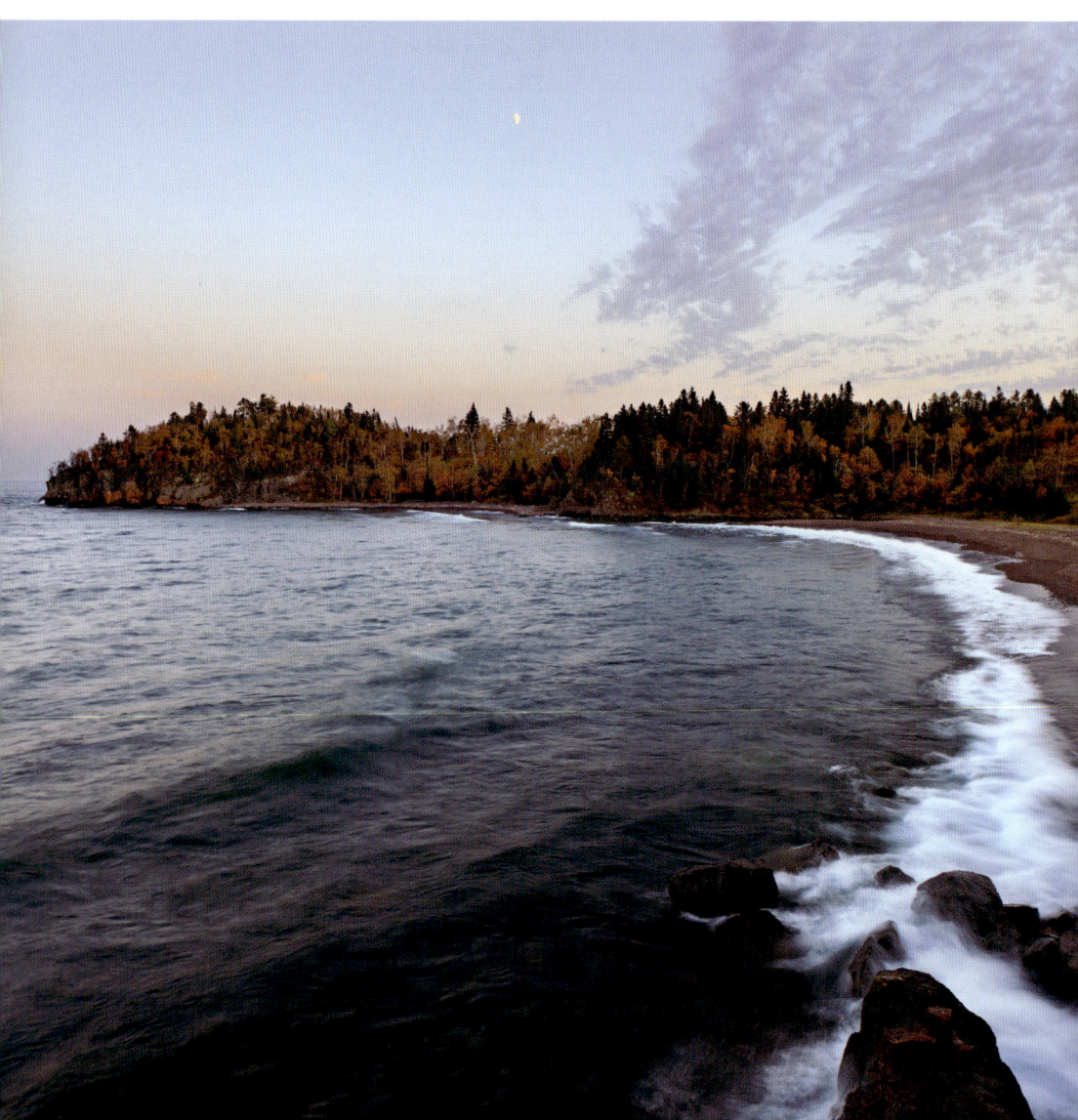

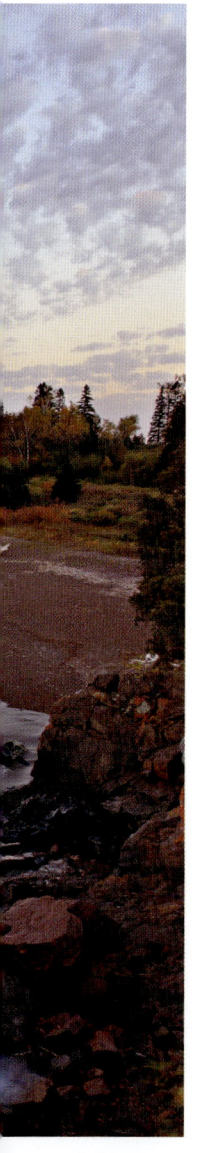

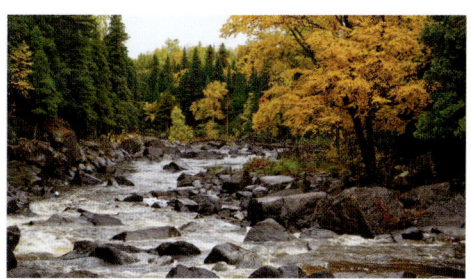

BEAVER RIVER ➤

Draining into Lake Superior's Beaver Bay, Beaver River exhibits the classic characteristics of a North Shore stream, including a large, exposed basalt bedrock and several cascading waterfalls within the last few miles of its 23.4-mile-long course. While not contained within the boundaries of a state park, its largest series of falls can be easily enjoyed from the pedestrian walkway on the north side of the Highway 61 bridge over the river. The most upstream of the cascades, Glen Avon Falls, is accessed from an unmarked area along County Highway 3, just west of Lax Lake Road. Other falls can be seen from a portion of the Superior Hiking Trail that follows the river.

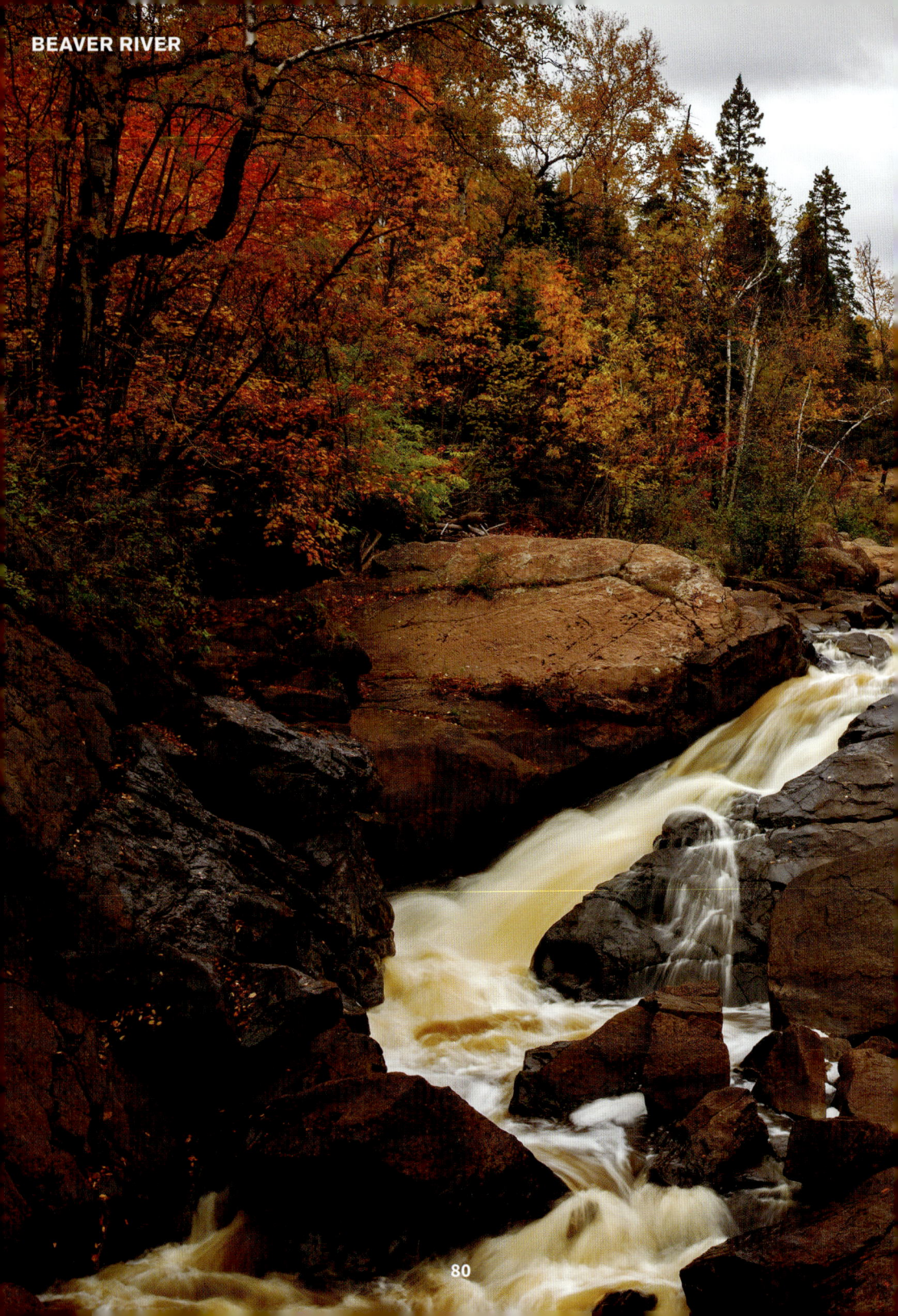

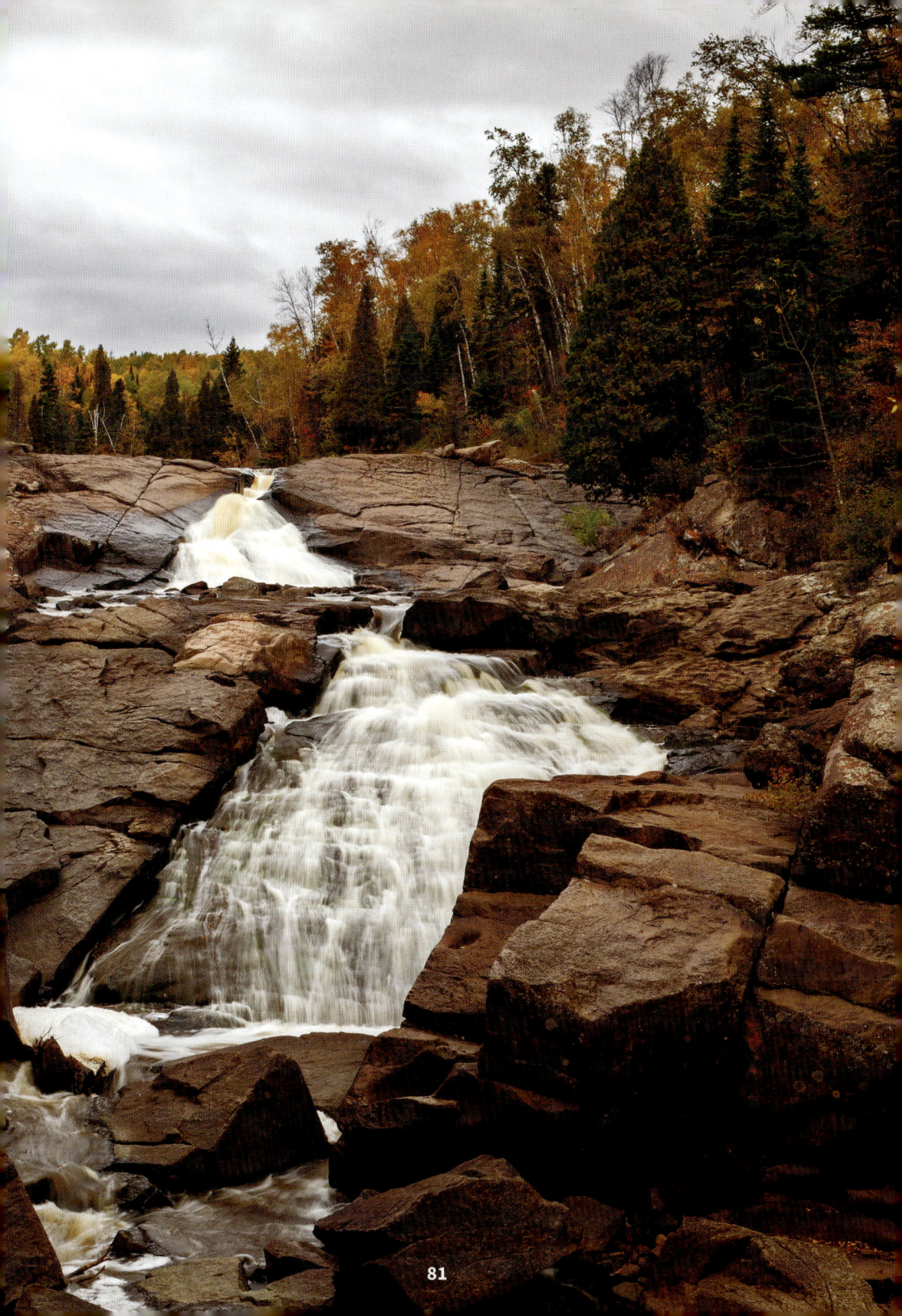

SILVER BAY MARINA

Owned by the Minnesota Department of Natural Resources and operated by the City of Silver Bay, this 110-slip safe harbor and marina serves as a public access to Lake Superior as well as a launching point for several charter boats offering scenic cruises and fishing excursions. About 40 feet beneath the surface of the water, near the west breakwall, lies the wreck of the *Hesper*, a steamship that sank in a spring storm in 1905. Other marina amenities include a deck and gazebo, an adjacent city park with a picnic area, and modern restrooms.

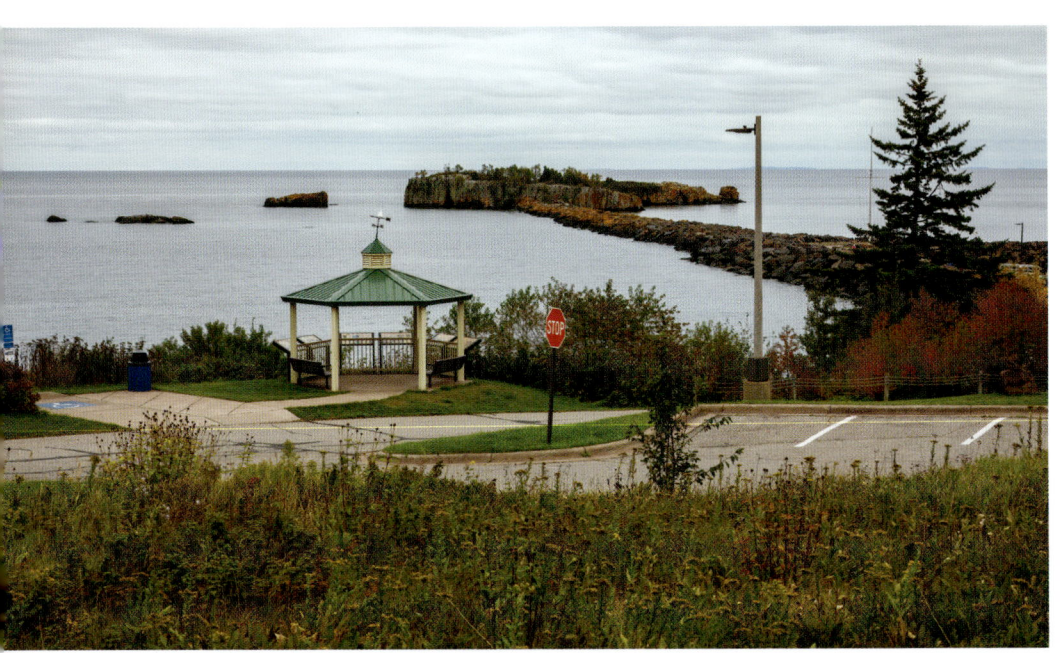

ROCKY TACONITE

An anthropomorphic pair of taconite pellets named Rocky Taconite greets visitors to the city of Silver Bay, the youngest settlement on the North Shore. Silver Bay was founded in 1954 as a company town for the expansive taconite plant operated by Reserve Mining (now Cleveland-Cliffs Inc.). The development of pelletized taconite processing technology was instrumental in the continuation of America's steel industry after the supply of high-grade iron ore was fully mined by the end of World War II. Dedicated in 1964, the 12-foot statue stands as a proud symbol of the city's heritage.

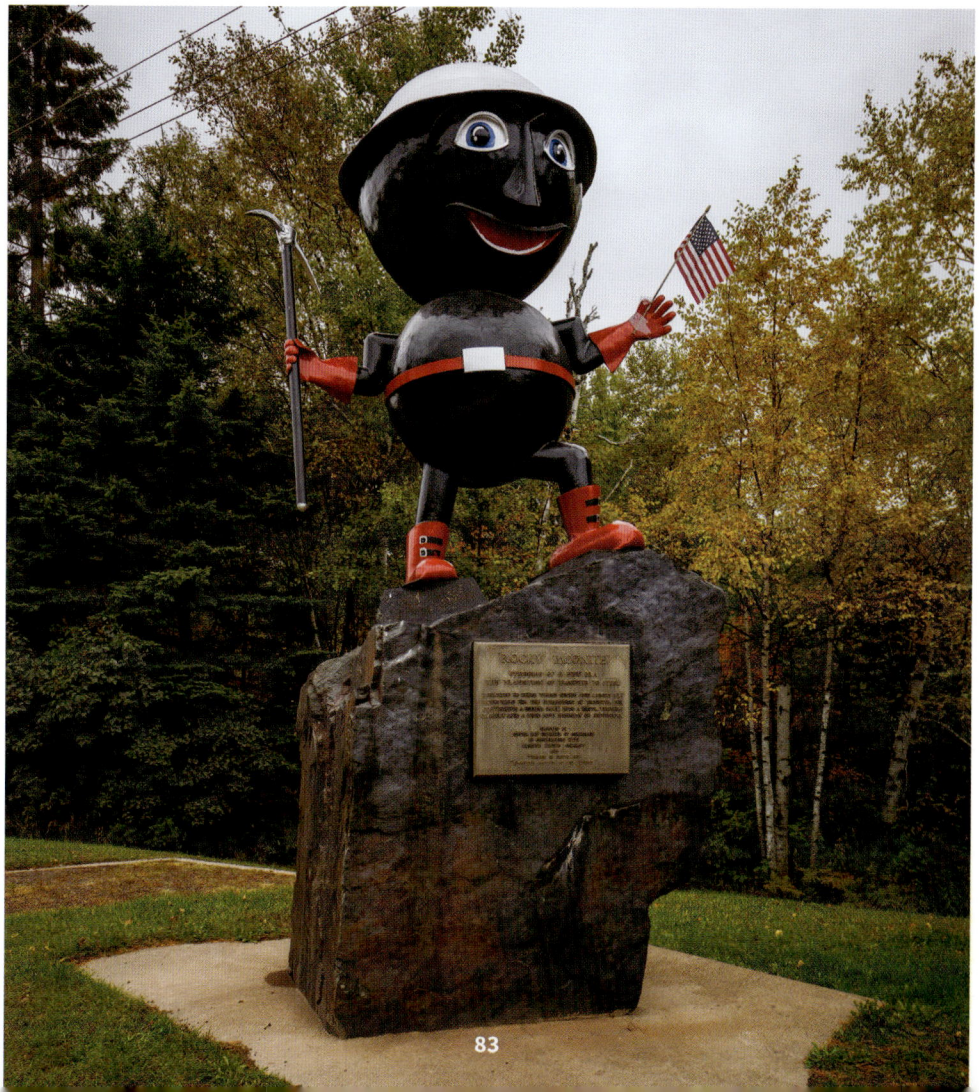

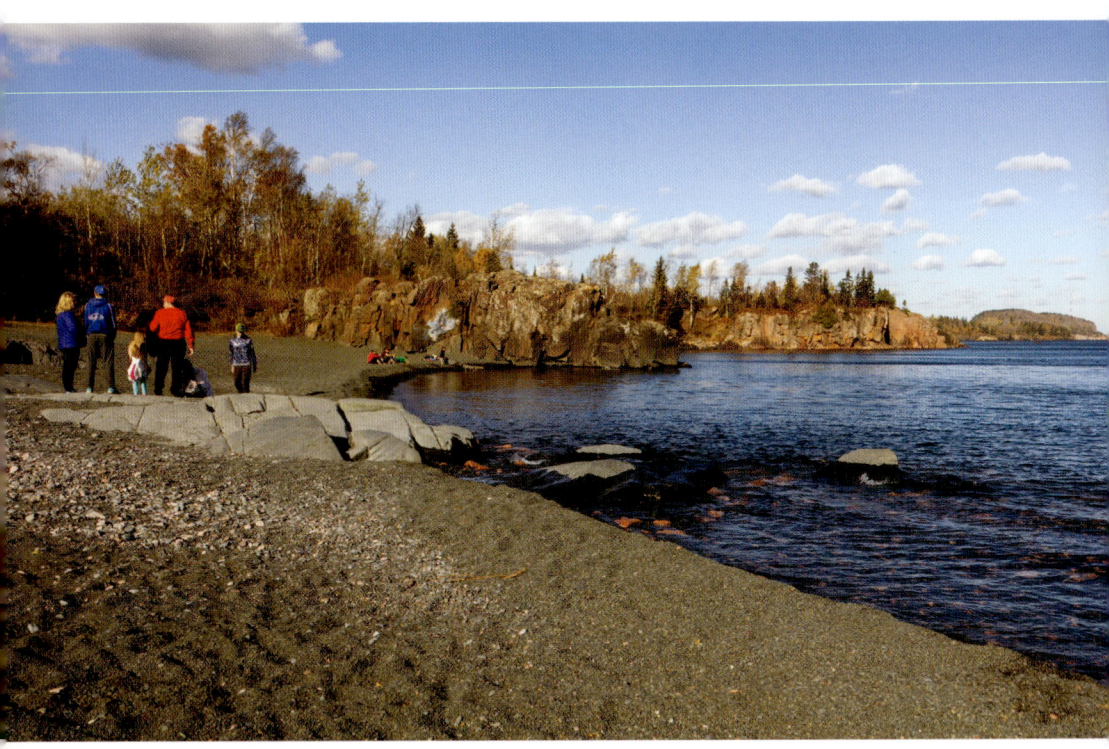

BLACK BEACH

Not long ago, Black Beach was a semi-secret refuge on Lake Superior, utilized primarily by residents of Silver Bay and savvy tourists. On private land owned by the local taconite processing plant, it officially became a public beach in 2015, following a lease agreement between the plant, the Minnesota Department of Natural Resources, and the City of Silver Bay. The beach, also known as Onyx Beach, is named for its unique black sand, which originated from the massive dumping of taconite tailings (waste products of production) from the nearby plant into Lake Superior from the 1950s through the 1970s.

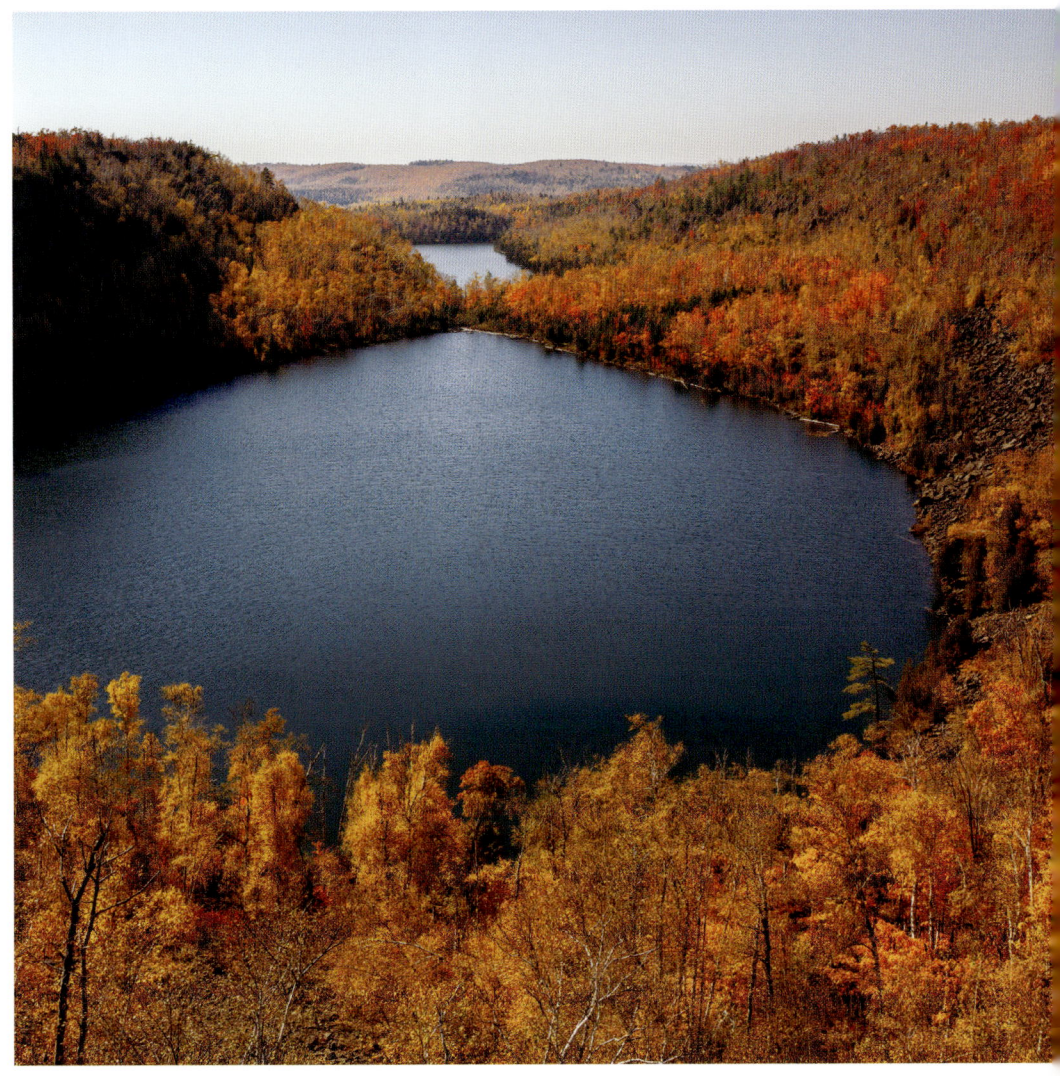

BEAN AND BEAR LAKES

Also known as the Twin Lakes Trail, a ruggedly challenging 6.8-mile loop on the western end of Tettegouche State Park brings hikers to a ridgeline showcasing breathtaking views of Bean and Bear Lakes, each set within a deep valley below. During autumn, the surrounding red and gold foliage contrasts beautifully with the deep blue of the alpine-like lakes on a sunny day. Several relatively flat rocky overlooks provide excellent perches to relax or enjoy a picnic lunch.

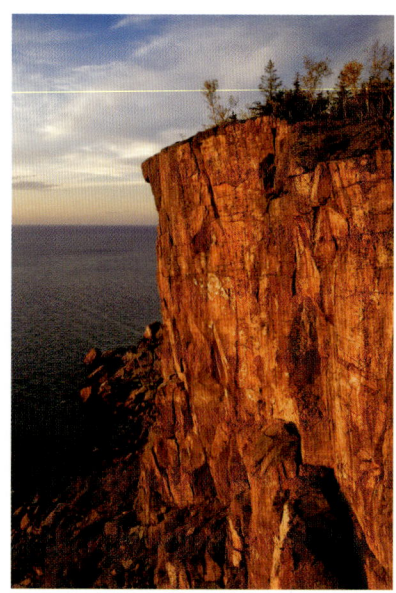

PALISADE HEAD

Towering as much as 300 feet over Lake Superior and with a 180-foot cliff face, Palisade Head offers some of the best panoramic views of Lake Superior and the Sawtooth Mountains. As a noncontiguous part of Tettegouche State Park, a winding narrow road from Highway 61 leads to a parking and viewing area at the top. The cliff face, offering several challenging routes, is a favorite of experienced rock climbers in the region. As with Shovel Point, the large rocky outcrop just to the north, Palisade Head is primarily composed of rhyolite, a volcanic rock highly resistant to erosion.

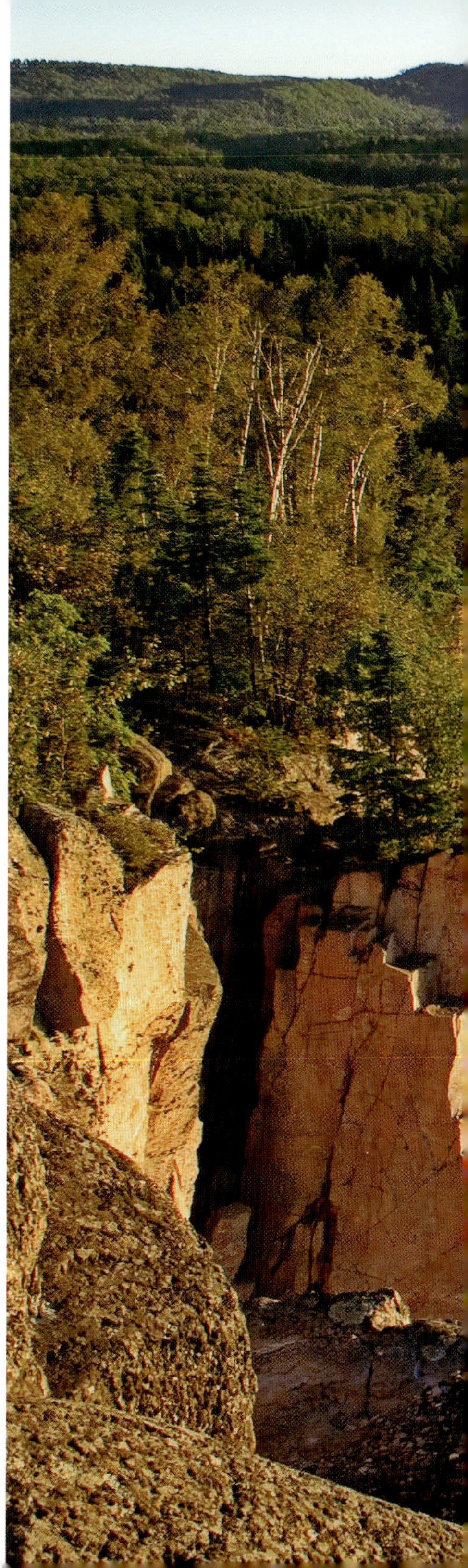

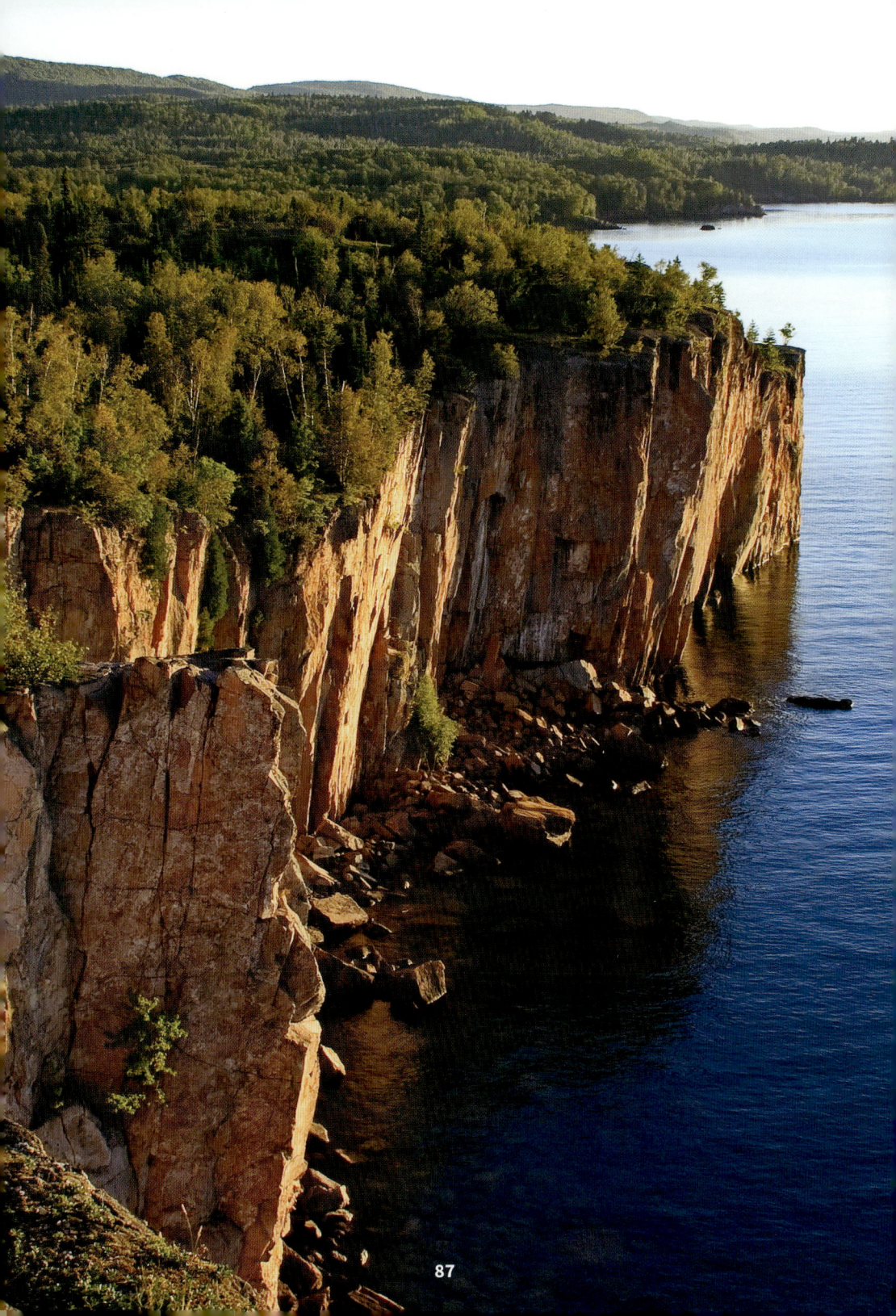

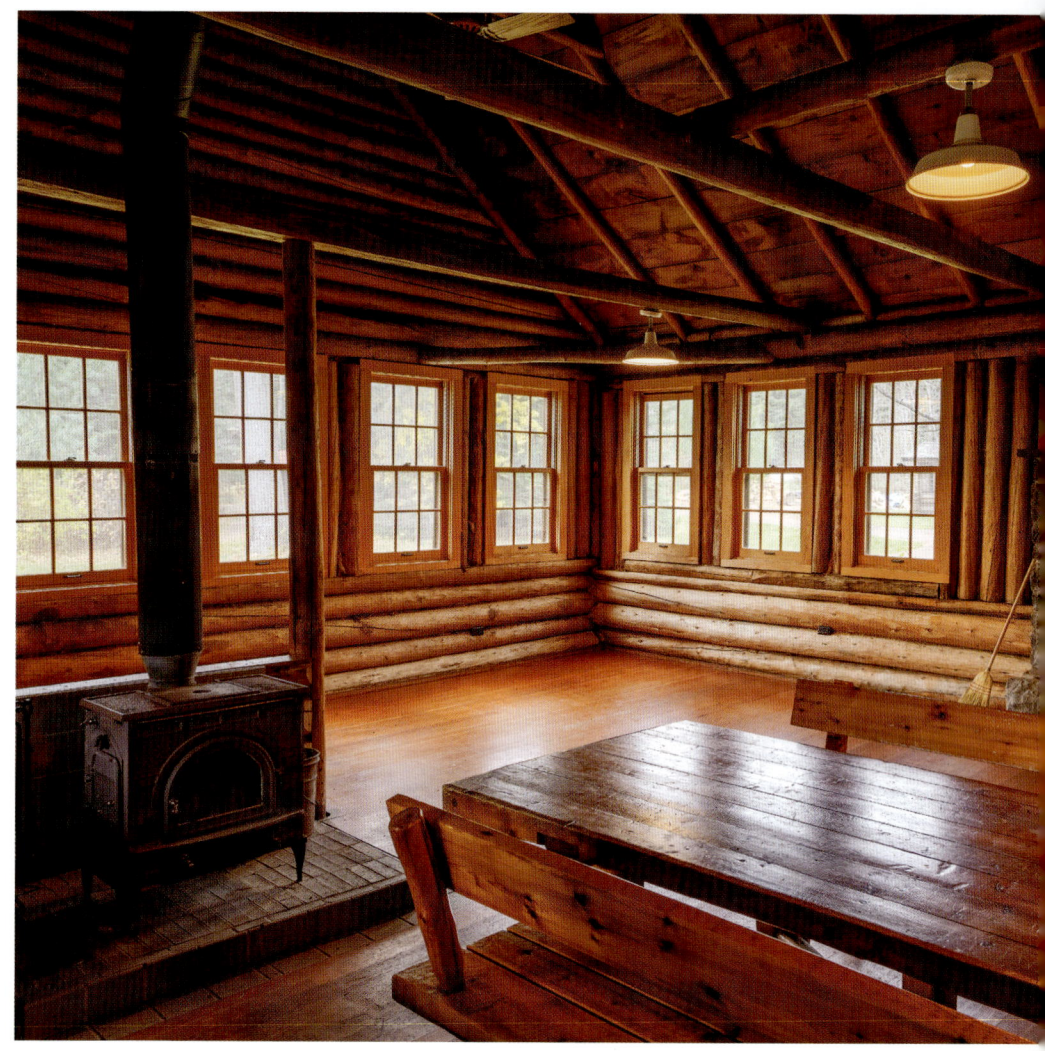

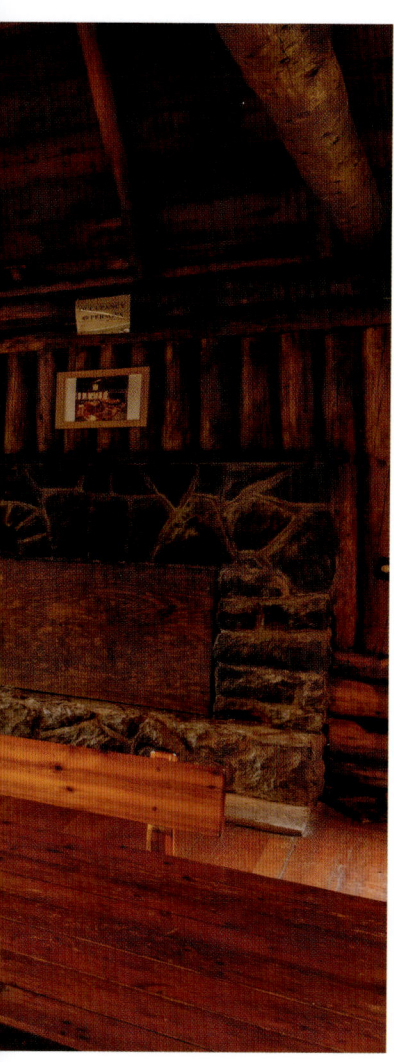

HISTORIC TETTEGOUCHE CAMP

In 1895, Michigan-based logging business Alger, Smith & Co. purchased land and set up a logging camp within what is now Tettegouche State Park. Much of the area was logged, leaving only a small section of the majestic old-growth red and white pines. Land containing the untouched pines was sold to a group of Duluth businessmen, who became known as the "Tettegouche Club." The group established an exclusive retreat on the site while promoting conservation of the land. In 1979, after exchanging hands a few times, the property was sold to the State of Minnesota and combined with Baptism River State Park to form Tettegouche State Park as we know it today. The historic Tettegouche Lodge is available for day use, and the restored cabins can be rented for overnight stays. However, all gear and supplies must be carried in on the 1.7-mile hike from the parking area on Lax Lake Road or a longer walk from the main park trailhead.

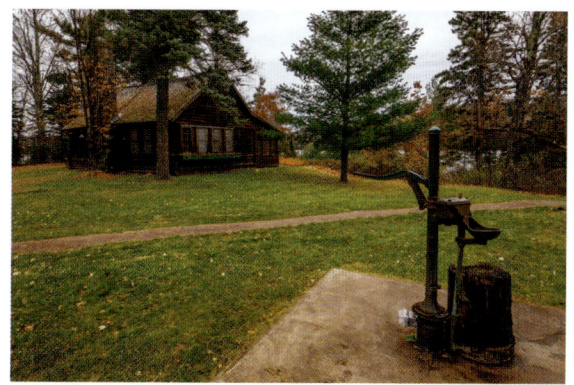

SHOVEL POINT AND SEA STACK

Like Palisade Head to the south, Shovel Point consists of a large rocky outcrop extending outward into Lake Superior. A 1.2-mile round-trip, moderately difficult trail from the Tettegouche State Park visitor center takes hikers to a viewing platform at the tip of the point. Along the way, a spur trail to the right leads to a beach below with excellent views of Shovel Point, as well as a small sea stack (a column of rock in the sea), which was once part of a famous sea arch that unexpectedly collapsed in August 2010.

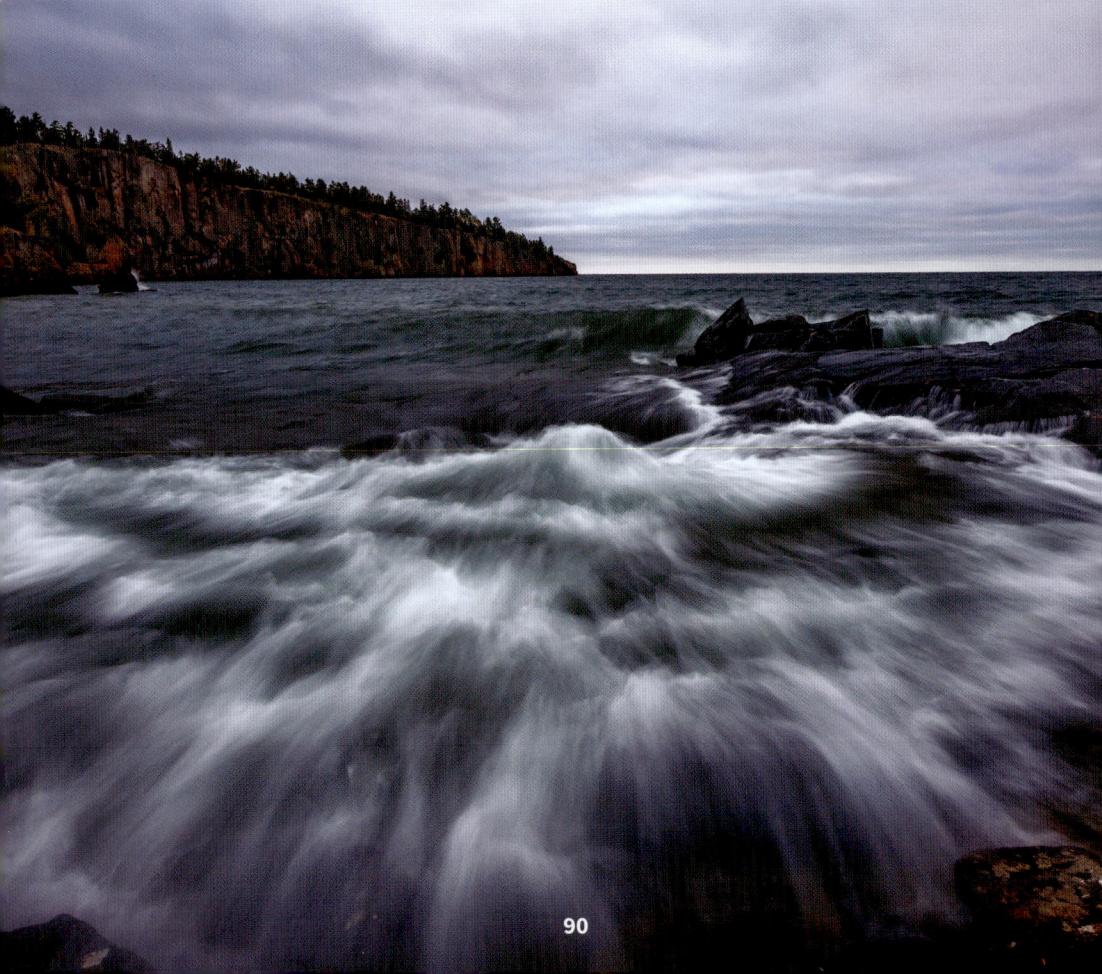

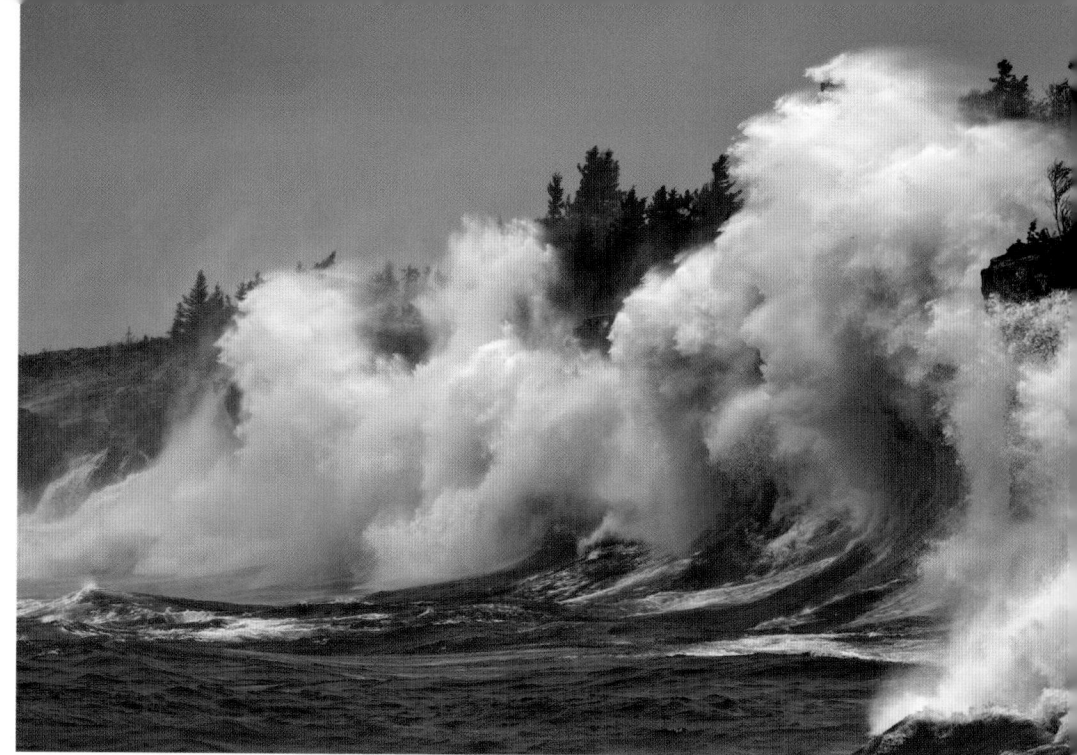

CRYSTAL BAY

With its exposed east-facing cliff faces, Crystal Bay is among the best locations on the North Shore to witness the power of Lake Superior gales as huge waves slam against the rocky shore. On calmer days, the beach offers a quiet spot to enjoy the beauty of the lake and view a sea cave within the cliff to the north, which can be explored by kayak. Crystal Bay is also the location of 3M's short-lived mining operation in the early 1900s, which failed to yield the valuable corundum the company's founders were seeking and nearly bankrupted the startup company. Crystal Bay Beach is reached via a short but steep trail from Highway 61, just east of Crystal Creek.

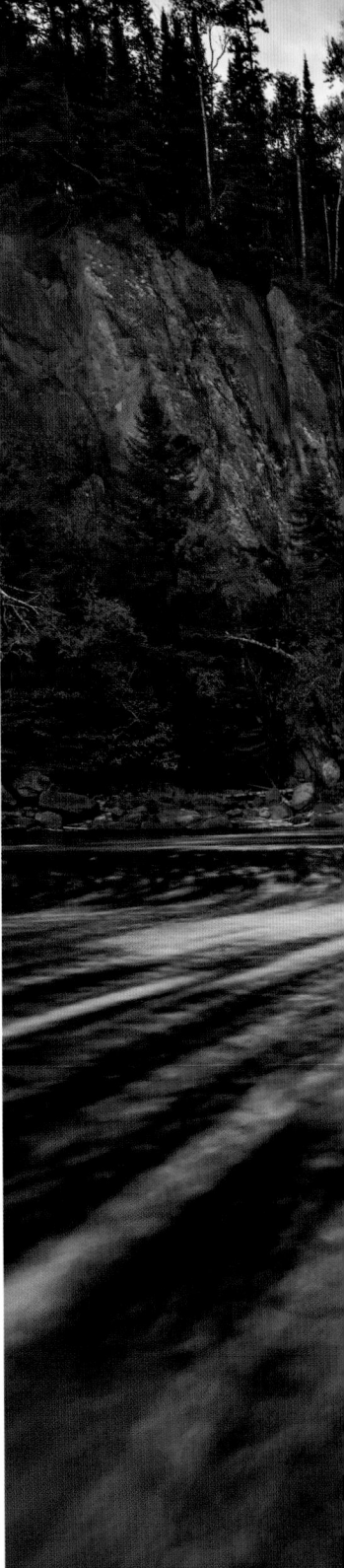

BAPTISM RIVER HIGH FALLS

The aptly named High Falls of the Baptism River, in Tettegouche State Park, plunges 60 feet in a single cascade, making it the highest waterfall entirely within Minnesota. A moderately difficult 0.7-mile one-way trek from the trail center takes hikers over a suspension bridge and to the base of the massive falls. This hike is often combined with Two Step Falls, about a half mile downstream.

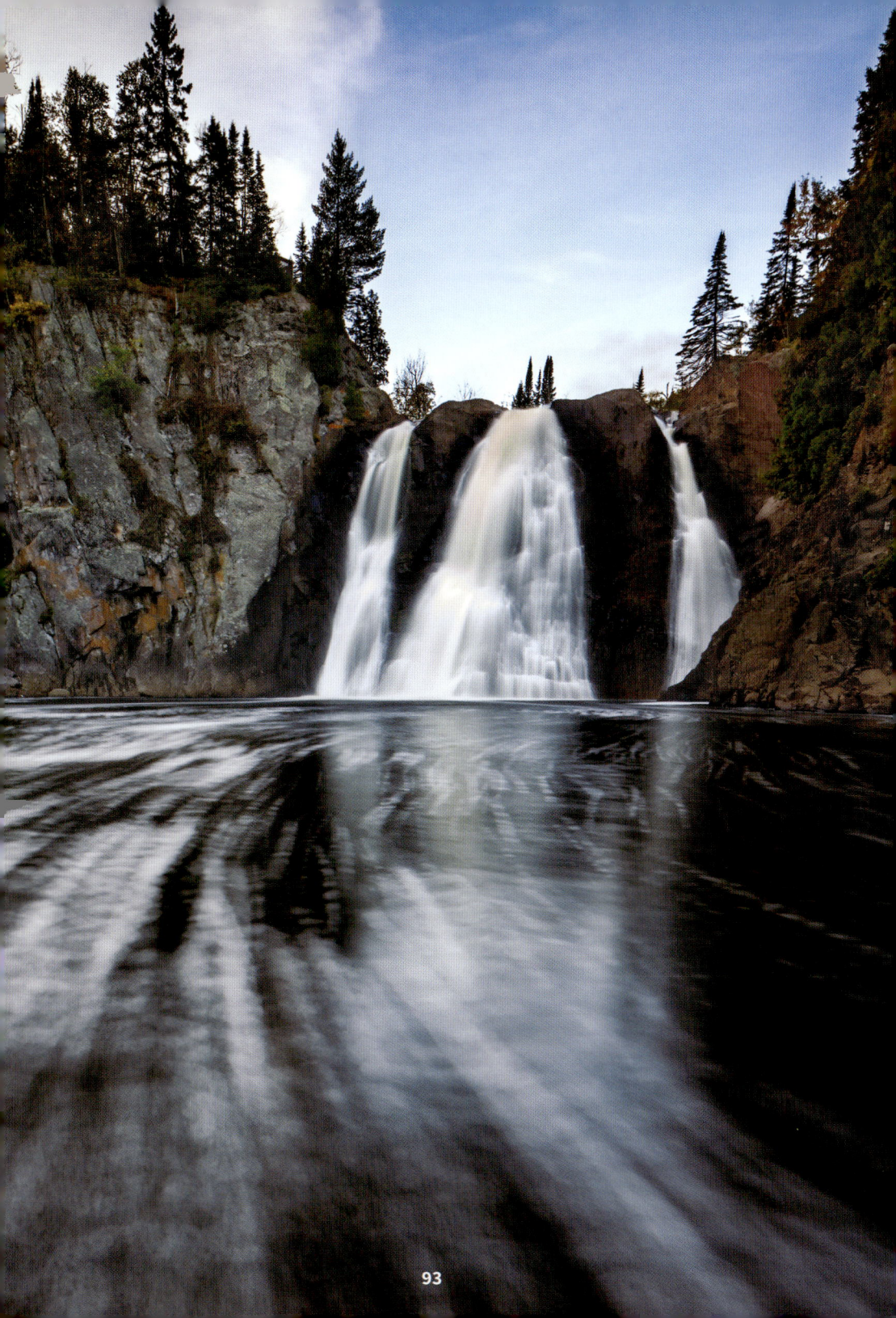

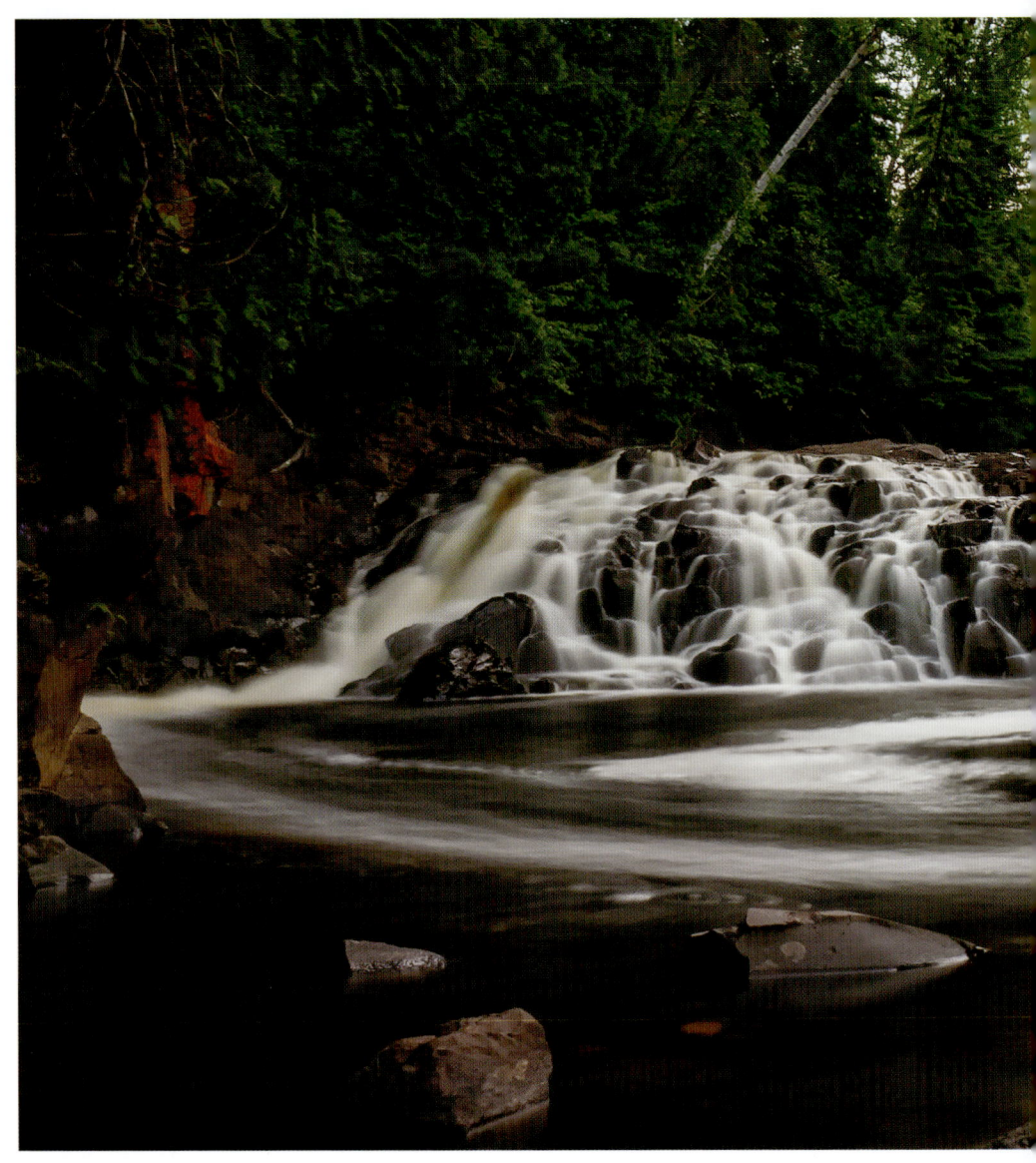

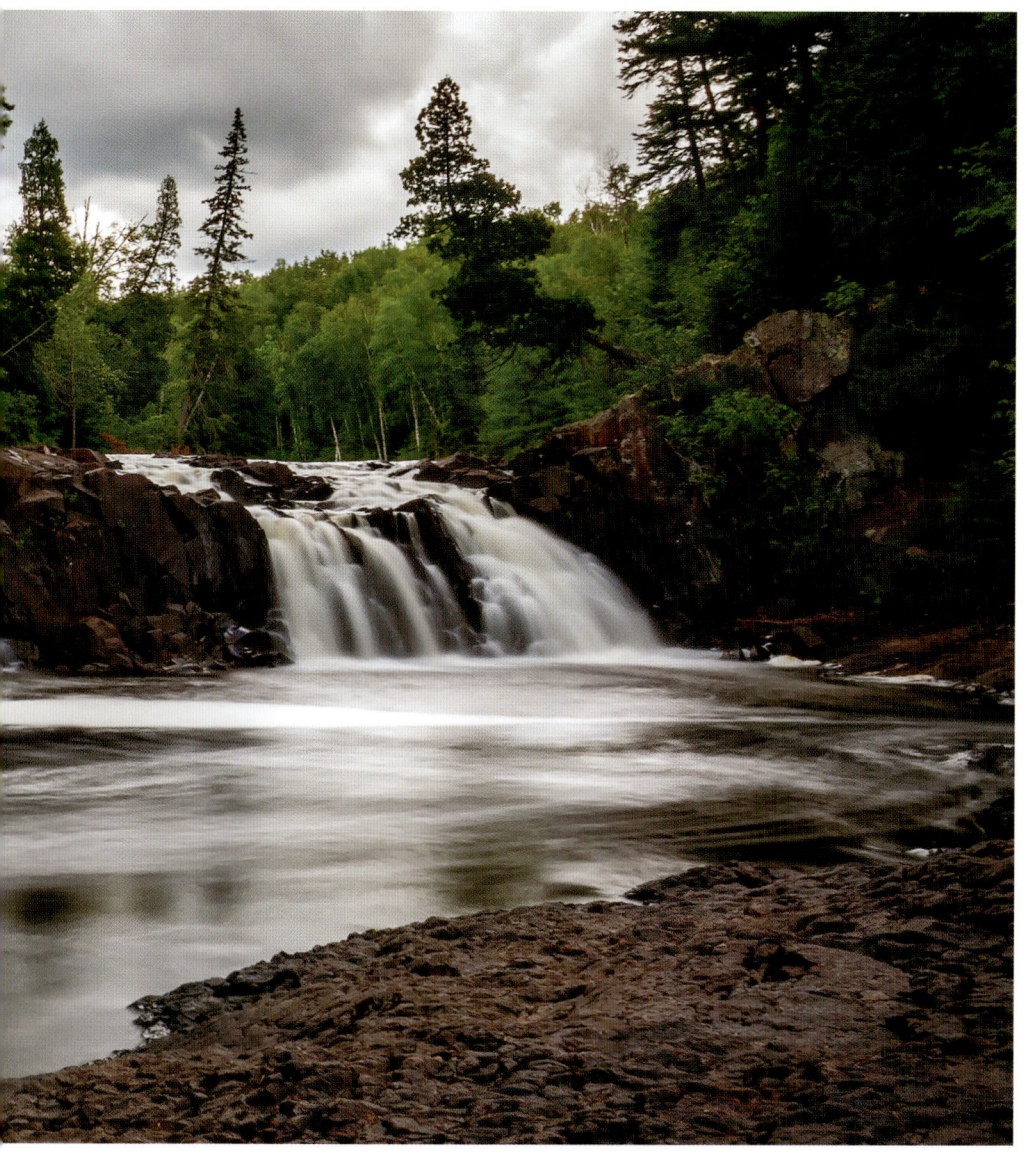

TWO STEP FALLS

While much less impressive than High Falls, Two Step Falls consists of two separate cascades, each dropping about 15 feet. This set of waterfalls can be accessed from trails on either side of the river. The shortest route is from the main trailhead, through the campground, and down the 175 steps to the falls.

ILLGEN FALLS

Off the beaten path and not accessible from the main area of Tettegouche State Park, Illgen Falls appears much larger than its 35-foot drop suggests, especially during high water on the Baptism River. Its power is best appreciated from a rocky overlook bordering the falls, at the end of a short path leading from a small parking area adjacent to Highway 1.

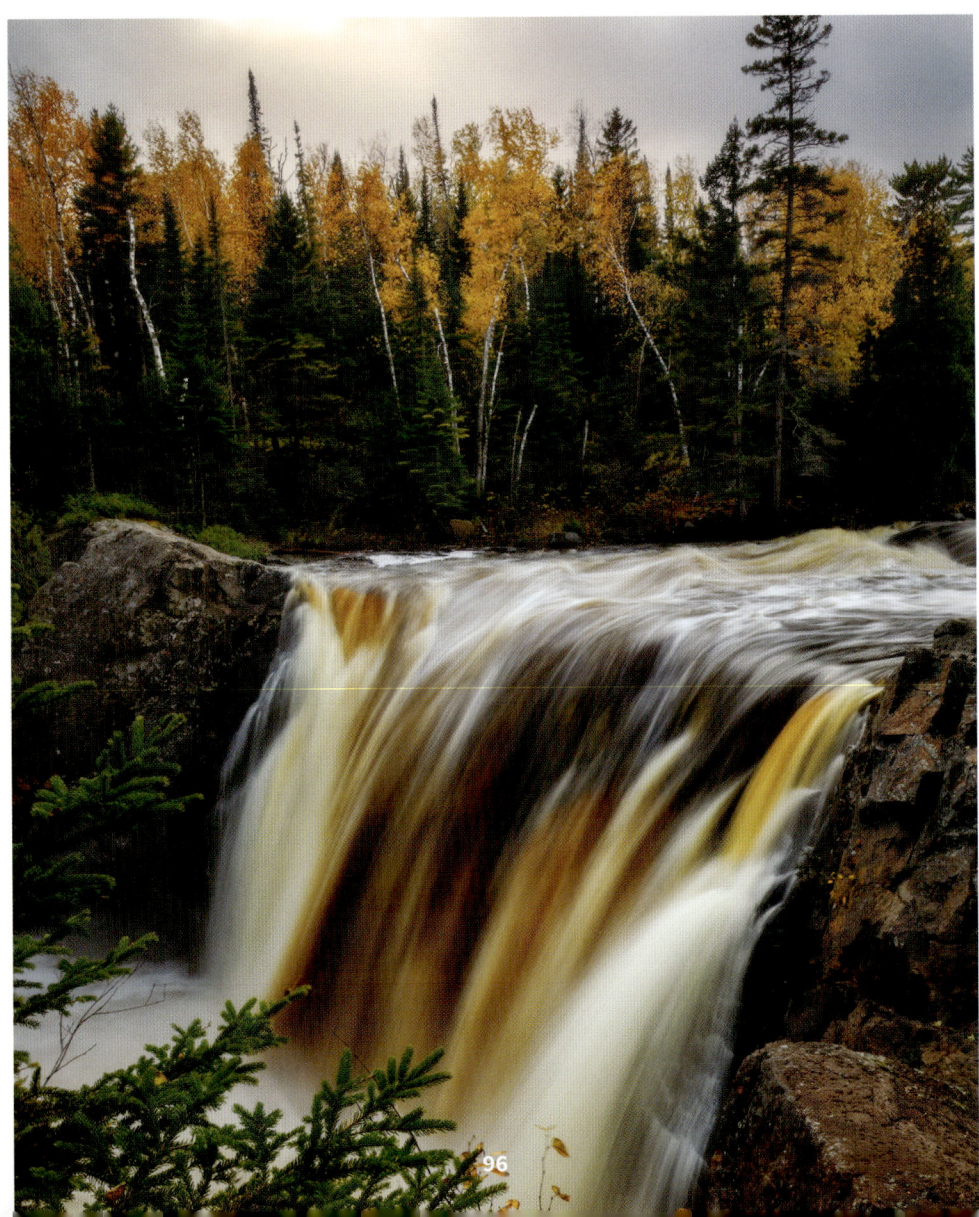

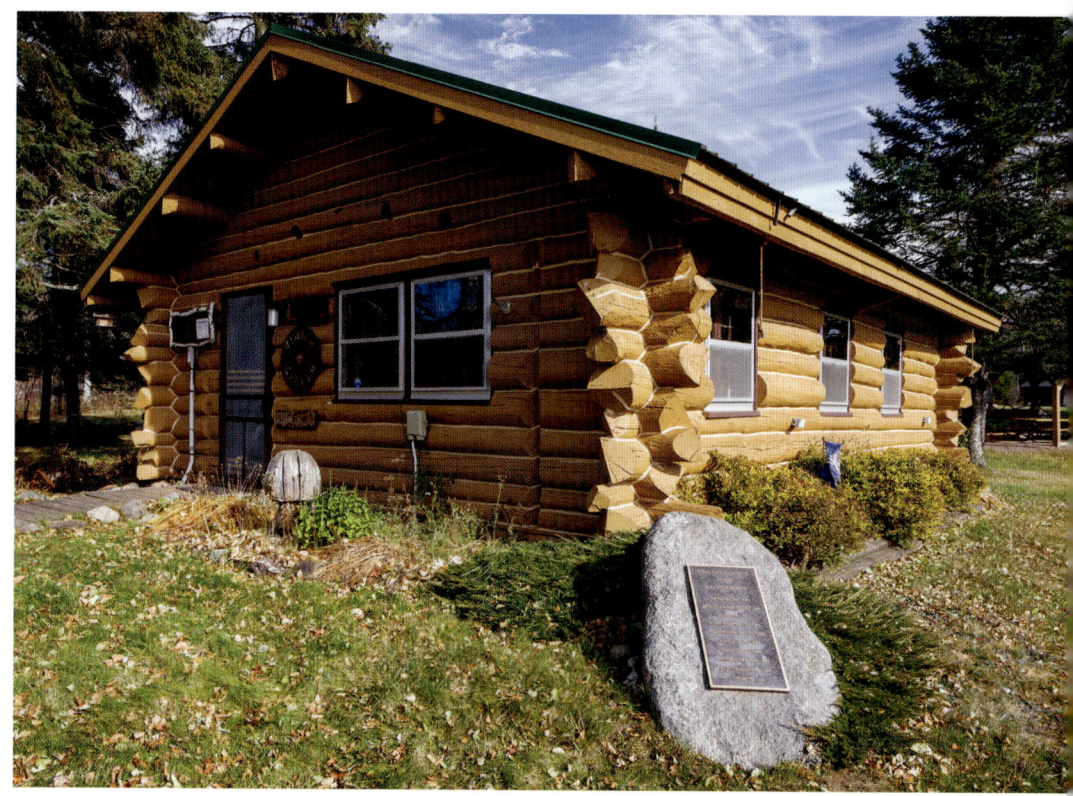

FINLAND MINNESOTA HERITAGE SITE

Acquired by Finland Minnesota Historical Society in 1986 after years of vacancy, the heritage site consists of a 40-acre homestead once owned by John Pine, a bachelor who suddenly and mysteriously disappeared after leaving his home for a walk in 1960. Today, the site not only contains the well-preserved home of John Pine, but also several buildings and artifacts that were donated and moved to the homestead to help share the stories of pioneer life and the Finnish heritage of eastern Lake County.

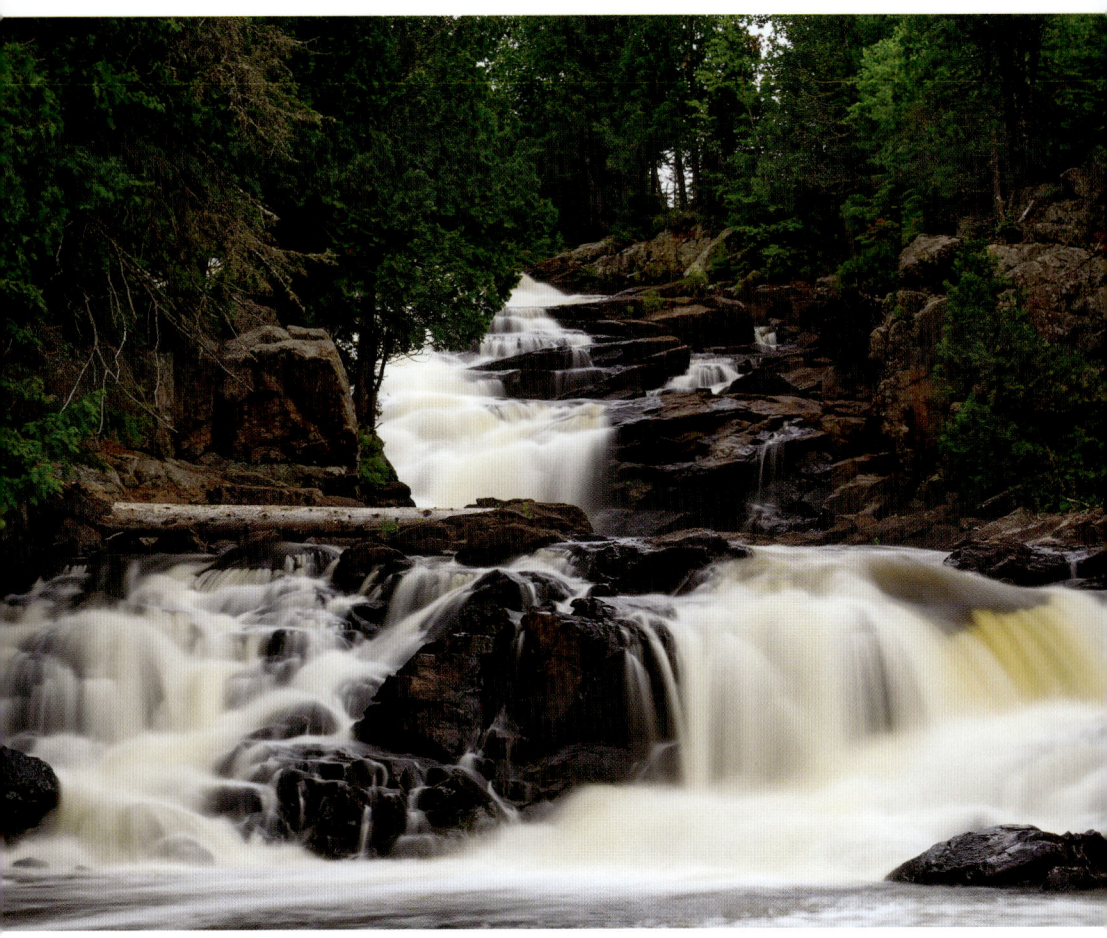

GEORGE H. CROSBY MANITOU STATE PARK

On land donated in 1955 by mining magnate George H. Crosby, the state park bearing his name has remained relatively undeveloped since its inception, containing Minnesota's first backpacking-only campground. A testament to its visionary organizers, the park maintains a wilderness-like setting to this day, with its dense boreal forest surrounding a wild volcanic gorge containing the Manitou River and its many cascades. Allowing only non-motorized watercraft, Benson Lake offers paddlers a taste of the Boundary Waters Canoe Area Wilderness several dozen miles to the north. It is also the only state park on Minnesota's North Shore not directly accessible from Highway 61.

CARIBOU FALLS STATE WAYSIDE

The preeminent attraction of the state wayside bearing its name, Caribou Falls drops 35 feet from a narrow gorge into a large pool at its base. A relatively level trail extends 0.7 mile from a parking area near Highway 61 to a set of wooden stairs leading down to the base of the falls. At the top of the stairs, the trail continues along the river gorge and intersects with the Superior Hiking Trail, offering opportunities for further exploration of the area.

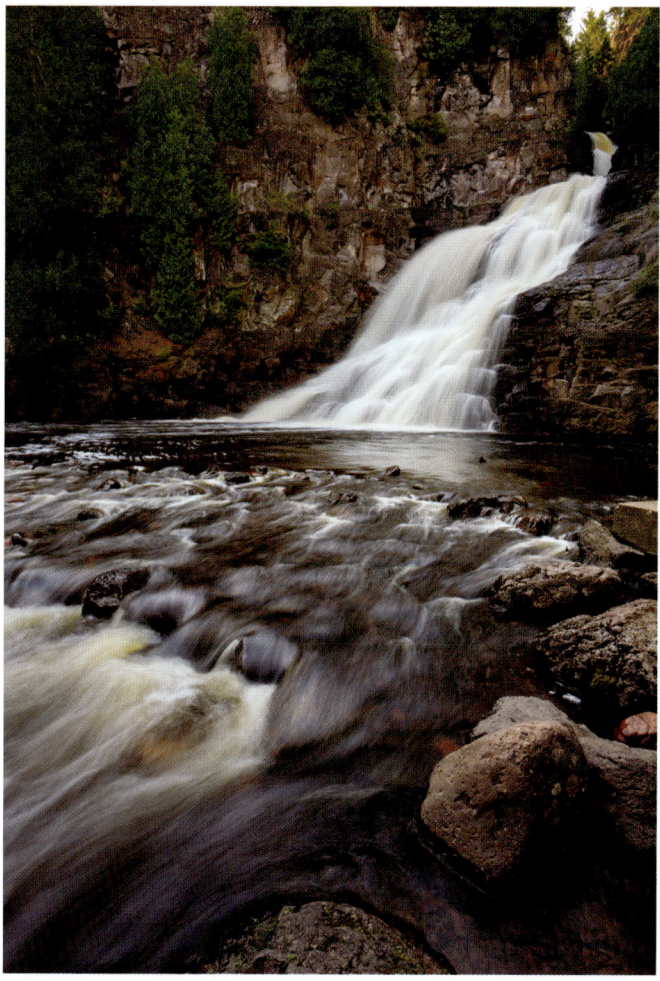

SUGARLOAF COVE

The site of a pulpwood rafting operation for Consolidated Papers Inc. during the middle part of the twentieth century, Sugarloaf Cove exemplifies the efforts made in restoring and preserving coastal land containing unique geology and diverse ecosystems. The 34-acre tract, established in 1993 and owned by Sugarloaf: The North Shore Stewardship Association and the Minnesota Department of Natural Resources, features a staffed nature center and 1-mile interpretive hiking trail that passes through new-growth pine plantations, rocky overlooks, and a cobblestone beach containing smooth multicolored rocks. About 10 acres of the land are a designated Scientific and Natural Area.

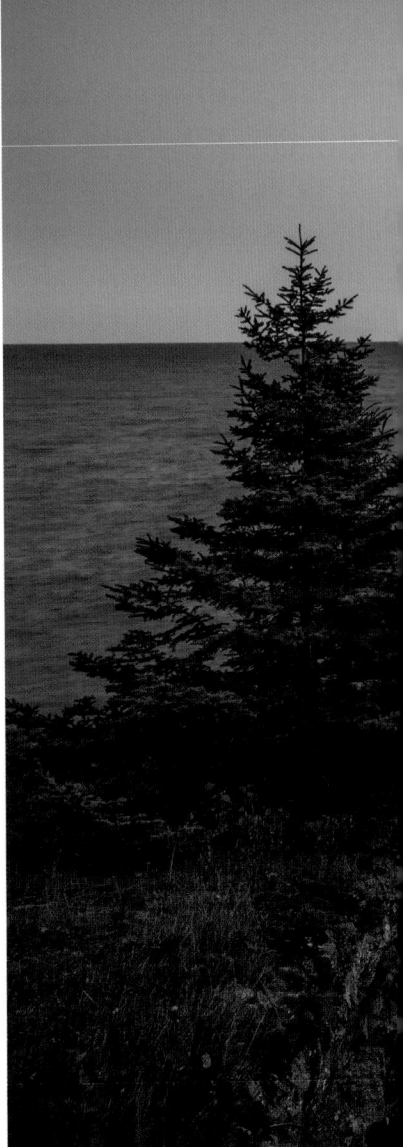

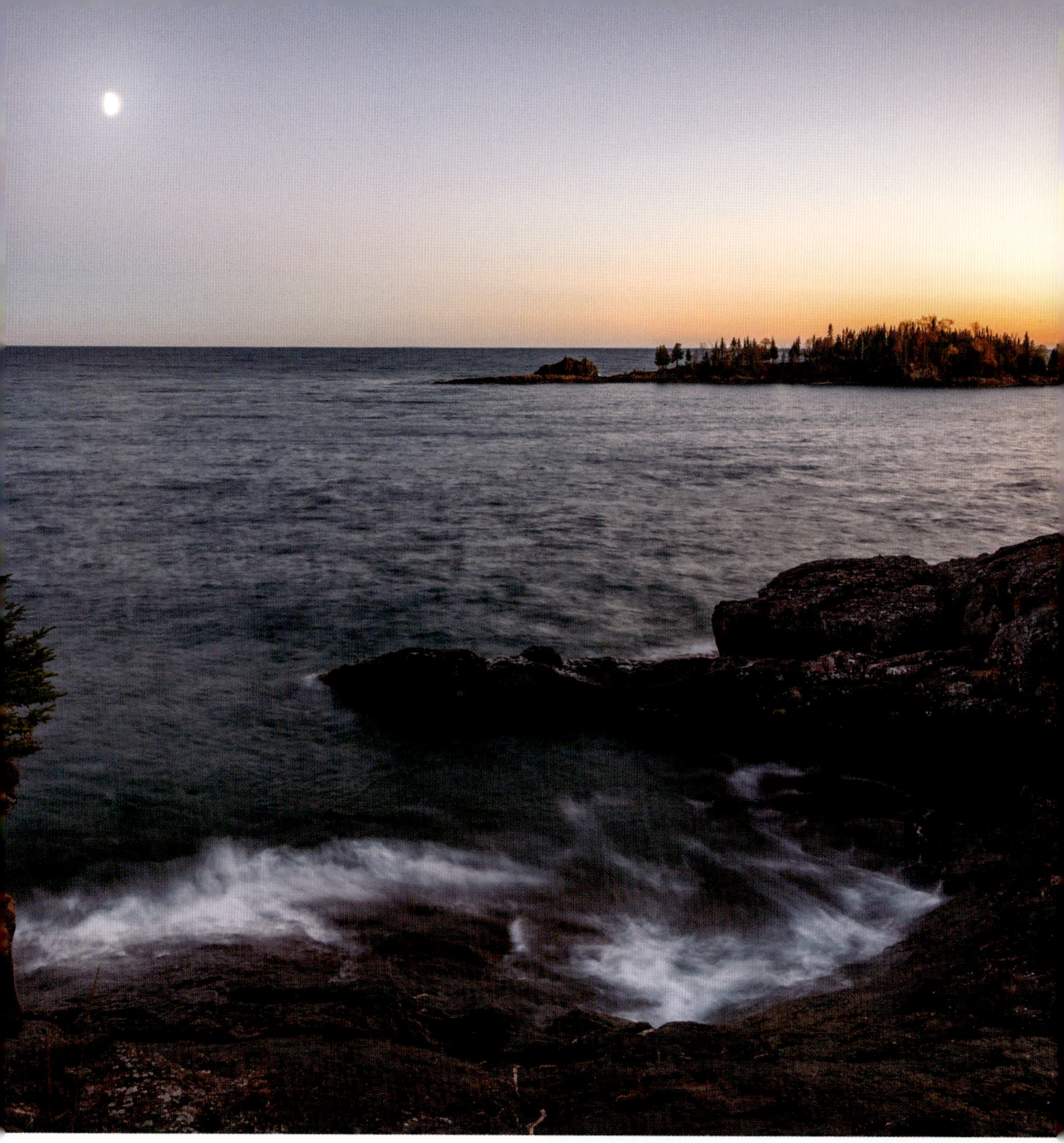

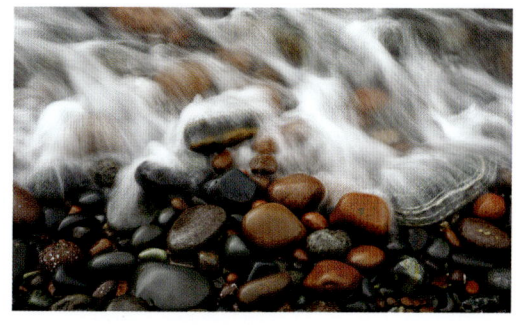

CROSS RIVER

Above the Highway 61 bridge in the town of Schroeder, the Cross River makes a long slide on volcanic basalt, and then it makes its final descent just below the bridge before meandering toward its mouth on Lake Superior. The upper "slide" portion of the falls is easily viewed from the pedestrian walkway on the north side of the bridge. The lower portion is found via a trail, with steps to a viewing platform, on the south side of the highway, near the Cross River Heritage Center. The heritage center, built in 1929 with a distinct Tudor-style architecture, offers exhibits focusing on the region's heritage and culture.

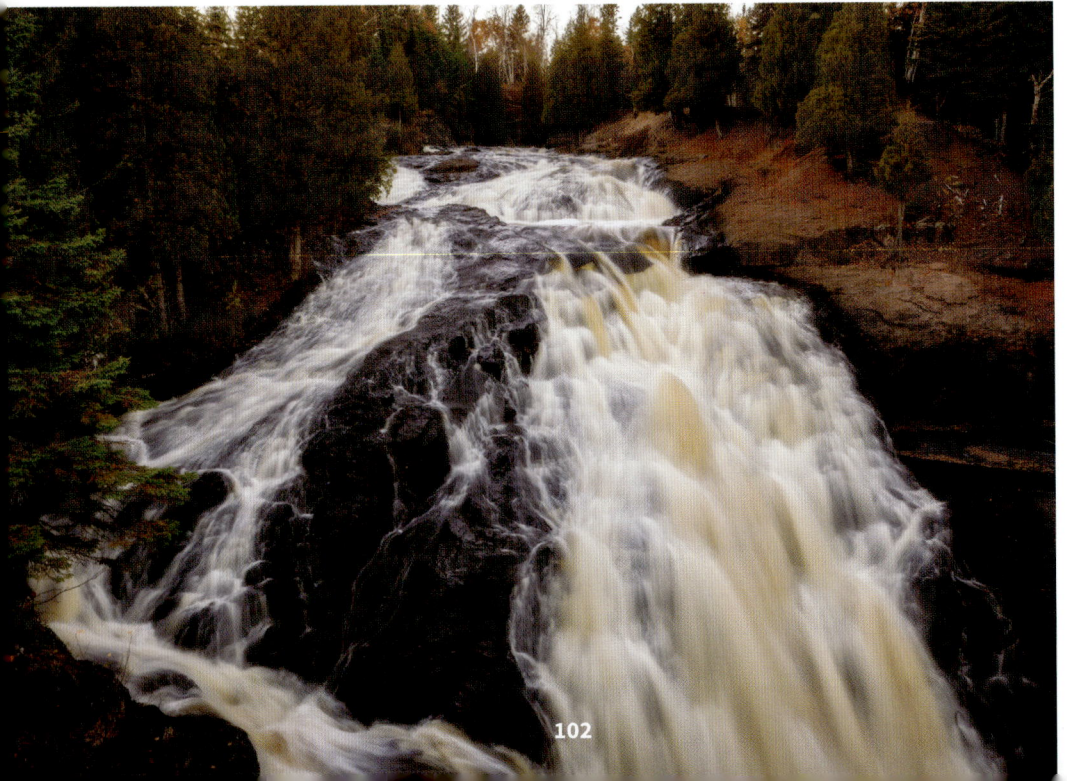

FATHER BARAGA'S CROSS

A Slovenian Catholic priest, Father Frederic Baraga settled and established missions in the Upper Great Lakes region, particularly in northern Michigan and Wisconsin. He was a grammarian of Native American languages and often traveled 100 miles by foot, snowshoes, or canoe to reach and minister to various tribes. In 1846, Father Baraga learned about an epidemic in Grand Portage, Minnesota, and to avoid a long, grueling 200-mile-long trek over land, he and a native guide decided to travel by boat over Lake Superior from the Apostle Islands to the Minnesota shore. Encountering a violent storm midway through their voyage, Baraga prayed for a safe landing and miraculously came ashore at the calm mouth of the present-day Cross River in Schroeder. In thanksgiving, he placed a wooden cross at the site, which was later replaced with the granite cross seen today.

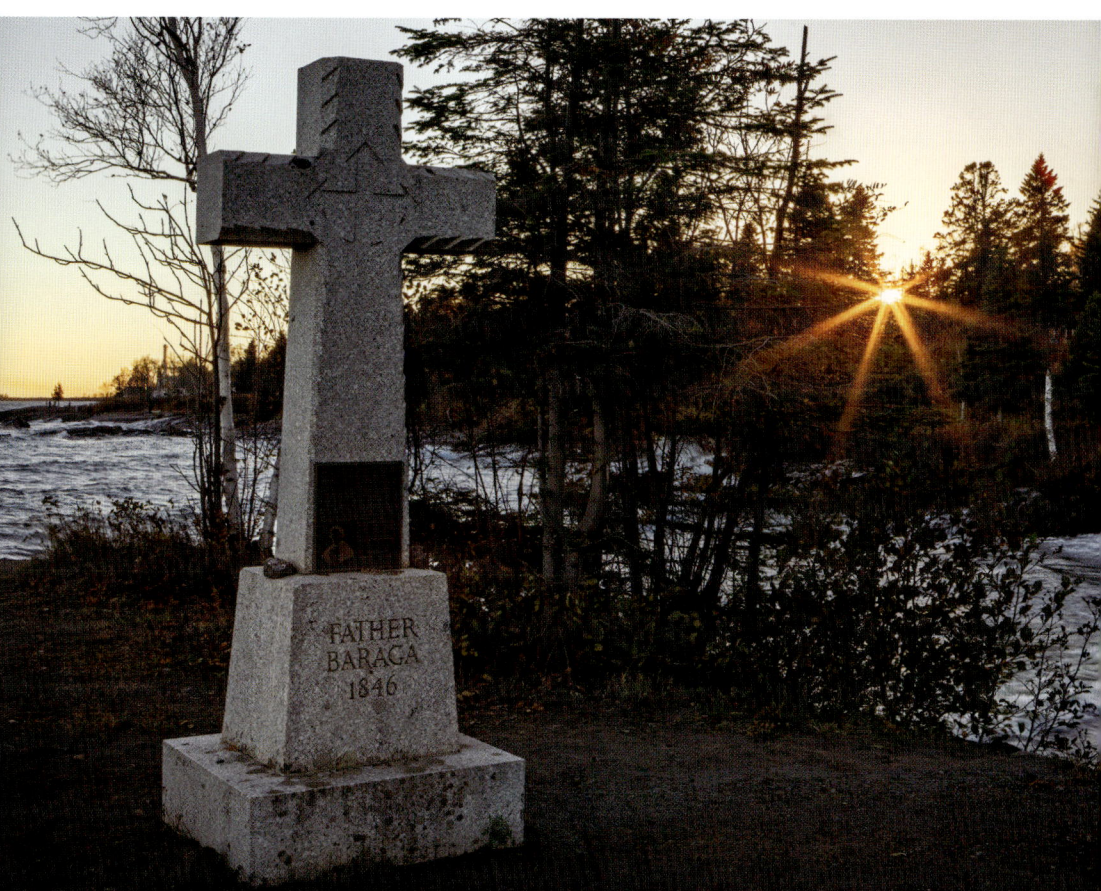

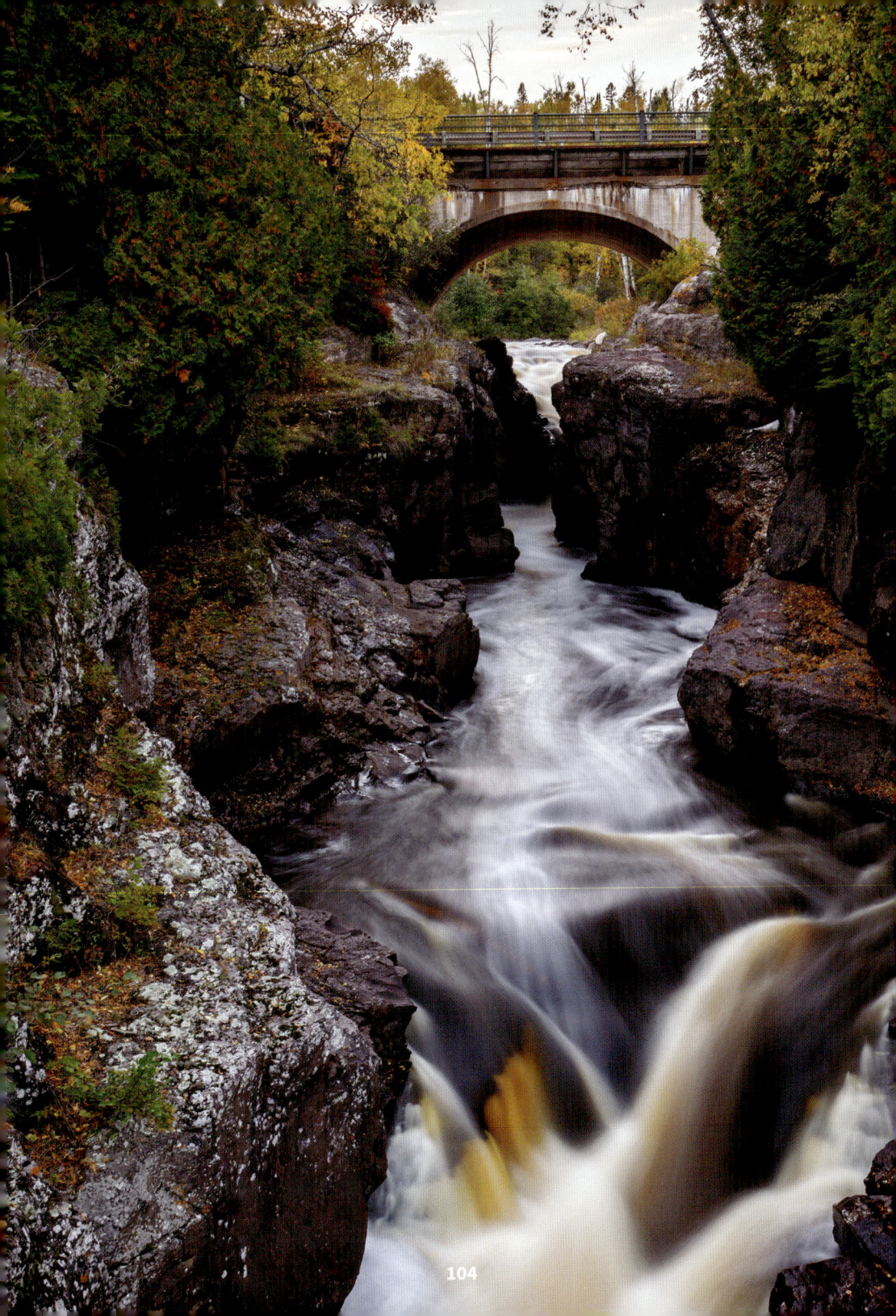

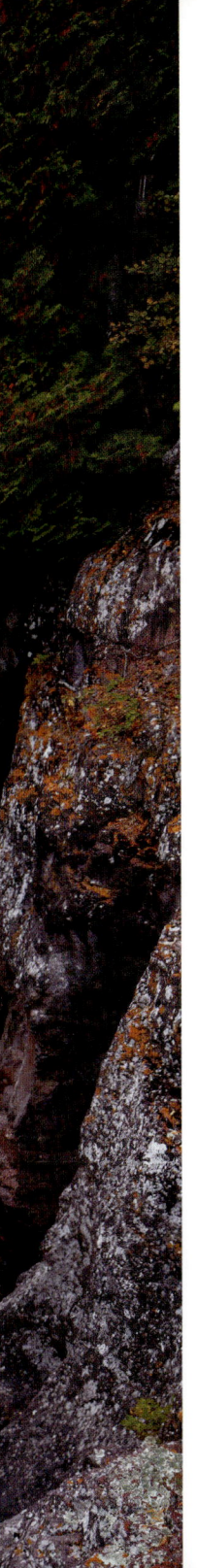
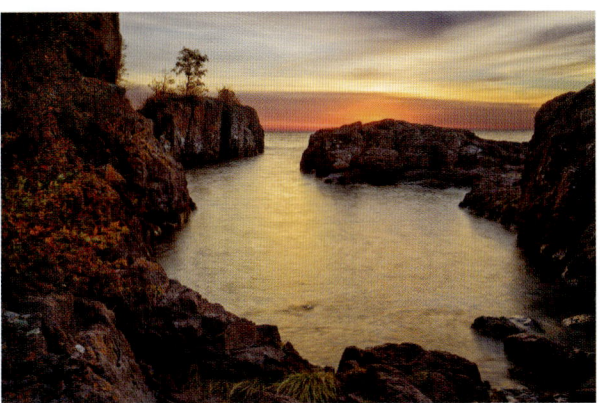

TEMPERANCE RIVER STATE PARK

Established in 1957, Temperance River State Park encompasses more than 5,000 acres of land, including the turbulent last mile of the Temperance River through a narrow, steep-walled gorge containing several waterfalls. Hiking trails follow both sides of the river, offering outstanding views of the deep gorge and outlet into Lake Superior. Unlike with most rivers, Temperance River's mouth lacks a sandbar, hence the stream's name by way of a pun on the word "bar." As rugged as the river gorge, the state park's Lake Superior shore contains numerous rock formations, as well as a beach with picnic area. Two drive-in campgrounds are separately located along the shore on each side of the river's mouth.

TOFTE PARK

Donated to the town of Tofte in 1922 by Elizabeth Tofte, daughter of John Tofte and one of the town's original settlers, this city park is a little-known gem, located right on the shore of Lake Superior. The well-manicured park's hidden treasures include 1,000 feet of Lake Superior shoreline, a boat launch, restrooms, paved trails, and a picnic shelter. A pair of nearly 100-year-old cobblestone bridges were meticulously built, using only red, white, and blue stones.

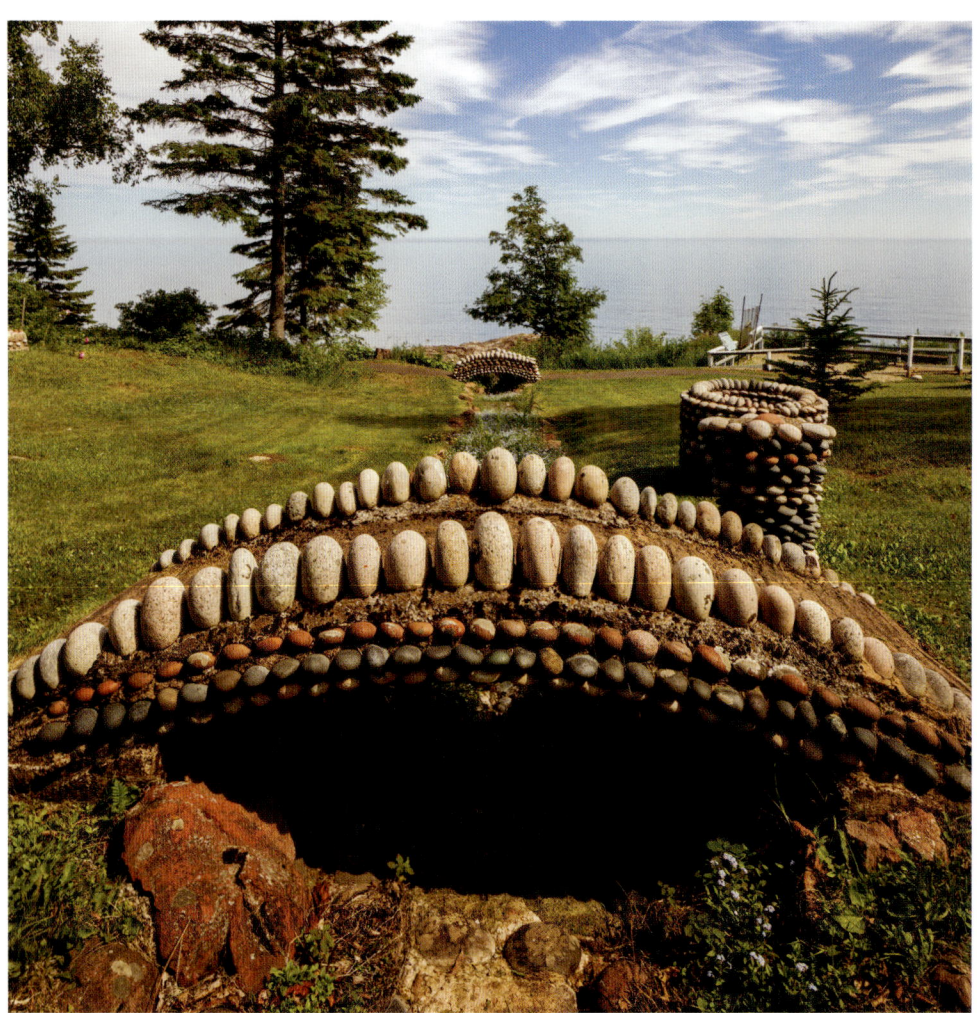

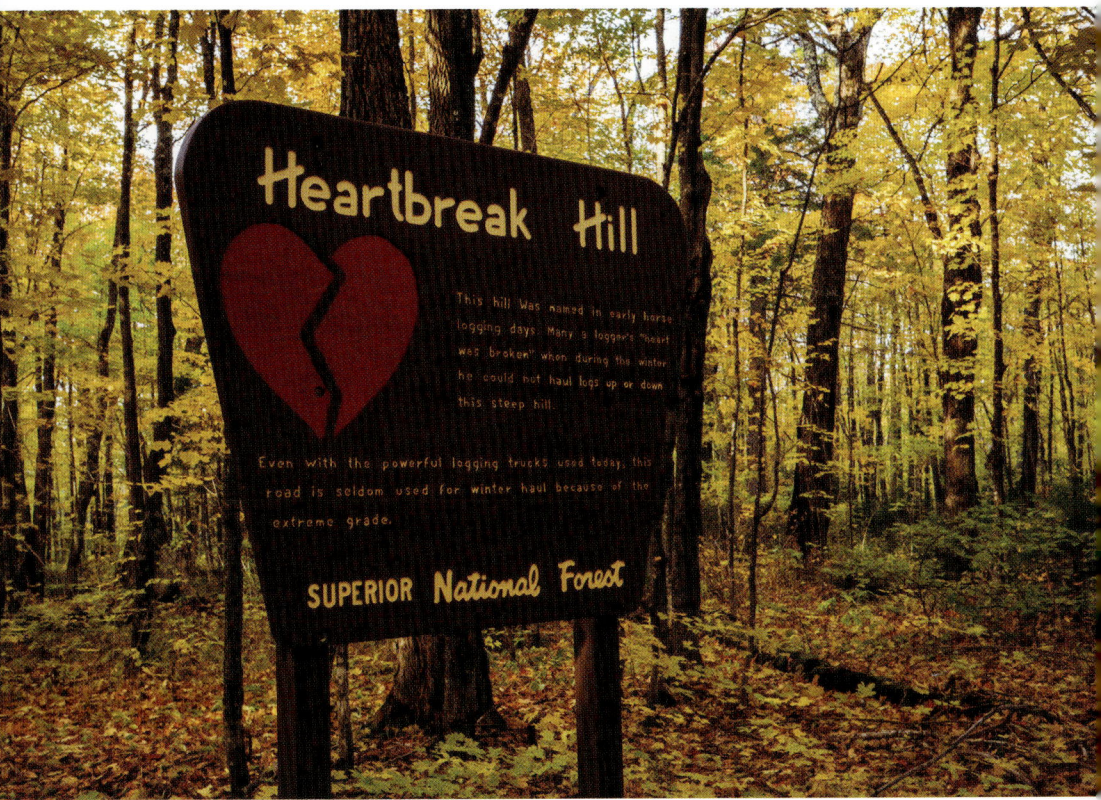

HEARTBREAK HILL AND FALL COLOR BACKROADS

Back in the horse-drawn logging days of the late 1800s and early 1900s, a stretch of forest road between the Sawbill Trail and Temperance River Road was given the name "Heartbreak Hill" due to the inability of horses to haul logs up and down the steep grade during winter, thus "breaking" a logger's heart. While there are several backroad circuits offering stunning displays of fall color in the Superior National Forest, this particular drive is a favorite of fall foliage seekers who enjoy driving among the dense canopies of maples.

Directions: The drive begins at the intersection of Highway 61 and Sawbill Trail and follows Sawbill Trail for 5.5 miles to a left turn at Six Hundred Road. Just after the turn, the route crosses the Temperance River and continues for 4.9 miles through the most colorful portion of the drive. A left turn at Temperance Road brings drivers back to Highway 61 in 5.1 miles.

CARLTON PEAK

Towering more than 900 feet above Lake Superior, Carlton Peak (elevation 1,526 feet) consists largely of anorthosite, a dense mineral that resisted the erosion caused by glaciers during the last ice age. While not the highest peak of the Sawtooth Range, its prominence provides some of the best panoramic views of Lake Superior and surrounding forest. In its early days of prospecting for the valuable mineral corundum, Minnesota Mining and Manufacturing (3M) blasted into Carton Peak, finding anorthosite instead. While not of use to the fledgling company, anorthosite was later quarried and used for local building projects. Access to the summit is possible via the Superior Hiking Trail, either from the Temperance River gorge area (6 miles round-trip) or from the Britton Peak parking area along the Sawbill Trail (3 miles round-trip).

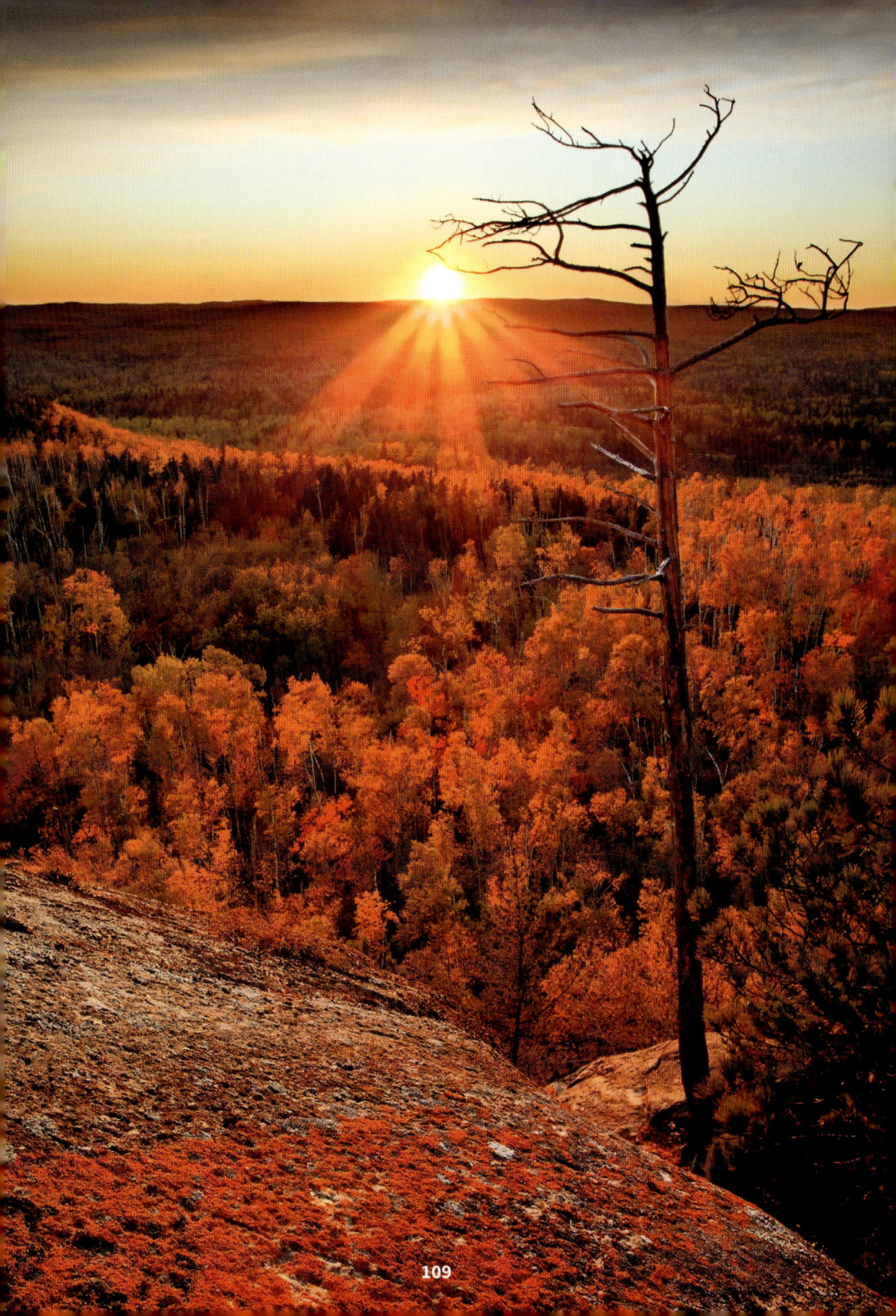

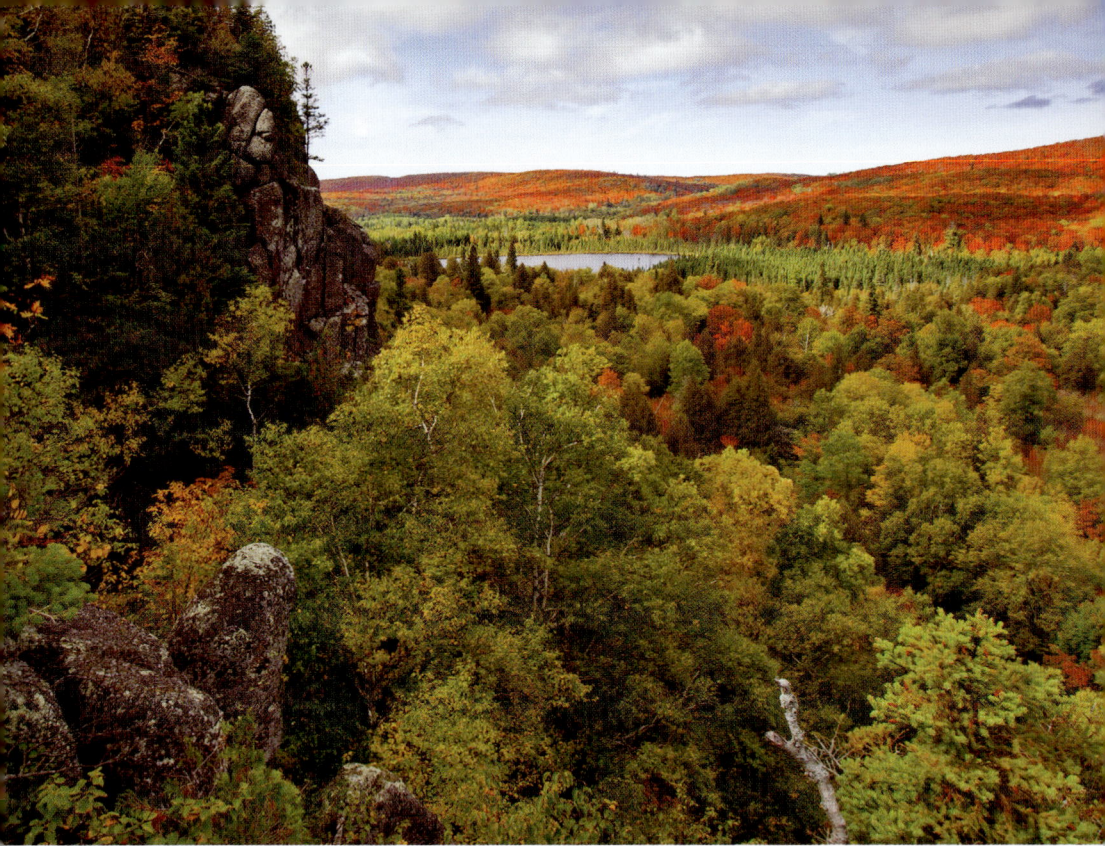

OBERG MOUNTAIN

Possibly the most popular hiking trail on the entire North Shore during fall, and a personal favorite of the author's, the 2.3-mile-long Oberg Mountain Loop offers majestic views in nearly all directions as hikers make their way around the top of the mountain, passing intermittently through maple forests and along exposed overlooks (use caution with children). The many overlooks provide bird's-eye views of Lake Superior, vast maple forest, and nearby Oberg Lake. The trailhead, shared with the LeVeaux Mountain Trail, is located 2 miles inland from Highway 61 on the gravel-surfaced Onion River Road. Onion River Road intersects Highway 61 about 5 miles northeast of Tofte.

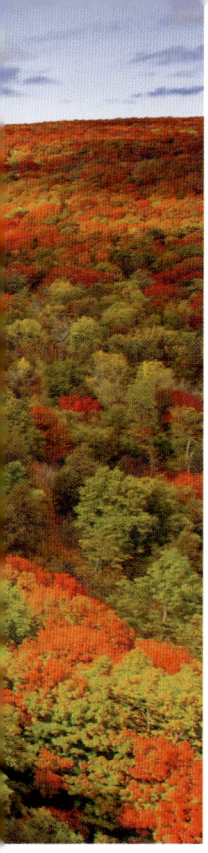

POPLAR RIVER

Rising from its source in Gust Lake, the Poplar River flows 21.7 miles to its mouth at Lutsen Resort on Lake Superior. The last 3 miles of the river follow a turbulent course with several waterfalls and numerous rapids as it descends toward the lake. The Poplar's flow has been modified by dams, and the river is one of the only North Shore streams to contain a hydroelectric plant, which was used in the 1920s and '30s to power the nearby Lutsen Resort and surrounding homes before electricity came to the region.

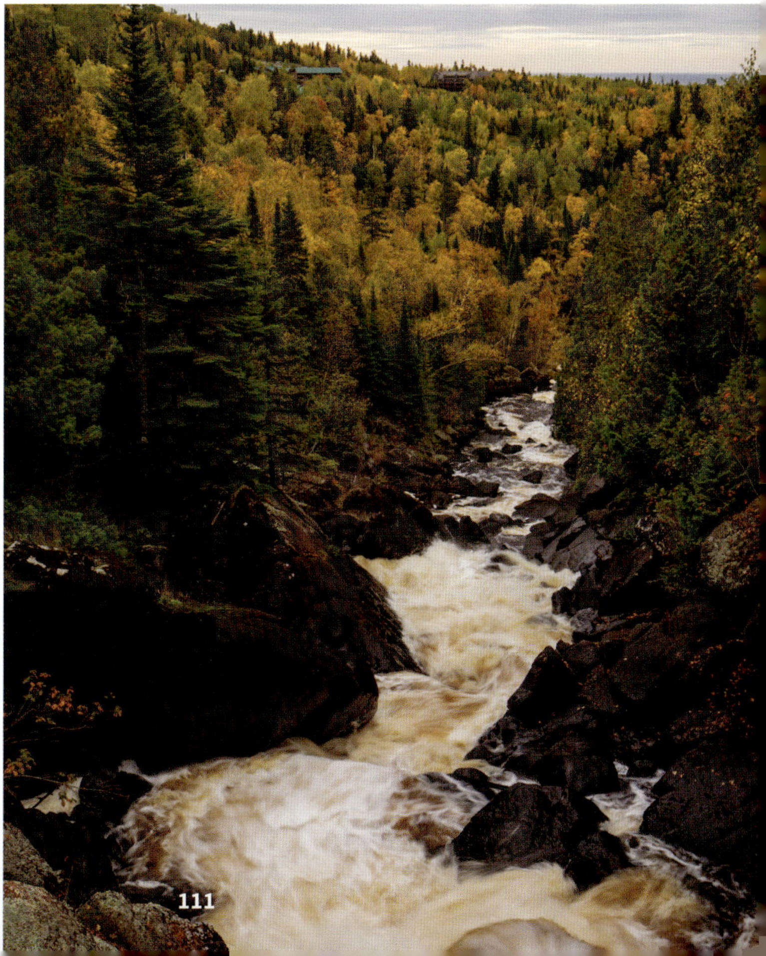

LUTSEN MOUNTAINS

One of the northernmost ski areas in the contiguous United States and the largest resort of its kind in the Midwest, Lutsen Mountains offers skiing and other snow sports on four separate mountains—Eagle, Moose, Mystery, and Ullr—from November into mid-April. The resort has been family owned and operated since its opening in 1948. It boasts the largest vertical drop—a respectable 1,088 feet—of any ski area in the Midwest and is the only Midwestern ski resort to operate a gondola. During the warm season, attractions at the resort include an alpine slide, scenic gondola rides, and several miles of hiking trails.

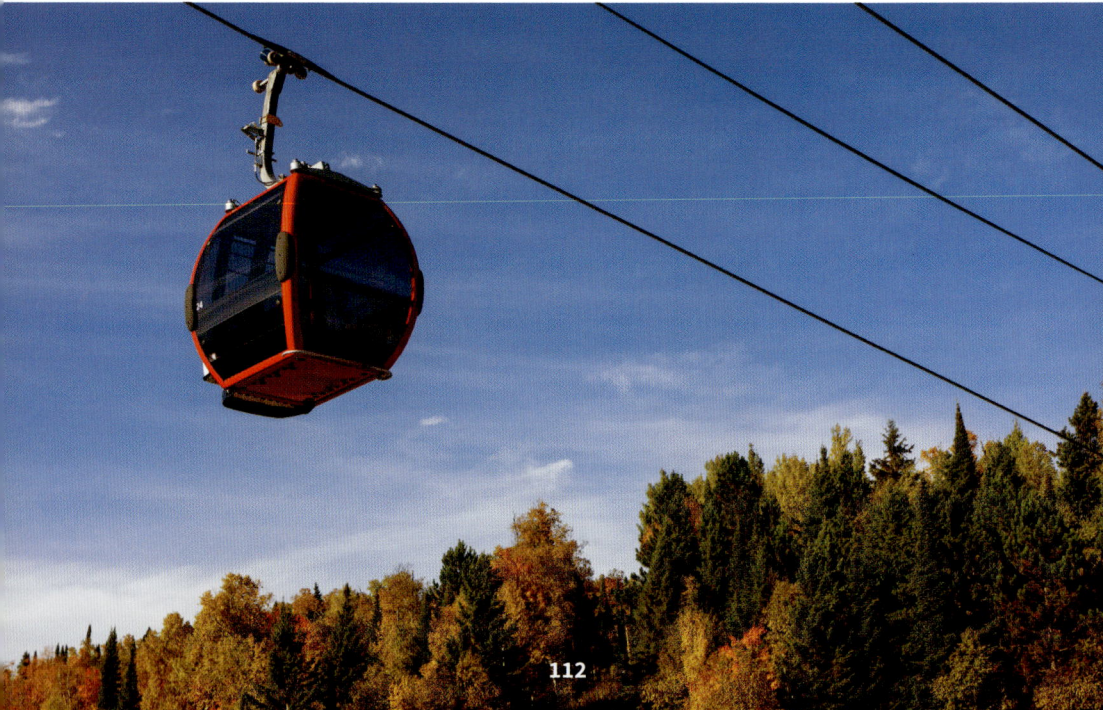

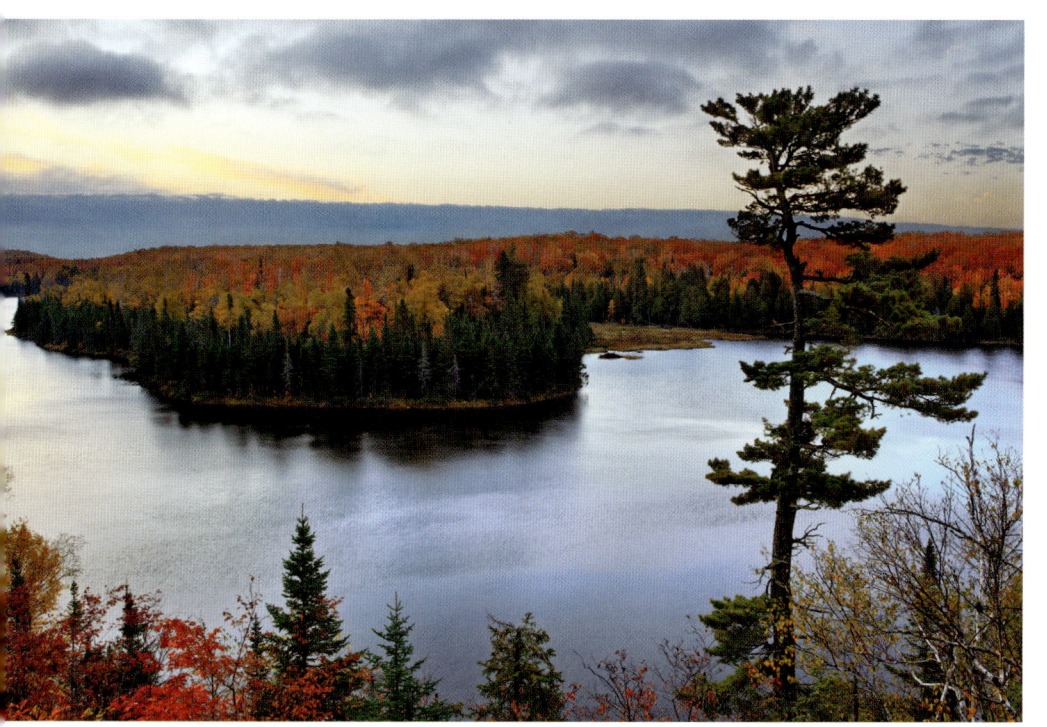

LAKE AGNES

The viewpoint at Hunter's Rock, overlooking Lake Agnes, exudes a Boundary Waters Canoe Area Wilderness-like aura (though in a setting much closer to civilization), with its several majestic pines and bald monolith perched above pristine waters. It is accessed via a spur trail of the Superior Hiking Trail heading west from the Caribou Trail trailhead (from Highway 61, drive 3.9 miles north on Caribou Trail, turn right onto White Sky Road and you'll see the parking area). Hunter's Rock also contains a backpacking campsite for hikers wishing to spend the night.

WHITE SKY ROCK

Offering panoramic views of Caribou Lake to the east, White Sky Rock sits high above the Caribou Trail at the terminus of a short spur trail. The trail is steep as much as it is short, with an elevation gain of 230 feet in 0.3 mile. While any time of the year offers tremendous views, fall is the best time to witness the sea of red and orange foliage surrounding the sky-blue surface of the lake. As with Lake Agnes, access to White Sky Rock is via the Superior Hiking Trail's Caribou Trail trailhead (from Highway 61, drive 3.9 miles north on Caribou Trail, turn right onto White Sky Road and you'll see the parking area). From the trailhead, walk the short distance to cross over Caribou Trail; at the next junction, veer to the right on White Sky Rock Trail, which will take you to the overlook.

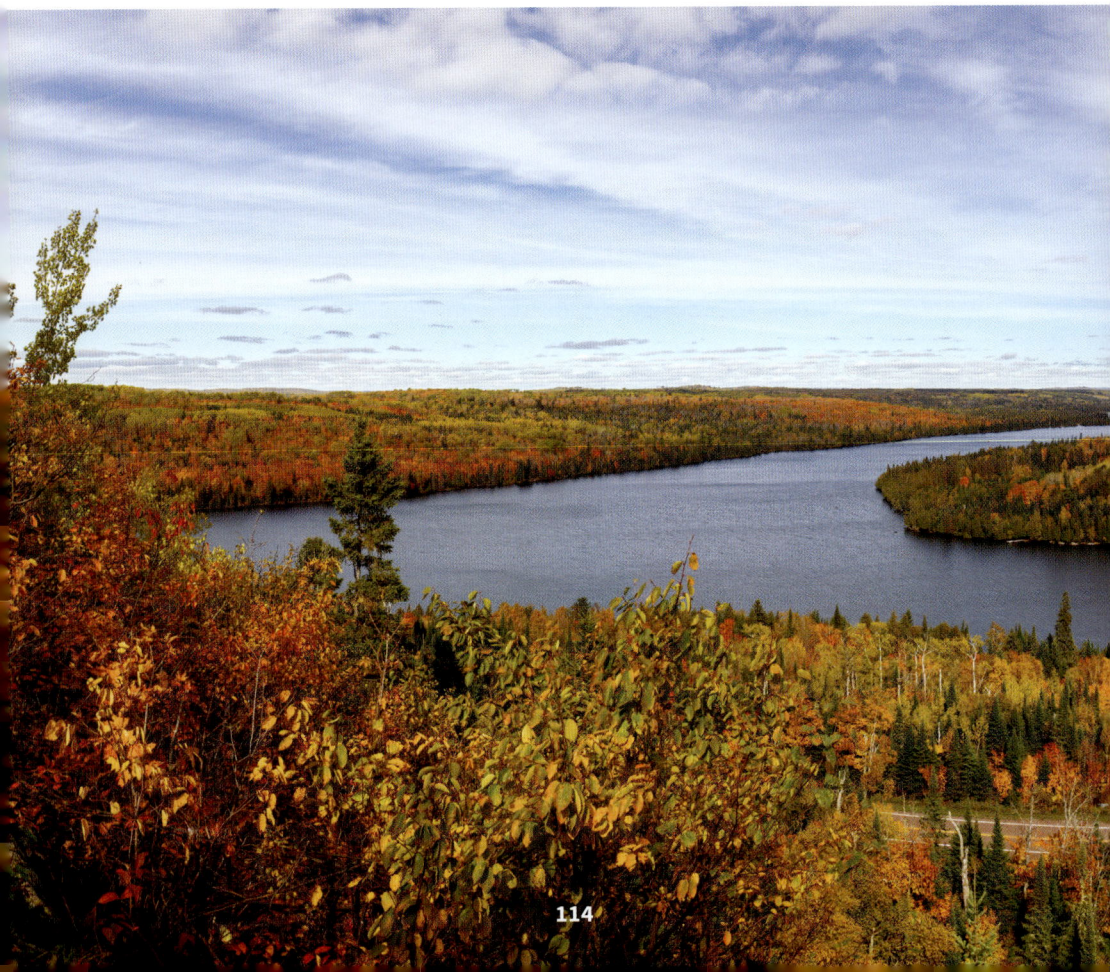

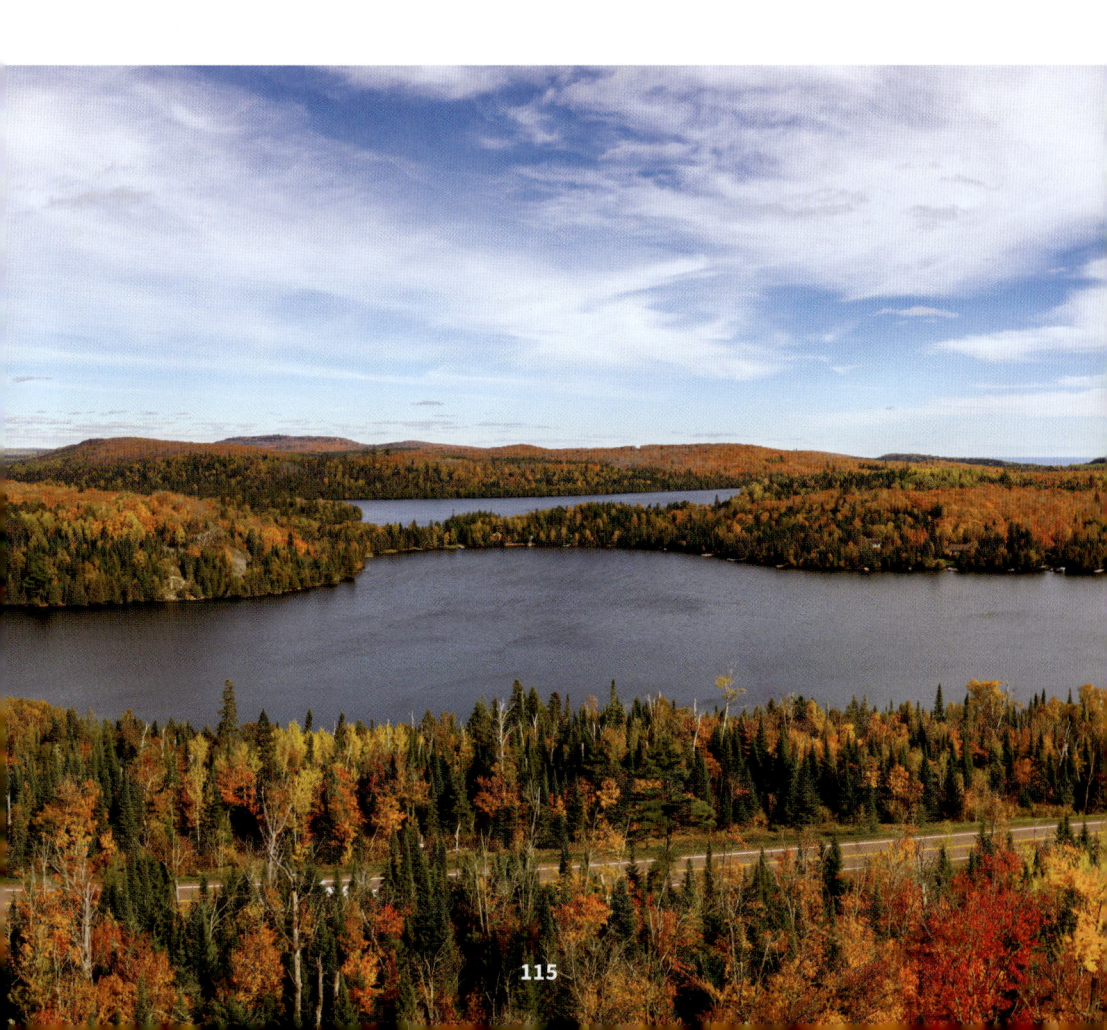

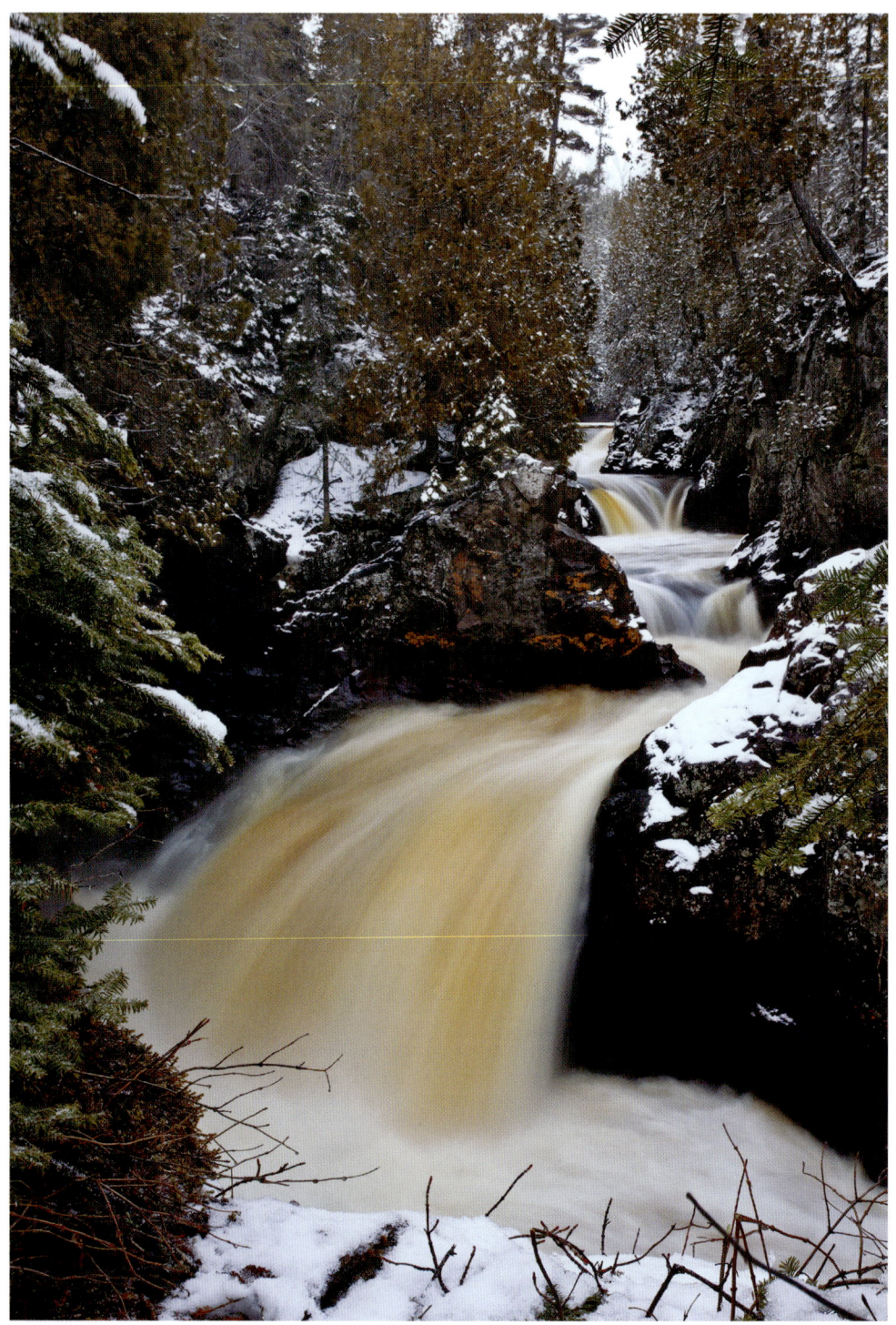

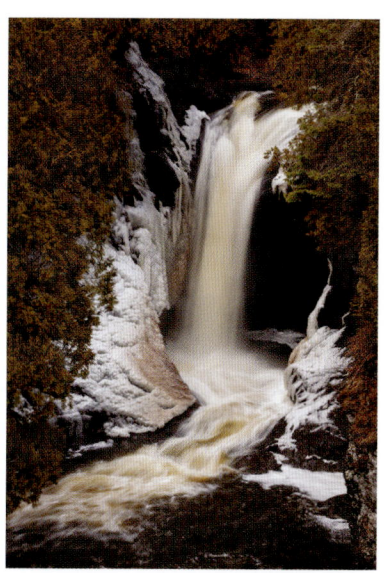

CASCADE RIVER STATE PARK

As the main feature of this state park, the Cascade River drops 900 feet over a series of ledges in its final 3-mile course toward Lake Superior. These graceful cascades, for which the river was named, make this portion of river arguably the most beautiful of any North Shore stream. The closest to Lake Superior, Cascade Falls, plunges nearly 30 feet, making it also the tallest waterfall in the park. A Civilian Conservation Corps camp built trails and structures here in the 1930s, many years before the park was officially designated in 1957. Besides the namesake river, the park's amenities include a drive-in campground with modern facilities, more than one mile of rugged Lake Superior shoreline with picnic areas, a picnic shelter, and several miles of hiking and skiing trails.

FALL RIVER

Due to their location outside of any established park and the lack of established infrastructure, the falls of the Fall River see few visitors, despite their beauty and proximity to Highway 61. While waterfalls exist on both sides of the highway, the tallest is on the Lake Superior side, plunging 30 feet into a pool before entering the lake. Access to the falls is somewhat limited, with only a narrow, often muddy footpath leading to an exposed ledge on the east side of the river overlooking the waterfall. Continuing farther for a straight-on view involves carefully navigating the rocky terrain to reach the small beach at lake level. A bridge for the paved Gitchi-Gami State Trail is slated for construction across the Fall River in 2019, just below the falls. The bridge's construction and any associated improvements will likely alter the accessibility and character of this area. Fall River is located about 2.5 miles west of downtown Grand Marais.

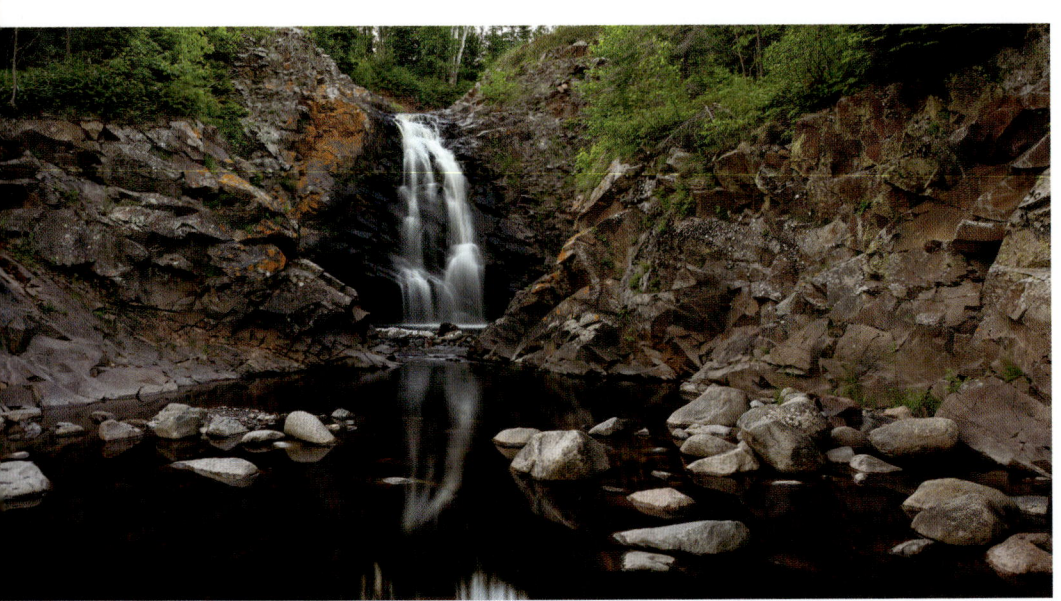

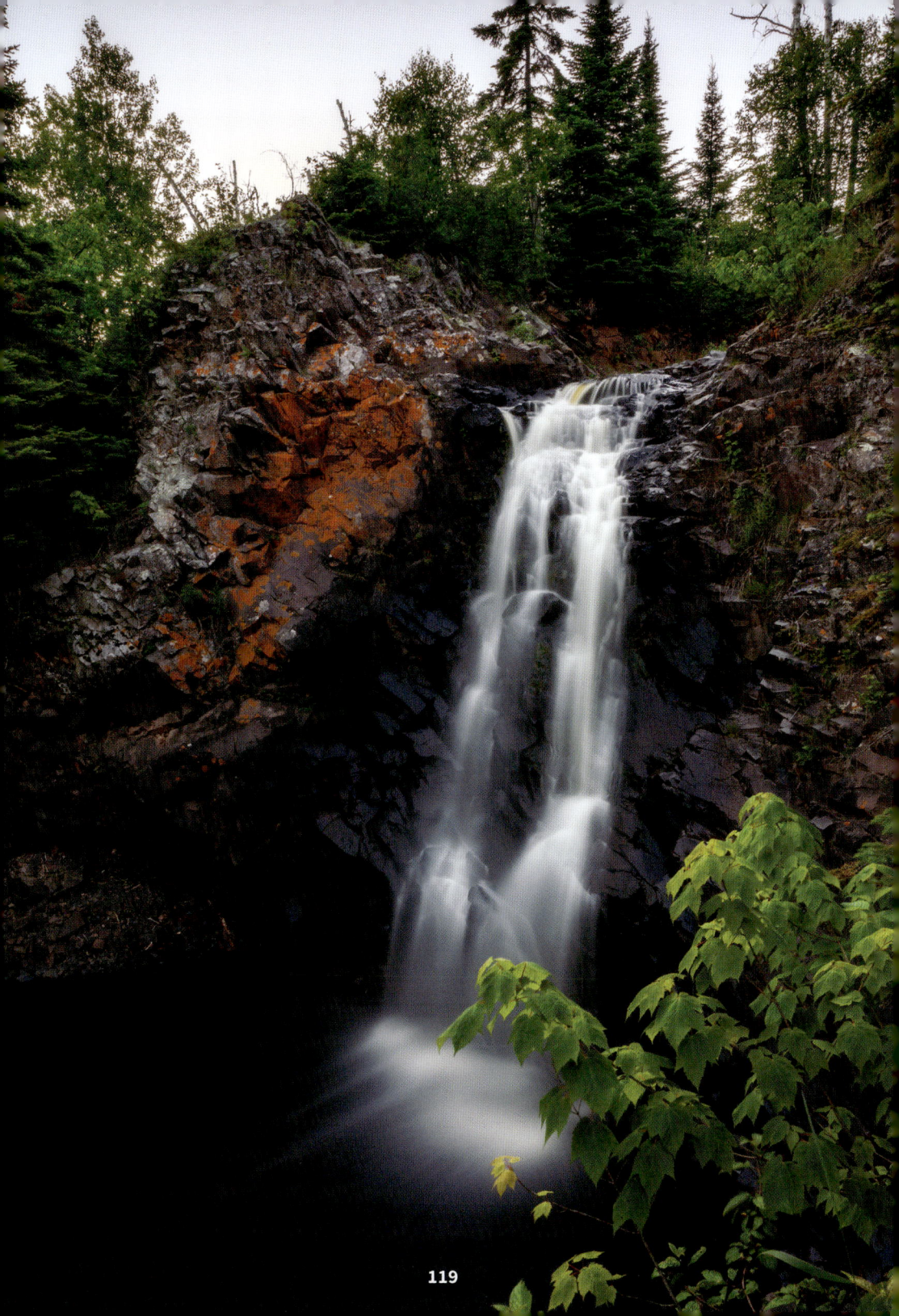

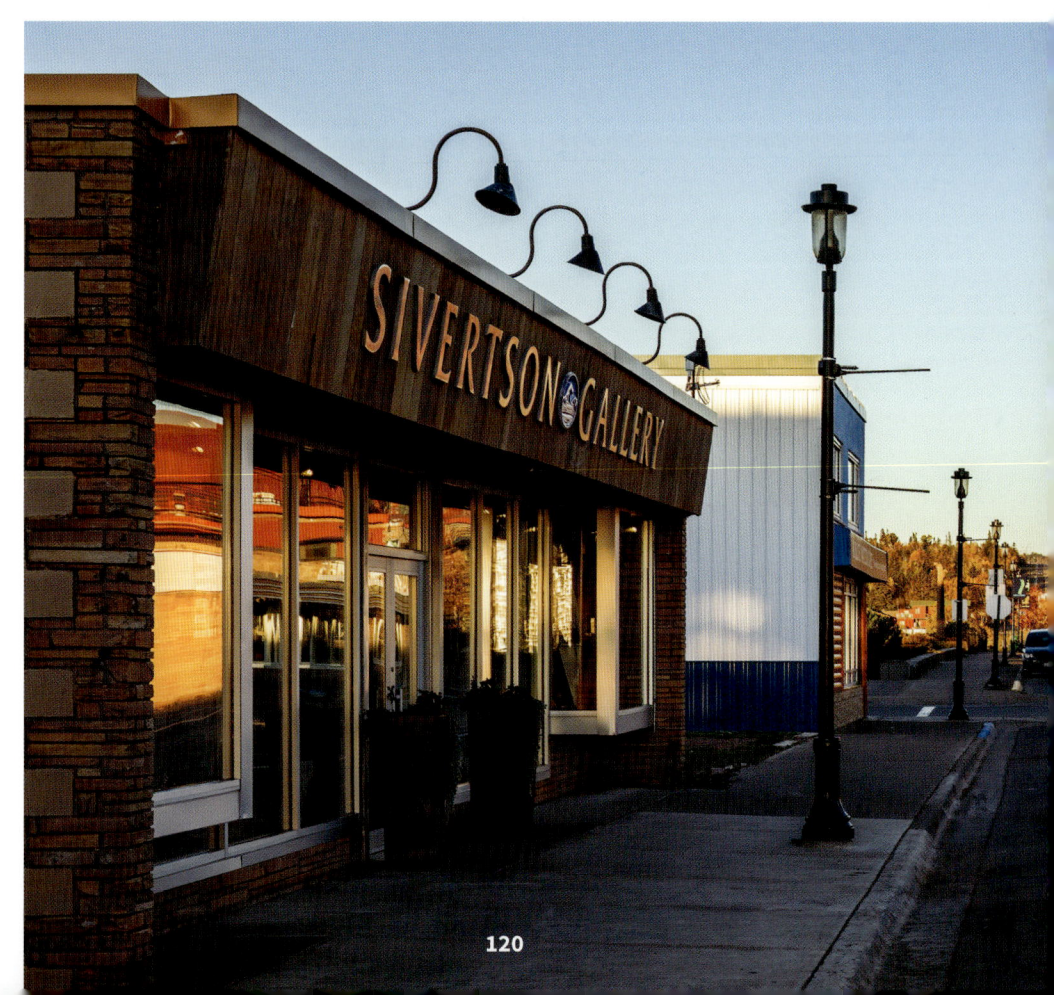

GRAND MARAIS

Originally inhabited by the indigenous Ojibwe people, in the 1700s French voyageurs established a fur-trading post here and named the village "Grand Marais," which is French for "Great Marsh." Today, the small community serves as a hub of arts, culture, and tourism on the upper reaches of Minnesota's North Shore and is a primary gateway to the Boundary Waters Canoe Area Wilderness via the Gunflint Trail. Grand Marais is home to a number of eclectic shops, galleries, and locally owned restaurants and also hosts several festivals and community events, including the juried Grand Marais Arts Festival in July, Fisherman's Picnic in August, and the Lake Superior Storm Festival in November.

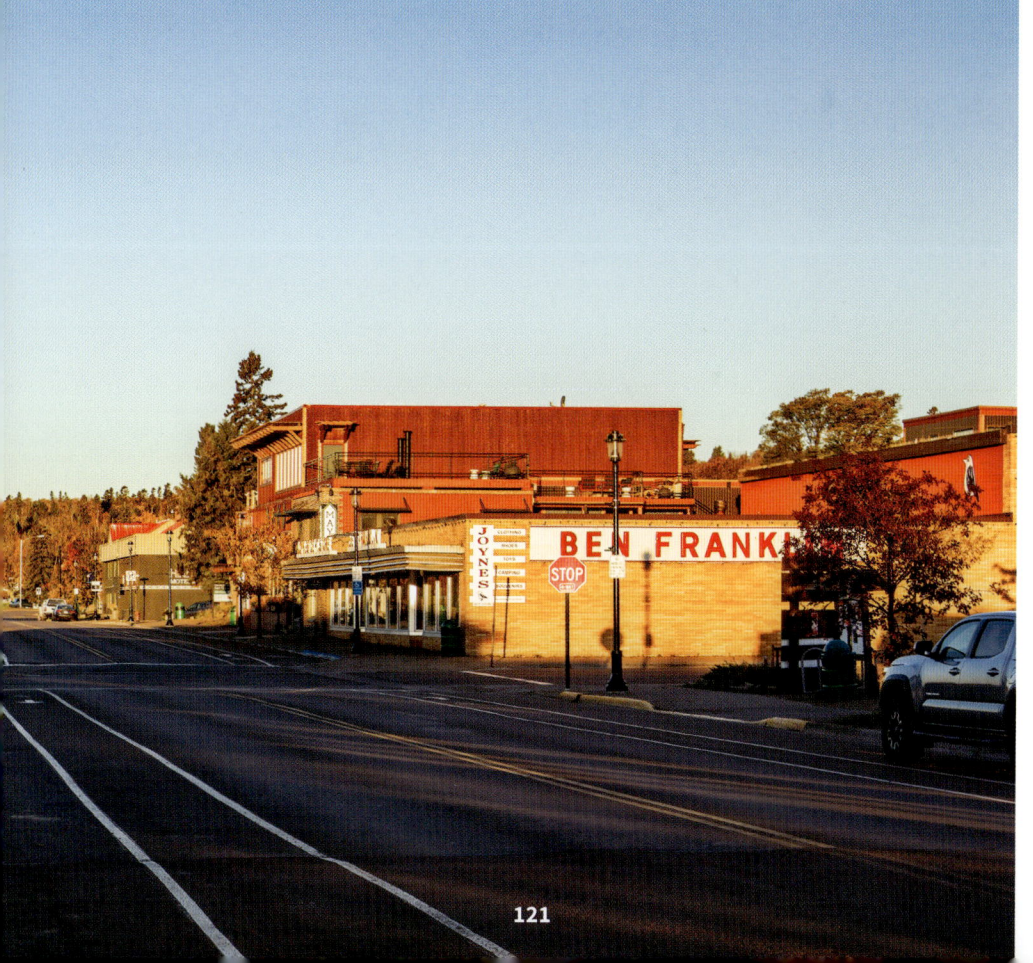

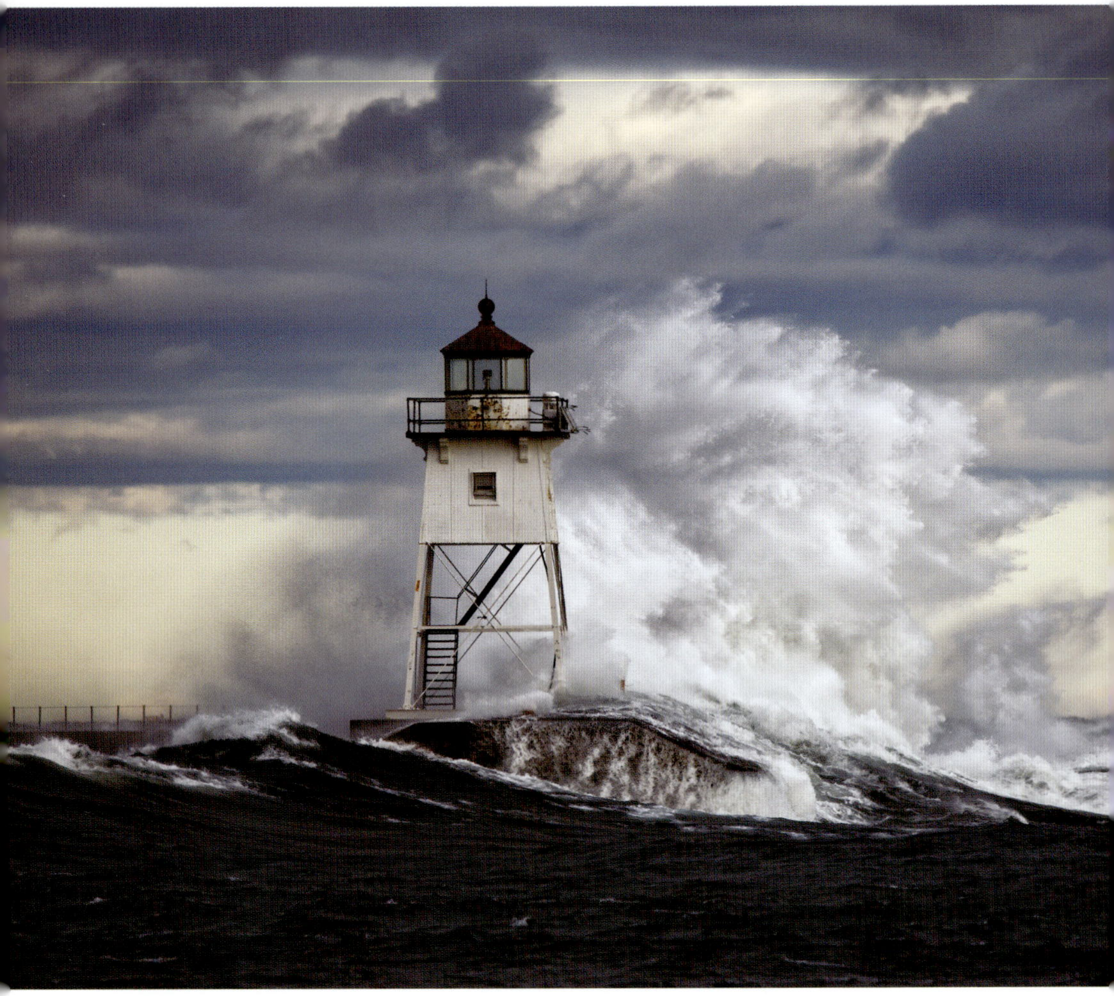

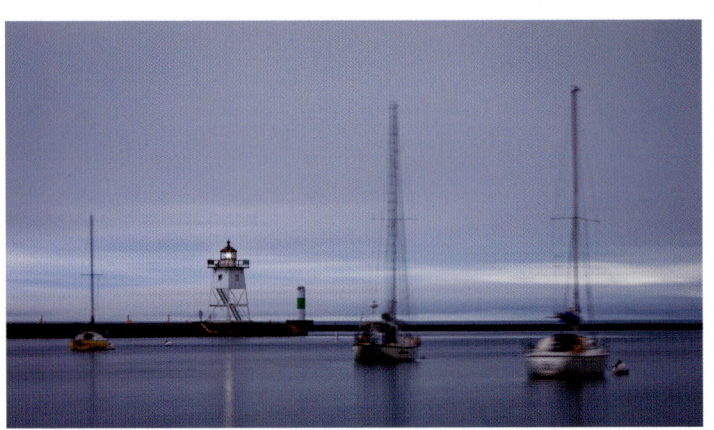

GRAND MARAIS HARBOR

Grand Marais enjoys some degree of protection from Lake Superior's infamous storms due to its natural harbor, enclosed in the east by Artists' Point. Man-made breakwaters were constructed in the late 1800s and early 1900s to offer greater shelter for recreational and fishing boats. At the end of the east breakwater stands the crown jewel of the harbor, the Grand Marais Light. Built in 1922, the modern steel-framed light replaced a fully enclosed 1880s-era timber-framed lighthouse that had been repeatedly damaged by storms. Its original Fifth-order Fresnel lens, replaced by a solar-powered lamp in 2012, is displayed at the Cook County History Museum, which itself served as the lighthouse keeper's residence until 1946.

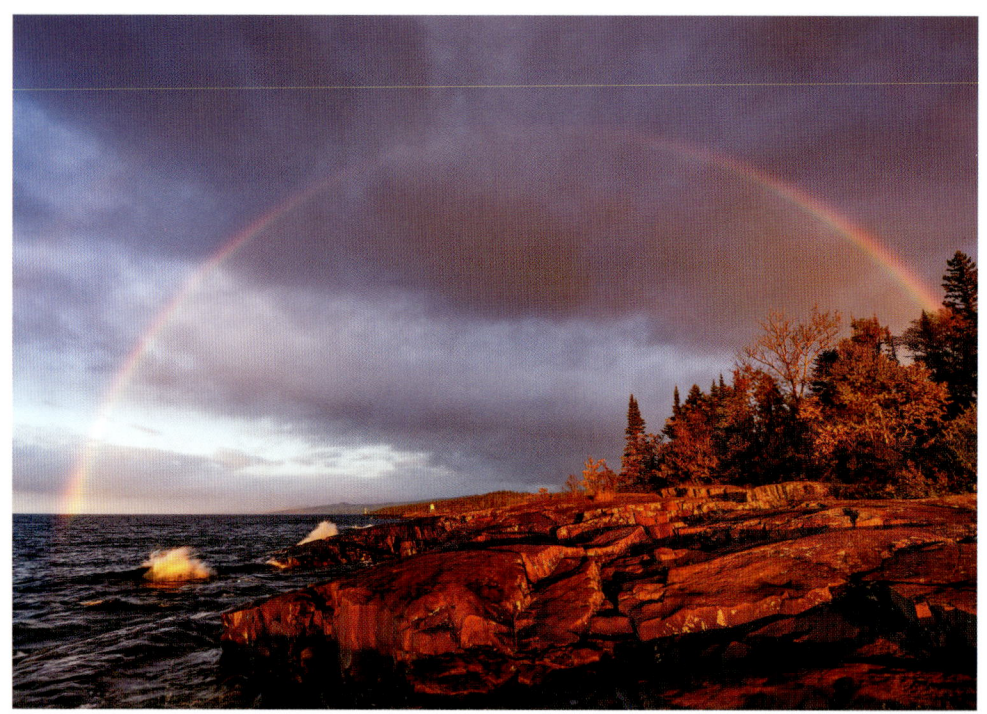

ARTISTS' POINT

Essentially an island that's connected to Grand Marais by a wide tombolo (a thin spit of gravel deposits that connect an island to the mainland), Artists' Point offers a wooded sanctuary with a rocky shoreline, complete with views of Lake Superior, the distant Sawtooth Mountains, and the Grand Marais Light. Because of its distinctively attractive and infinitely interpretable rugged landforms and wildly varying weather and surf conditions, the point has long provided inspiration for artists living in or visiting the region.

BEAVER HOUSE

Housed within an iconic downtown building with a giant walleye seemingly crashing through the roof, Beaver House has been selling live bait and an eclectic assortment of fishing lures in Grand Marais since 1964, when Bill Cronberg first opened it as a shoe repair and clothing business. Owned by the Cronberg family ever since, it is known for its Beaver Flicks, a special fishing lure invented by Marty Cronberg and supposedly guaranteed to catch any type of fish. The store's unique exterior also includes a few landscape murals and a sculpture depicting—you guessed it—beavers building a house.

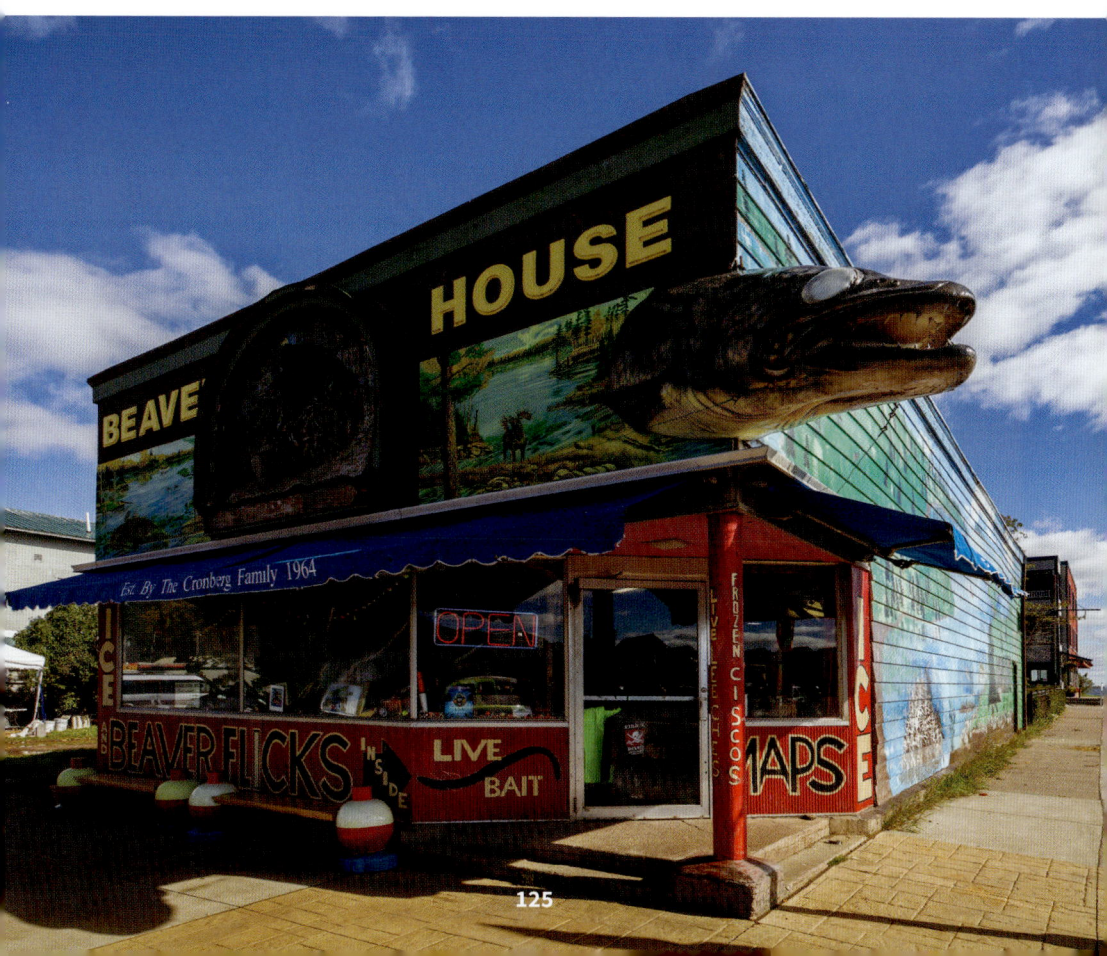

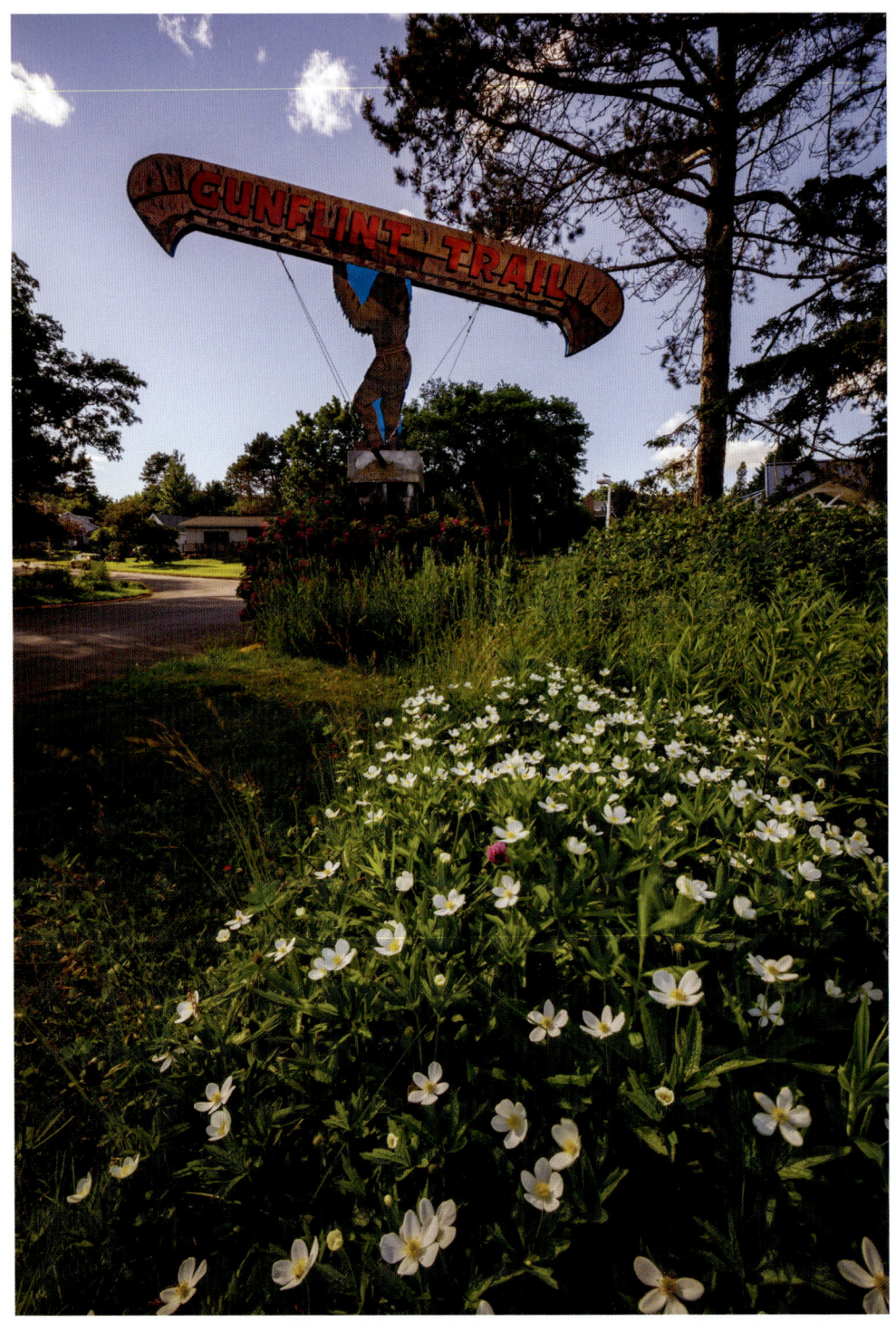

GUNFLINT TRAIL SIGN

On what began as a footpath connecting inland lakes to Lake Superior, the Gunflint Trail is now a paved two-lane road, extending 57 miles from Highway 61 on the east side of Grand Marais to its terminus near Saganaga Lake, on the Ontario border. Designated as a scenic byway, the route contains no cities or towns, but numerous side roads lead to resorts, campgrounds, lakes, hiking trails, and wildlife-viewing spots. It is a primary access road for many locations in the Boundary Waters Canoe Area Wilderness. Installed in the 1950s, the iconic Gunflint Trail signage near the library in downtown Grand Marais, depicting a voyageur carrying a canoe and a bear driving a motorboat, marks the road's former entrance.

This book does not cover the Gunflint Trail in detail, but instead highlights a few locations worth visiting within about a half-hour's drive from Grand Marais.

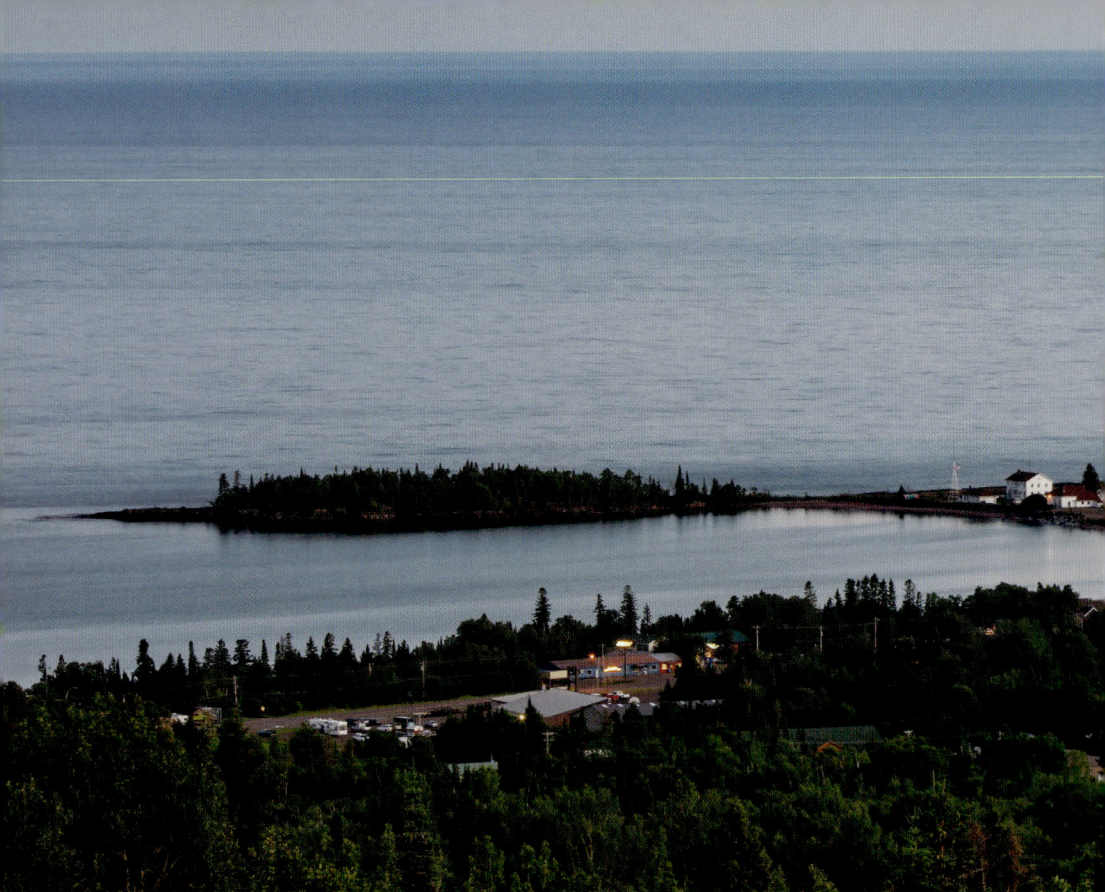

PINCUSHION MOUNTAIN

Providing gorgeous bird's-eye vistas of Artists' Point and the Grand Marais Harbor to the south, as well as views of the Devil Track River canyon to the north, Pincushion Mountain features 15 miles of trails for hiking, mountain biking, snowshoeing, and cross-country skiing. The Superior Hiking Trail also traverses the mountain, offering opportunities for longer treks. For those not wanting to venture far, the parking area near the trailhead offers more-than-adequate views of Grand Marais below. The Pincushion Mountain trailhead is located about 2.5 miles up the Gunflint Trail from Highway 61.

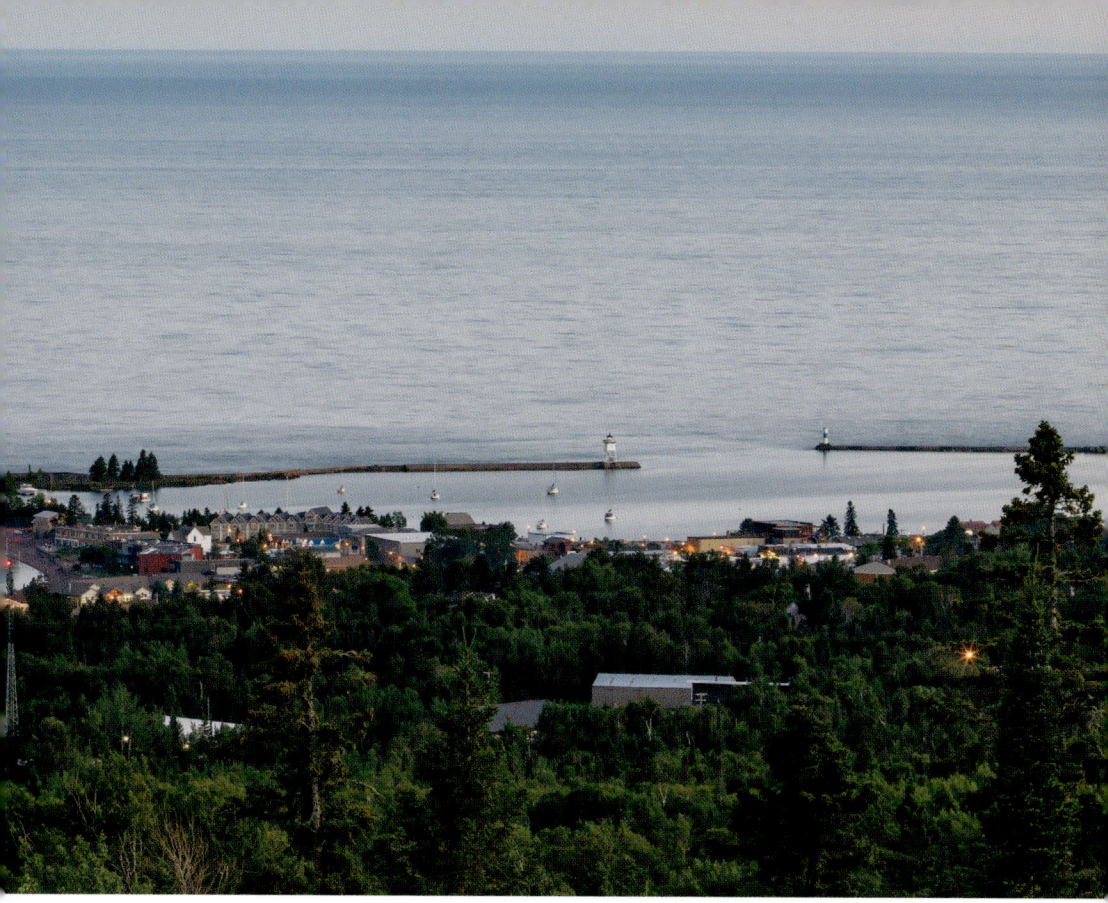

MAPLE HILL CHURCH

In the late 1800s, a small community of people settled atop the hill above Grand Marais, about 5 miles up the Gunflint Trail. The settlement became known as Maple Hill, and two schoolhouses, a town hall, a cemetery, and a church were built. The cemetery and church remain, although the church was rebuilt after an act of arson destroyed it in 1986. Today, Spirit of the Wilderness Episcopal Church conducts services in the rebuilt historic worship space. Fall is a great time to experience this quiet location while enjoying the eye-popping reds and oranges of the surrounding maple forest.

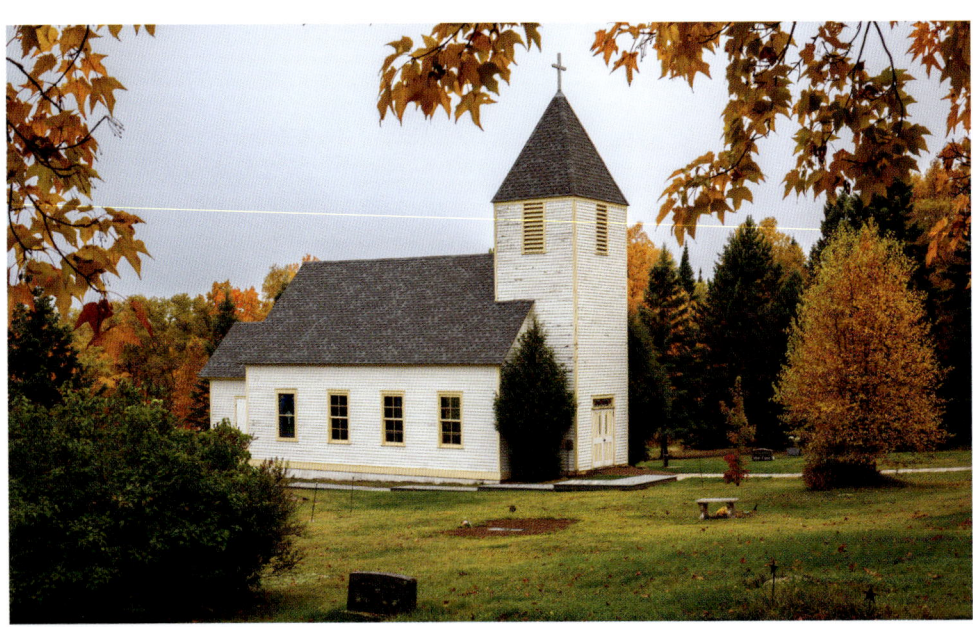

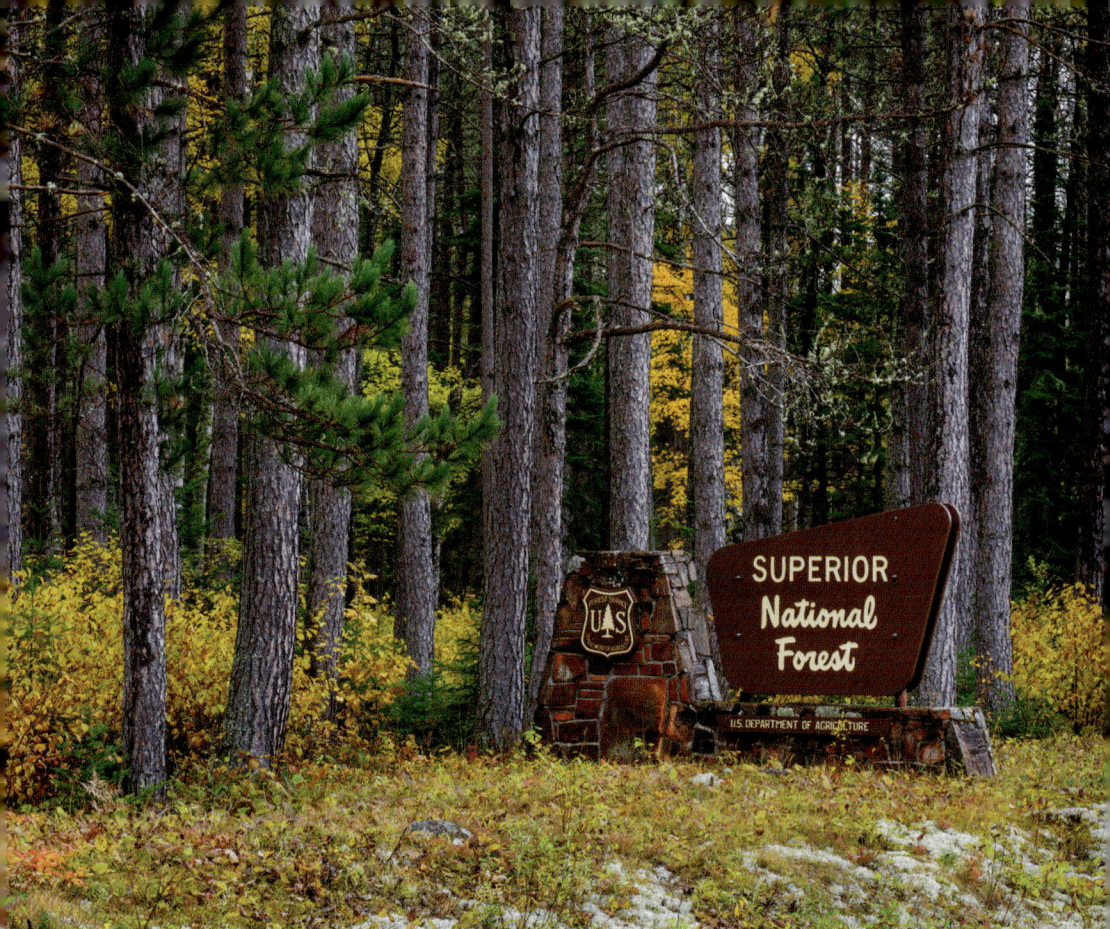

GEORGE WASHINGTON PINES

Established in 1932 when a Boy Scout troop from Grand Marais planted more than 22,000 Norway and white pines on 32 acres in the wake of a 1927 fire, George Washington Pines provides an opportunity to view a large plantation of towering pines and imagine what many of the North Shore's forests looked like before the logging era led to the mass harvest of old-growth pines around the turn of the twentieth century. A 2-mile loop trail passes through the majestic pine forest and is enjoyed by hikers during the warm seasons and cross-country skiers and snowshoers during the winter. Part of the Superior National Forest, the plantation is located just under 7 miles up the Gunflint Trail from Highway 61.

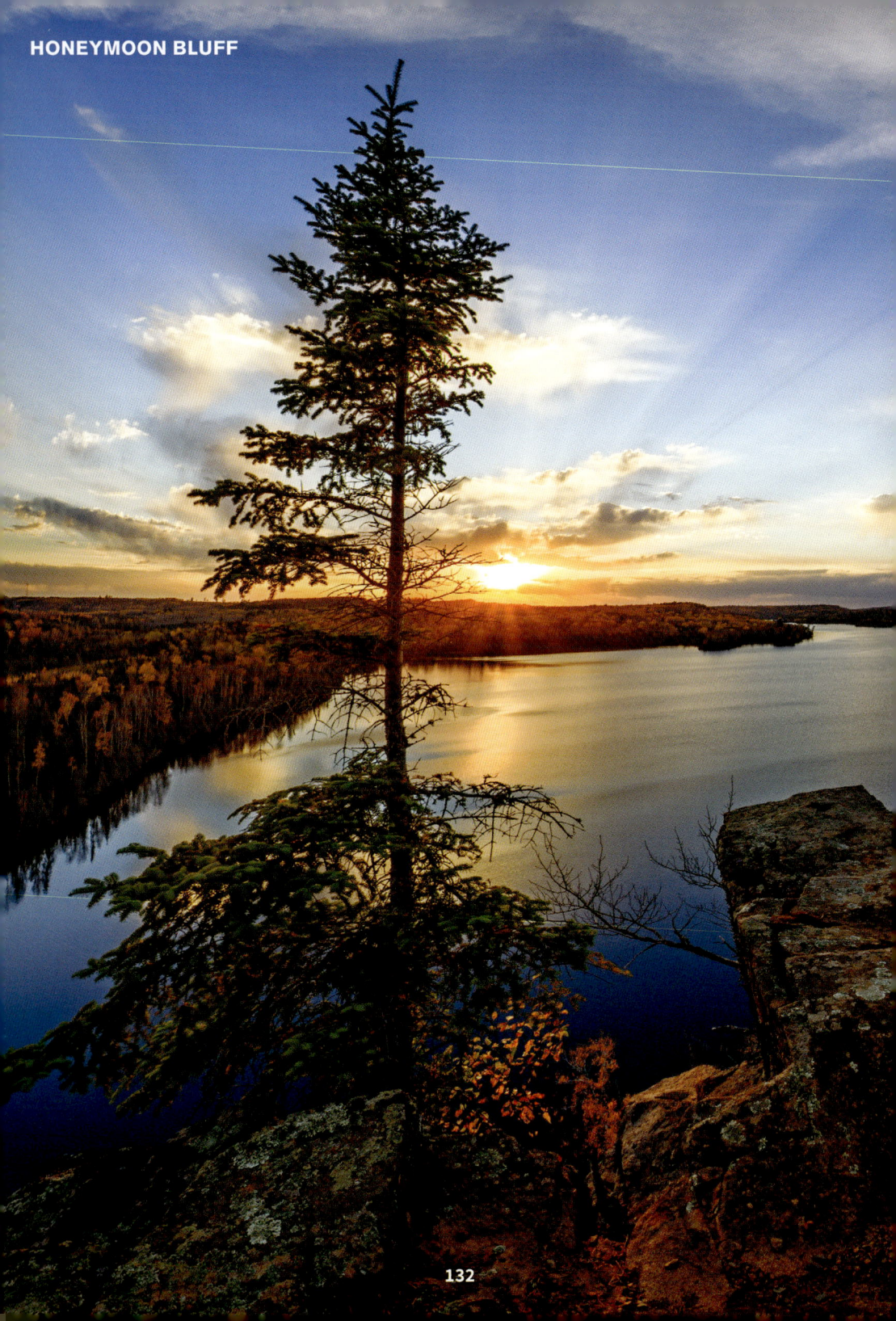

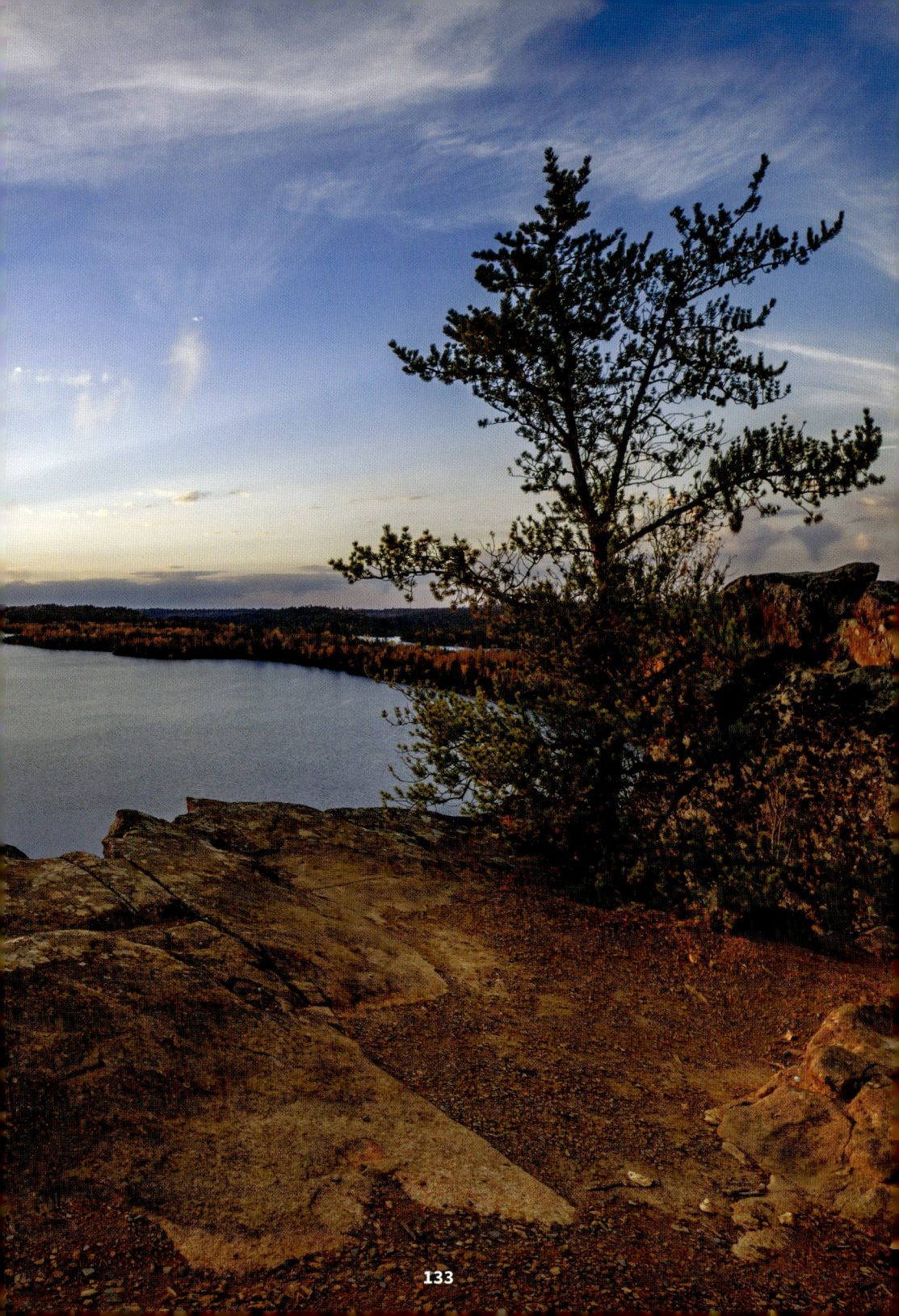

◄ HONEYMOON BLUFF/HUNGRY JACK LAKE

With its cliffside overlook of Hungry Jack Lake, Honeymoon Bluff offers exceptional views of the lake and surrounding boreal forest. While getting there involves a 30-mile drive from Grand Marais, once at the trailhead, the reward-to-effort ratio is very good. The viewpoint lies at the far end of a slightly steep 0.5-mile round-trip loop hike and provides a spectacular vantage to enjoy the sunset. To get there, travel 27 miles from Highway 61 on the Gunflint Trail, take a right at Clearwater Road, and proceed 2.2 miles to the trailhead.

KADUNCE RIVER

Passing through a deep, very narrow moss-covered canyon for much of the last mile of its 8.5-mile-long journey to Lake Superior, the Kadunce River exhibits a unique feel among North Shore steams. The easiest and safest way to enjoy a couple of the river's waterfalls is to hike the relatively gentle 1.1-mile out-and-back trail from the wayside rest on Highway 61. The trail follows the east side of the gorge, ascending high above the river. Approximately 0.5 mile into the hike, a clearing on the left provides a view of Heart of the Earth Falls, arguably the most beautiful on the river. Proceeding a bit farther on the trail offers views of a few more small cascades and takes hikers to a wooden bridge that crosses the river. At this point, the spur trail from Highway 61 intersects with the main Superior Hiking Trail. Unless you're continuing farther, turn around and return to the highway on the same trail.

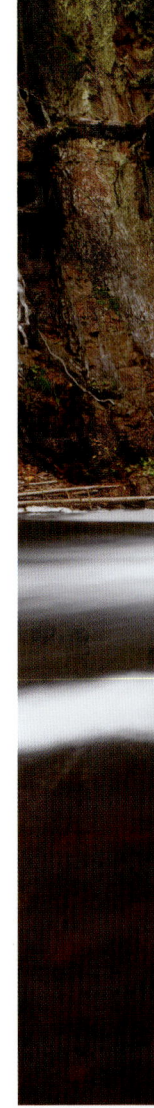

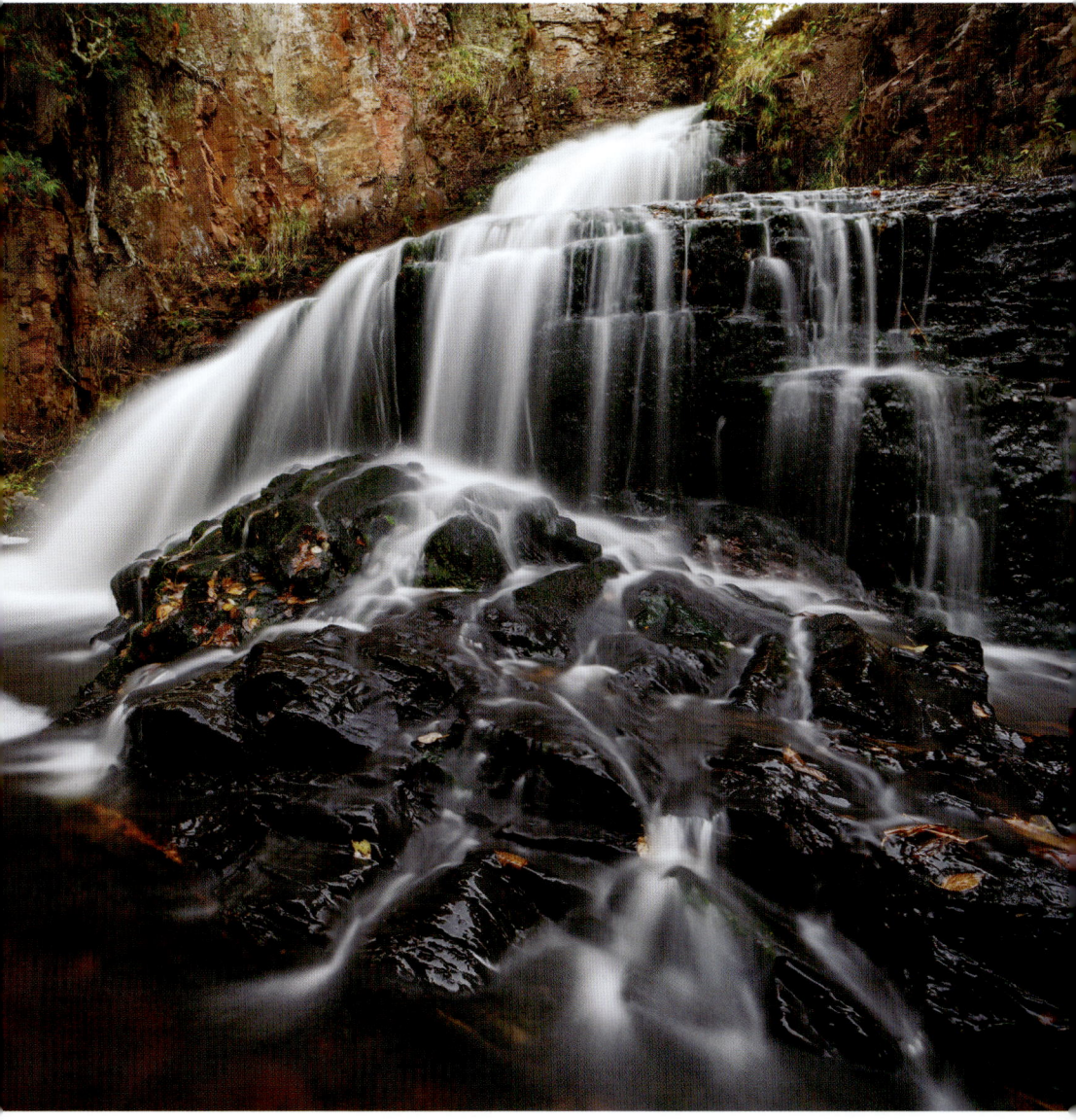

SUPERIOR HIKING TRAIL LAKEWALK

Even though the 310-mile Superior Hiking Trail is named after Superior, the Great Lake it loosely follows, only about 1.6 miles of it lies near the water's edge. Known as the Lakewalk (not to be confused with Duluth's Lakewalk), the lone segment that closely hugs the shoreline offers an easy hike along cobblestone beaches and ancient volcanic rock. Near the eastern end of this hike, a very photogenic island, populated with a cluster of trees, sits just offshore. Sometimes the island is connected to the mainland by a tombolo. The trail crosses Highway 61 at two locations—on the west end between highway mile markers 120 and 121 and on the east end between markers 121 and 122. Park on the shoulder of the highway near either trail junction.

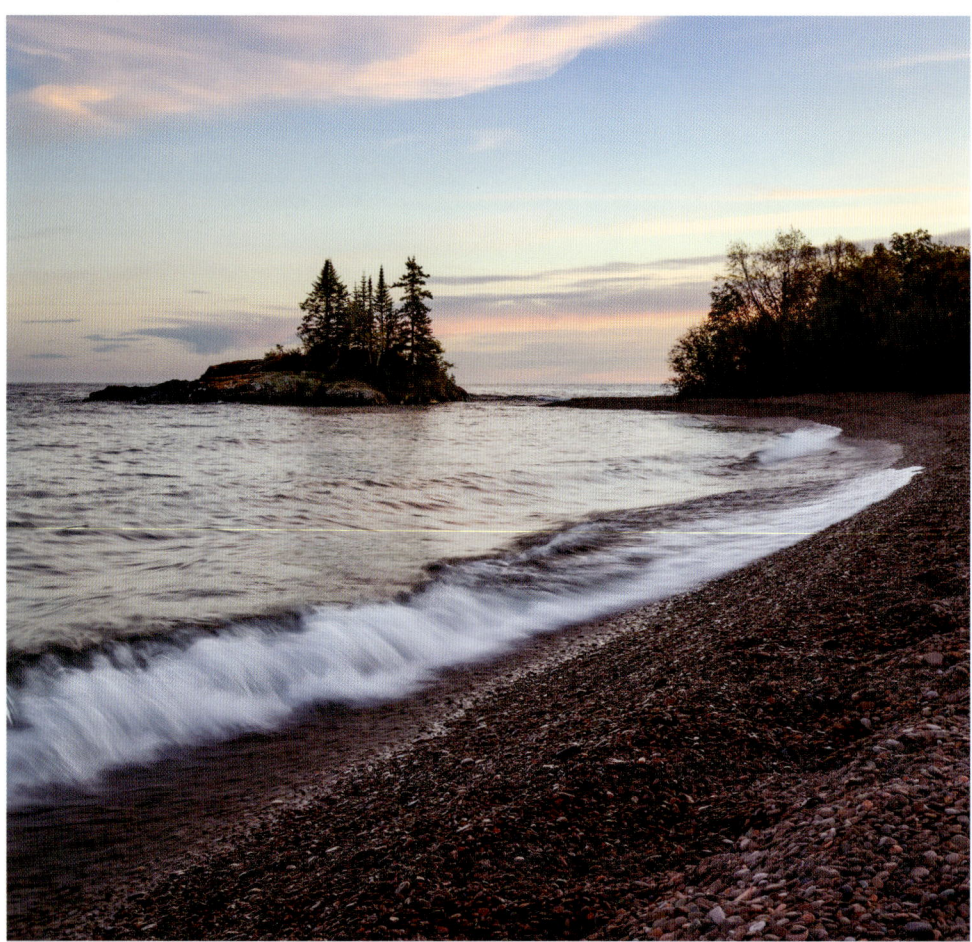

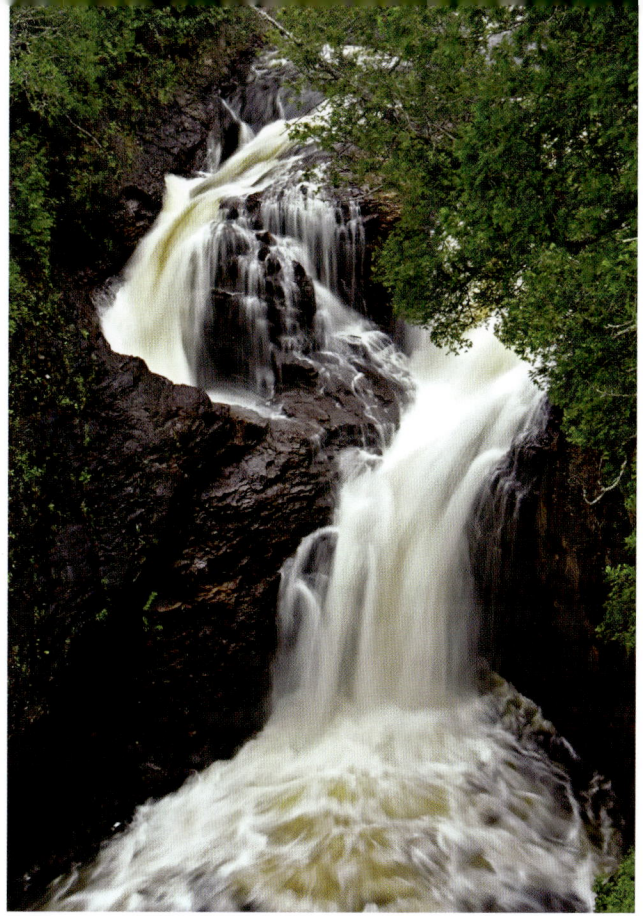

JUDGE C.R. MAGNEY STATE PARK

Named for Clarence R. Magney, a former mayor of Duluth and a Minnesota Supreme Court justice who played a major role in advocating for state parks and waysides on the North Shore, Judge C.R. Magney State Park contains more than 4,000 acres surrounding the lower stretches of the Brule River. The park is renowned for the Devil's Kettle, an enigmatic waterfall in which half of the river plunges 50 feet over a conventional cascade while the other half drains into a large pothole with an outlet that has never been found. The long-standing mystery was partially solved in 2016, when researchers conducted flow studies and determined that drainage from the pothole must exist within a short distance downstream from the falls. A trek to the falls involves a relatively strenuous 2-mile round-trip hike over steep terrain and more than 170 stairs. A short distance downstream of Devil's Kettle Falls lies the more archetypical 25-foot Upper Falls of the Brule River.

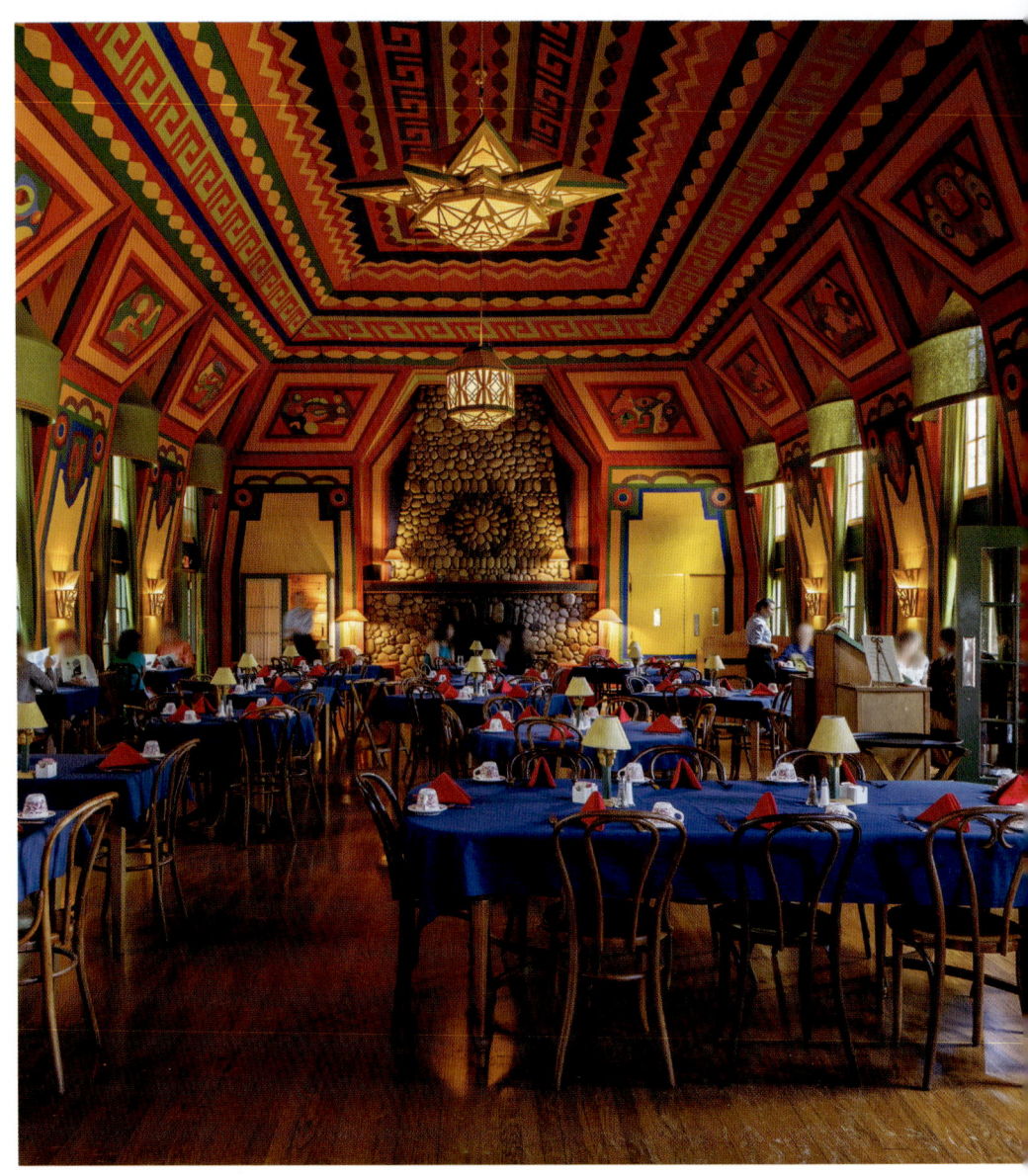

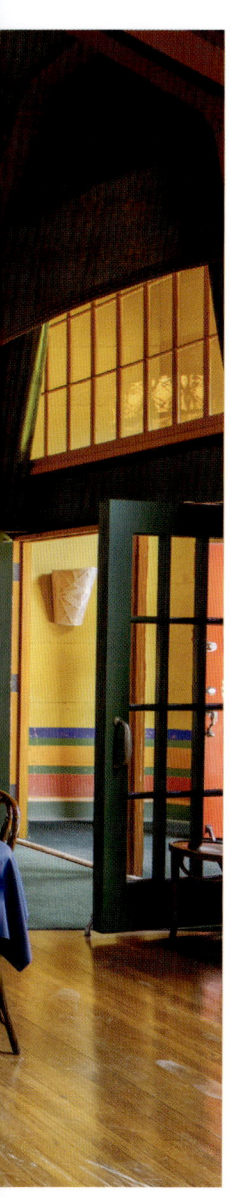
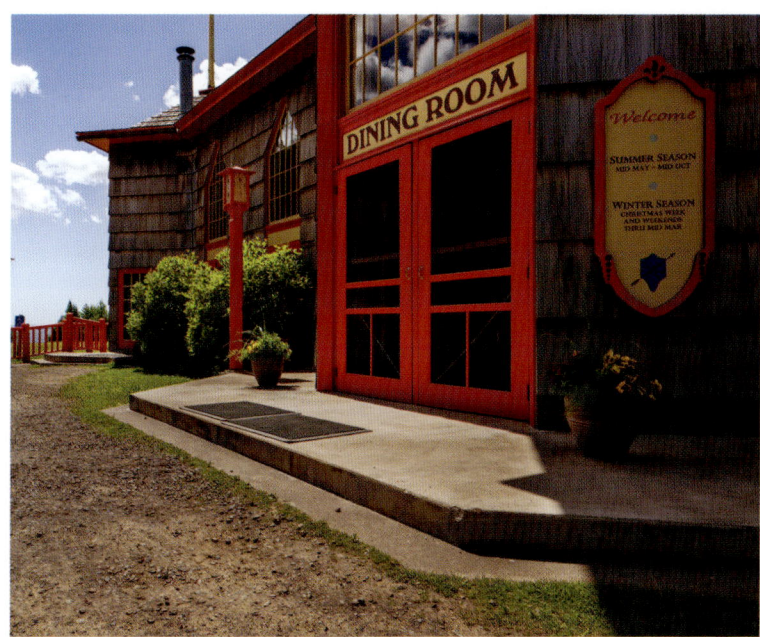

NANIBOUJOU LODGE

Built in the late 1920s as part of what was to become a large private club on the North Shore of Lake Superior, Naniboujou Lodge now serves as a lodging and fine dining venue for visitors to the region. First envisioned as an exclusive club that attracted the likes of Babe Ruth, Jack Dempsey, and Ring Lardner, the club folded during the Great Depression and ownership changed hands multiple times over the subsequent decades. Listed on the National Register of Historic Places, the well-preserved lodge contains a large, architecturally stunning dining room, including Minnesota's largest native-rock fireplace and a colorfully painted interior featuring Cree Indian designs with a notable Art Deco influence.

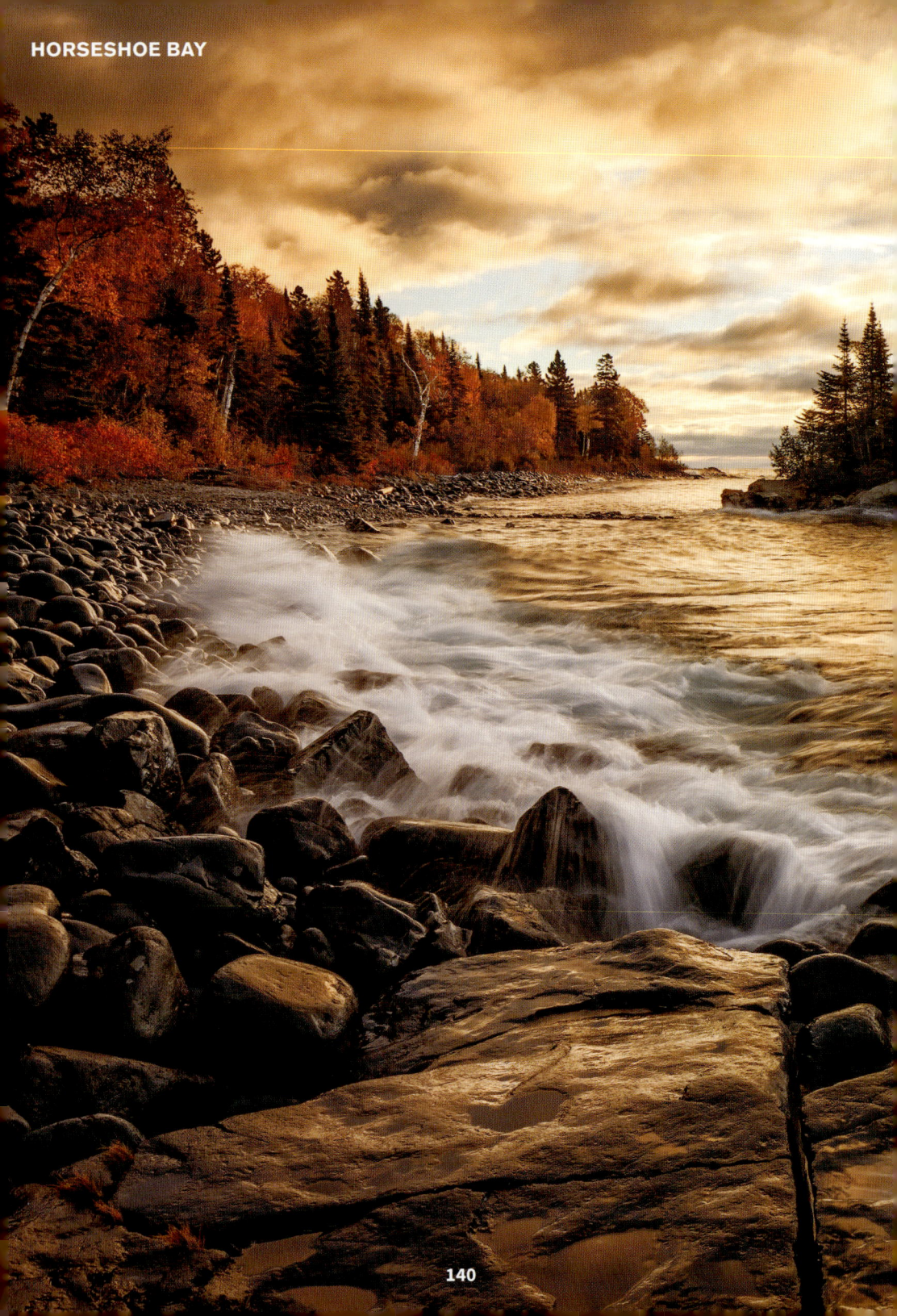
HORSESHOE BAY

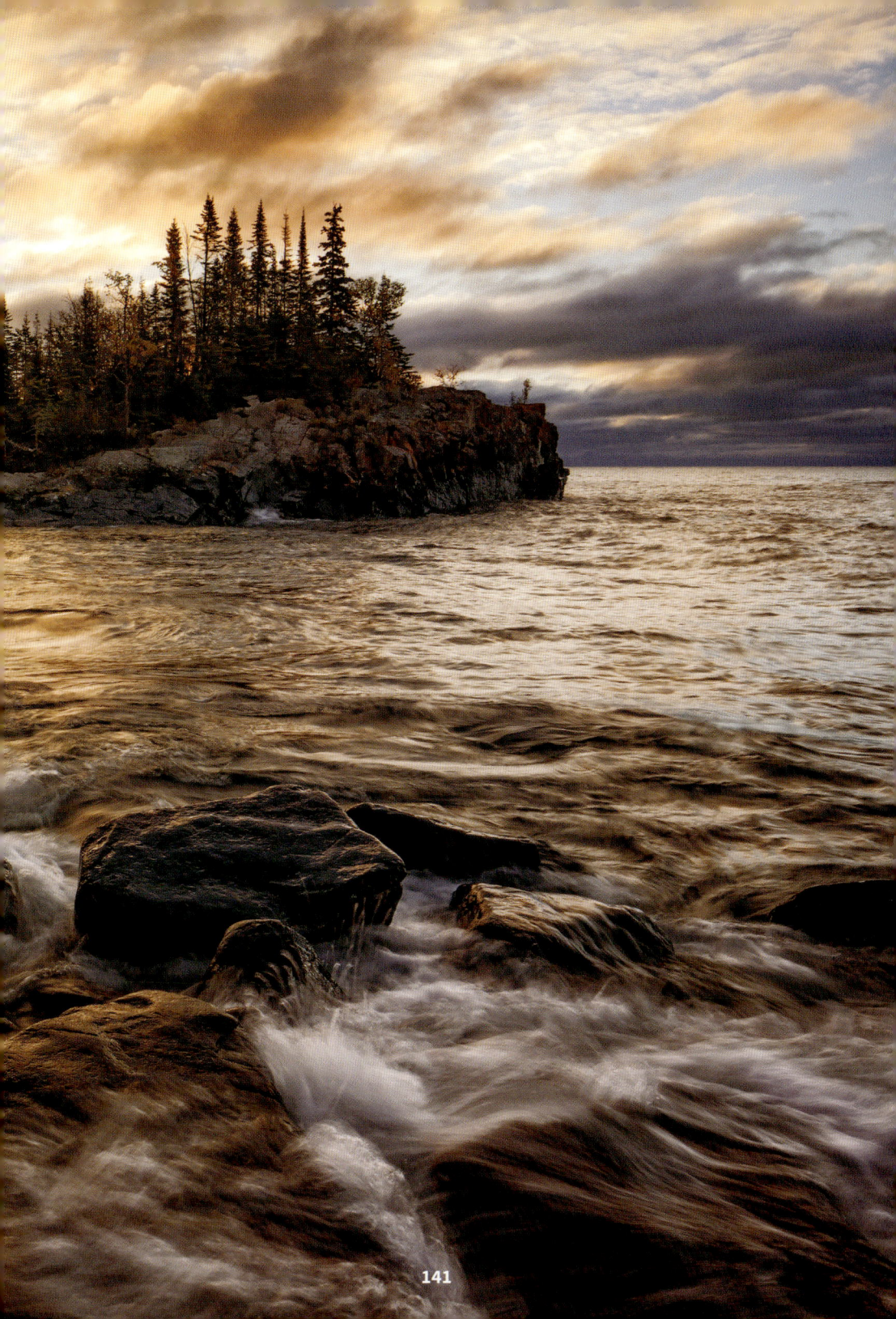

◄ HORSESHOE BAY

The site of a remote small craft harbor managed by the Minnesota Department of Natural Resources, the Horseshoe Bay area also includes a small campsite and the second of three scenic, just-offshore rock islands between Grand Marais and Grand Portage. The campsite is available for use by kayakers paddling the Lake Superior State Water Trail. The island, located just east of the bay, is quite forested for its size and a visual treat by itself. The mixed cobblestone and volcanic bedrock beach offers a front-row seat for enjoying the solitude of this area. Horseshoe Bay is located 1.8 miles northeast of the village of Hovland on Highway 61.

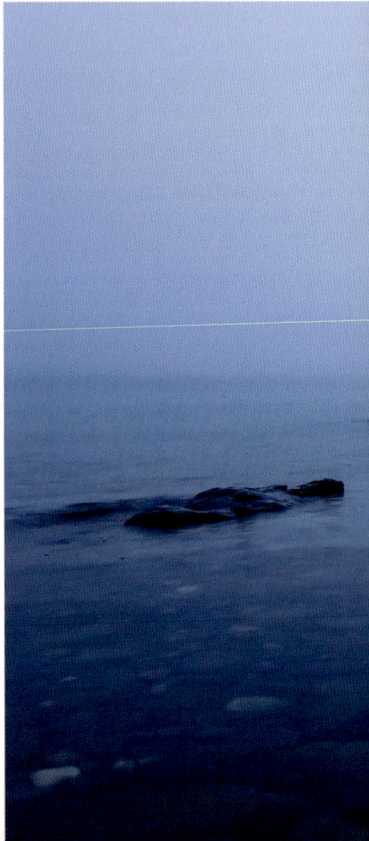

HOLLOW ROCK

Located just offshore of a small resort bearing its name, Hollow Rock seems more like an offshore arch than an island. Its unique form was most likely made possible by fractures in the middle of the rock that gave way to speedier erosion and chunks of rock being carved away over time by the power of Lake Superior. The adjacent Hollow Rock Resort maintains several cottages of various sizes and configurations that can be rented through Grand Portage Lodge. Hollow Rock is located just north of the Hollow Rock Creek crossing on Highway 61. Visitors to Hollow Rock should take extra care in respecting the privacy of guests occupying the resort.

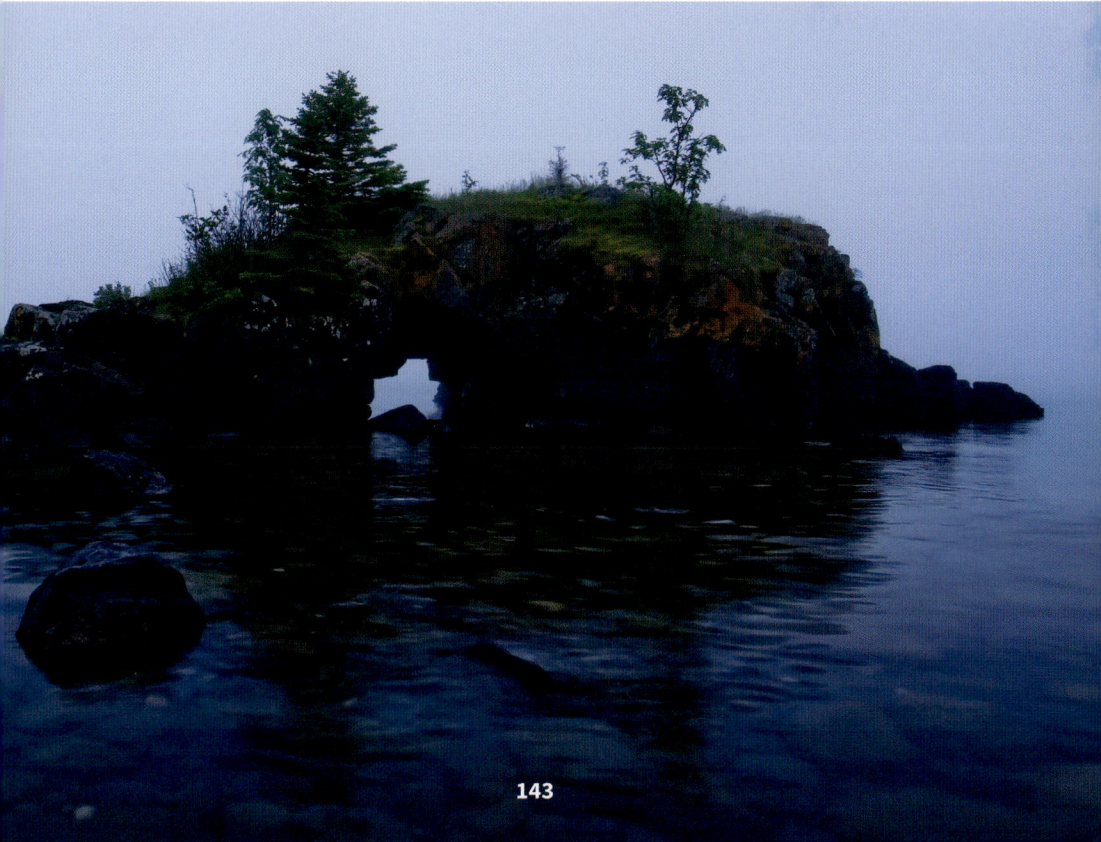

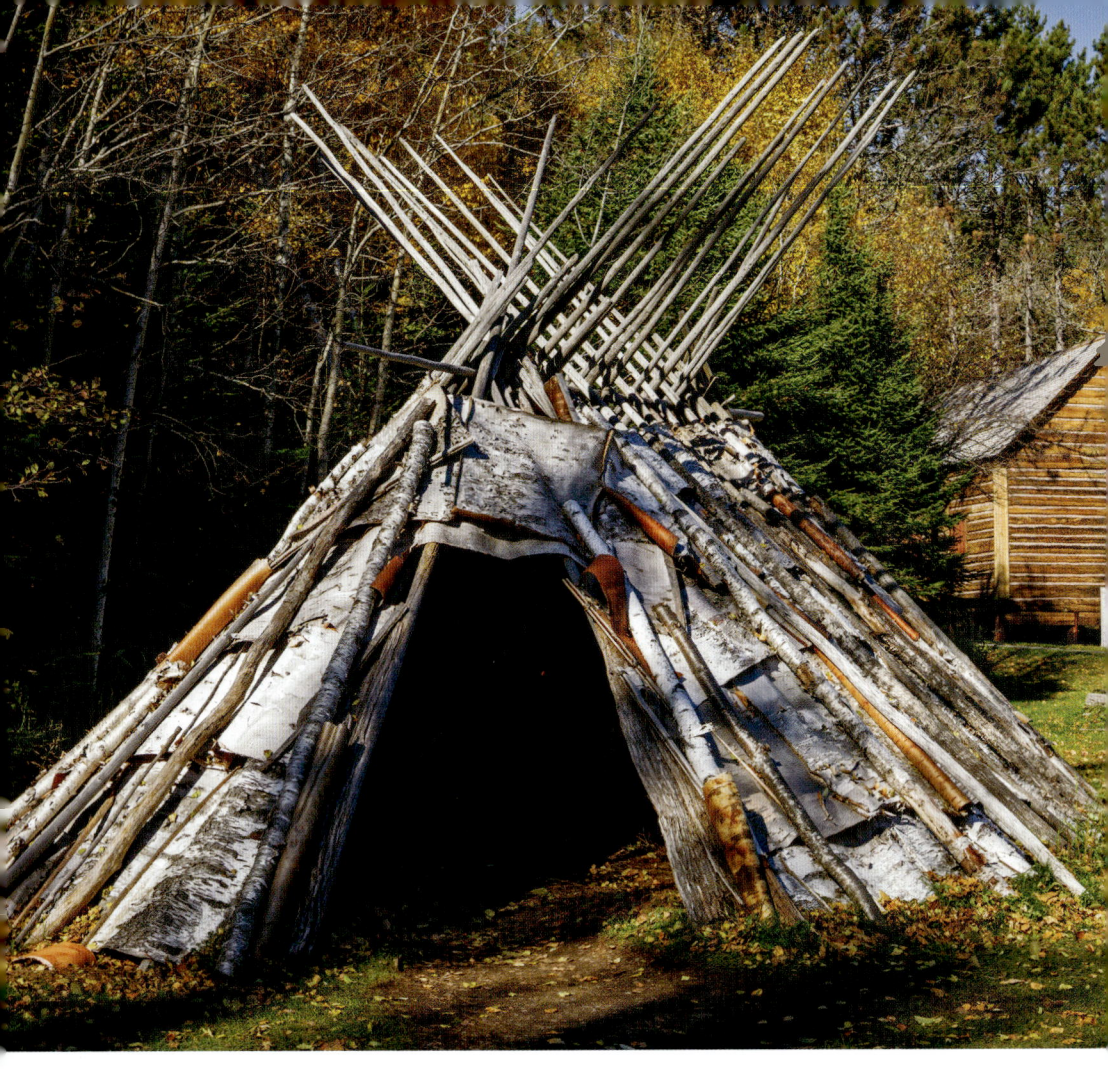

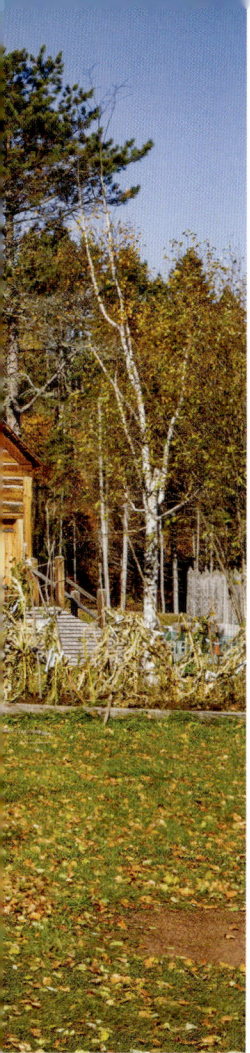

GRAND PORTAGE NATIONAL MONUMENT

Established as the Grand Portage National Historic Site in 1951 and designated a national monument seven years later, the site preserves a once-vital and bustling center of fur-trading activity and shares the heritage of the local Ojibwe people. The reconstructed North West Company trading post, including a great hall, kitchen and other buildings, provides an authentic look at the region's fur-trading past. The monument also preserves the 8.5-mile-long Grand Portage Trail and the site of Fort Charlotte on the Pigeon River. Each second weekend of August, the monument hosts Rendezvous Days, a celebration of Grand Portage's rich heritage held in conjunction with a pow wow by the Grand Portage Band of Ojibwe.

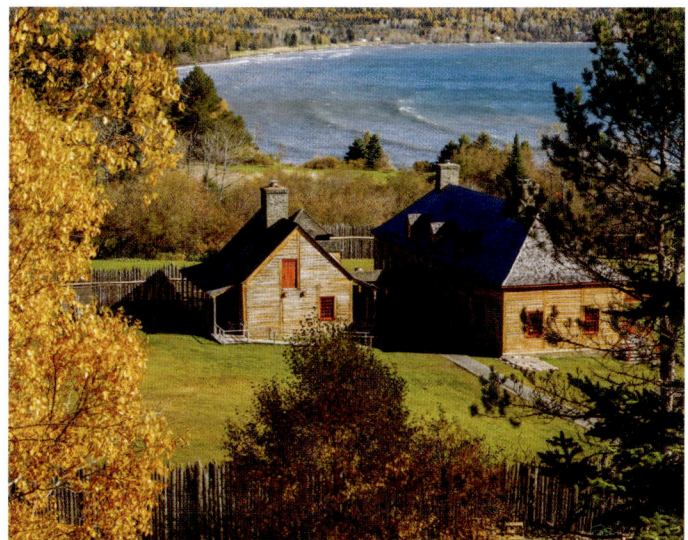

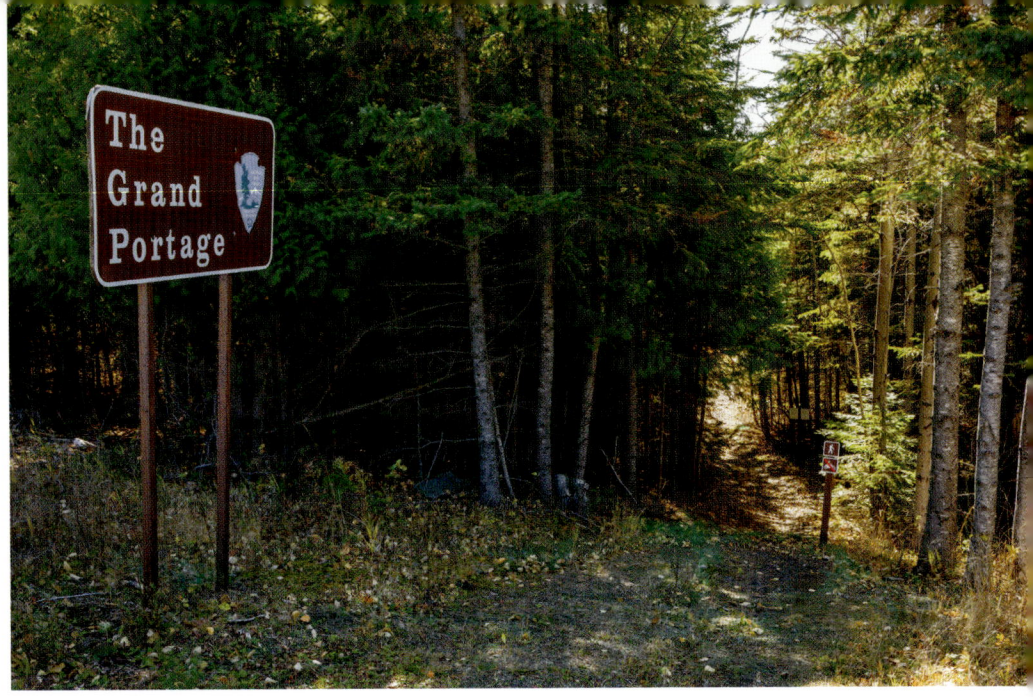

THE GRAND PORTAGE

Possibly used as many as 2,000 years ago as a seasonal migration route for indigenous peoples, The Grand Portage became a vital link in the 1700s for fur-trading voyageurs. The portage enabled them to transport their goods on the Great Lakes from hunting lands in the western interior of North America. The several miles of the Pigeon River closest to Lake Superior present numerous impassable canyons and waterfalls, creating the need for a portage route to access waterways farther west. Today, hikers can make the 8.5-mile trek from Lake Superior to Fort Charlotte, retracing the footsteps of the voyageurs more than 200 years ago.

MOUNT JOSEPHINE AND WAYSWAUGOING BAY OVERLOOK

Easily one of the finest overlooks on Lake Superior's North Shore in Minnesota, Mount Josephine provides majestic views of Pigeon Point, the Susie Islands, and—if the horizon is clear—20-mile-distant Isle Royale. The easiest approach for taking in the panoramic scene is by pulling off Highway 61 at the Wayswaugoing Bay Overlook, near mile marker 148. The overlook contains a parking area with a modern observation deck and pit toilets. For those with more time or energy, the best views can be had at the summit of Mount Josephine (elevation 1,342 feet), reached via a strenuous 2.5-mile-round trip hike. The trailhead for the hike is approximately 1 mile east of Grand Portage National Monument on Upper Road.

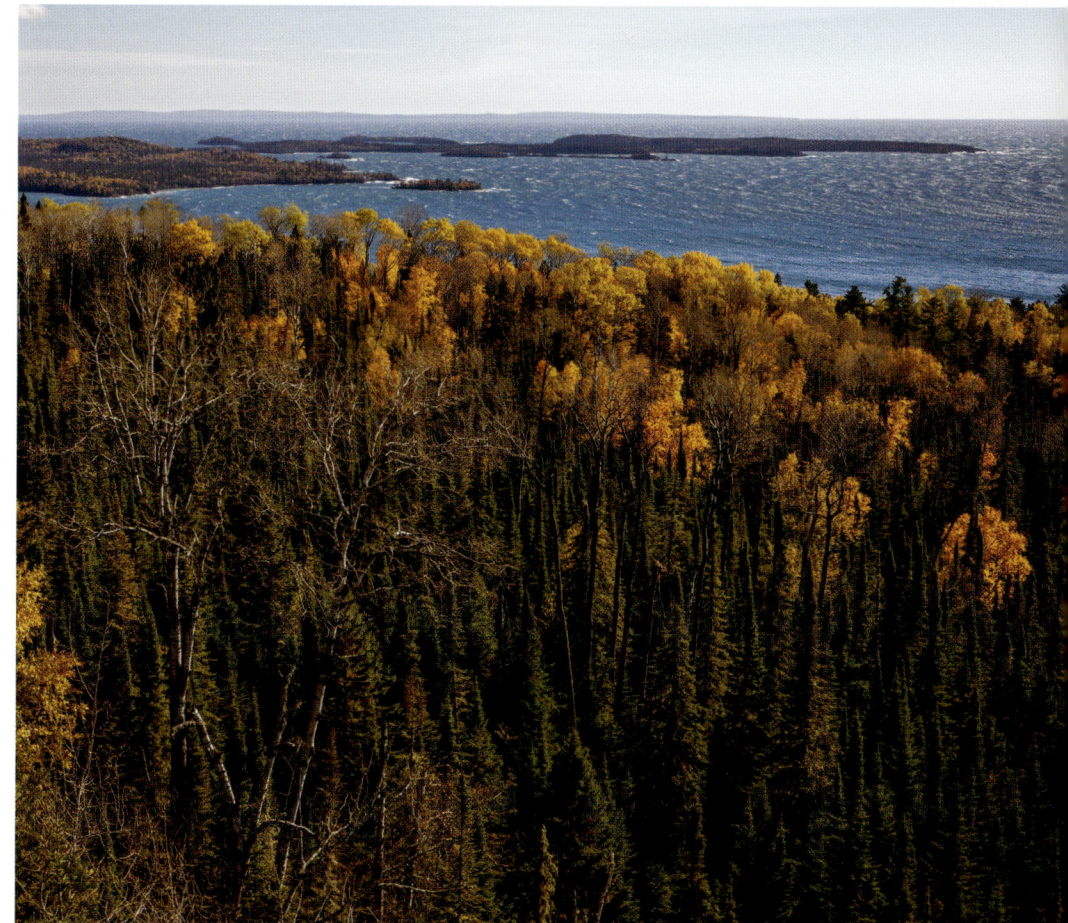

GRAND PORTAGE STATE PARK

Established in 1989, Grand Portage is one of Minnesota's newest state parks. Its signature attraction, High Falls of the Pigeon River, drops 120 feet, double the height of Minnesota's second-tallest waterfall. The 0.5-mile trail leading to the impressive falls is fully paved and wheelchair accessible with boardwalk viewing platforms. A much more challenging trail begins just before the start of the boardwalk and continues another 2.3 miles to the 20-foot Middle Falls. While there are no campground facilities, the day-use-only park features a modern visitor center, serving as both a highway rest area and Minnesota Travel Information Center.

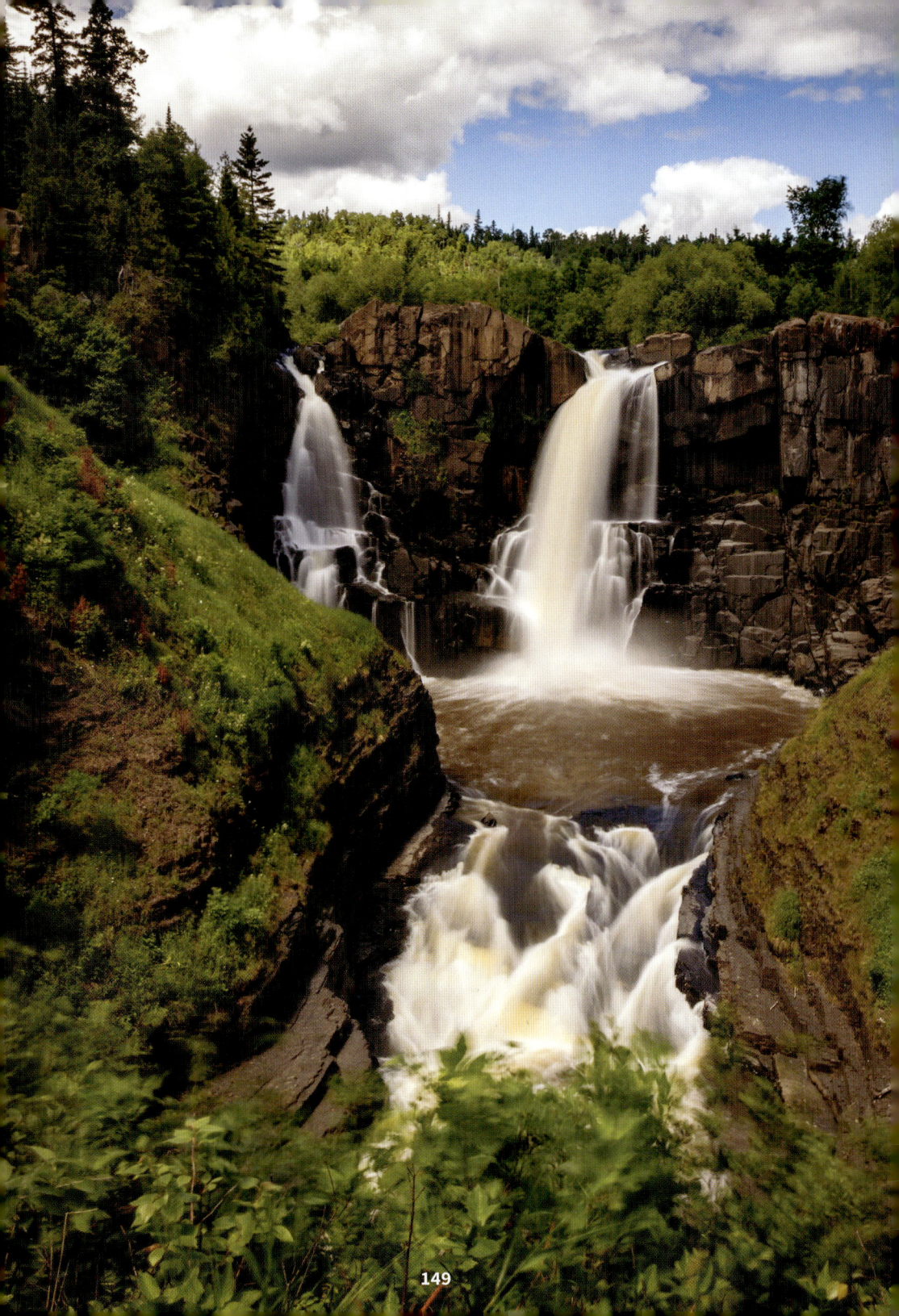

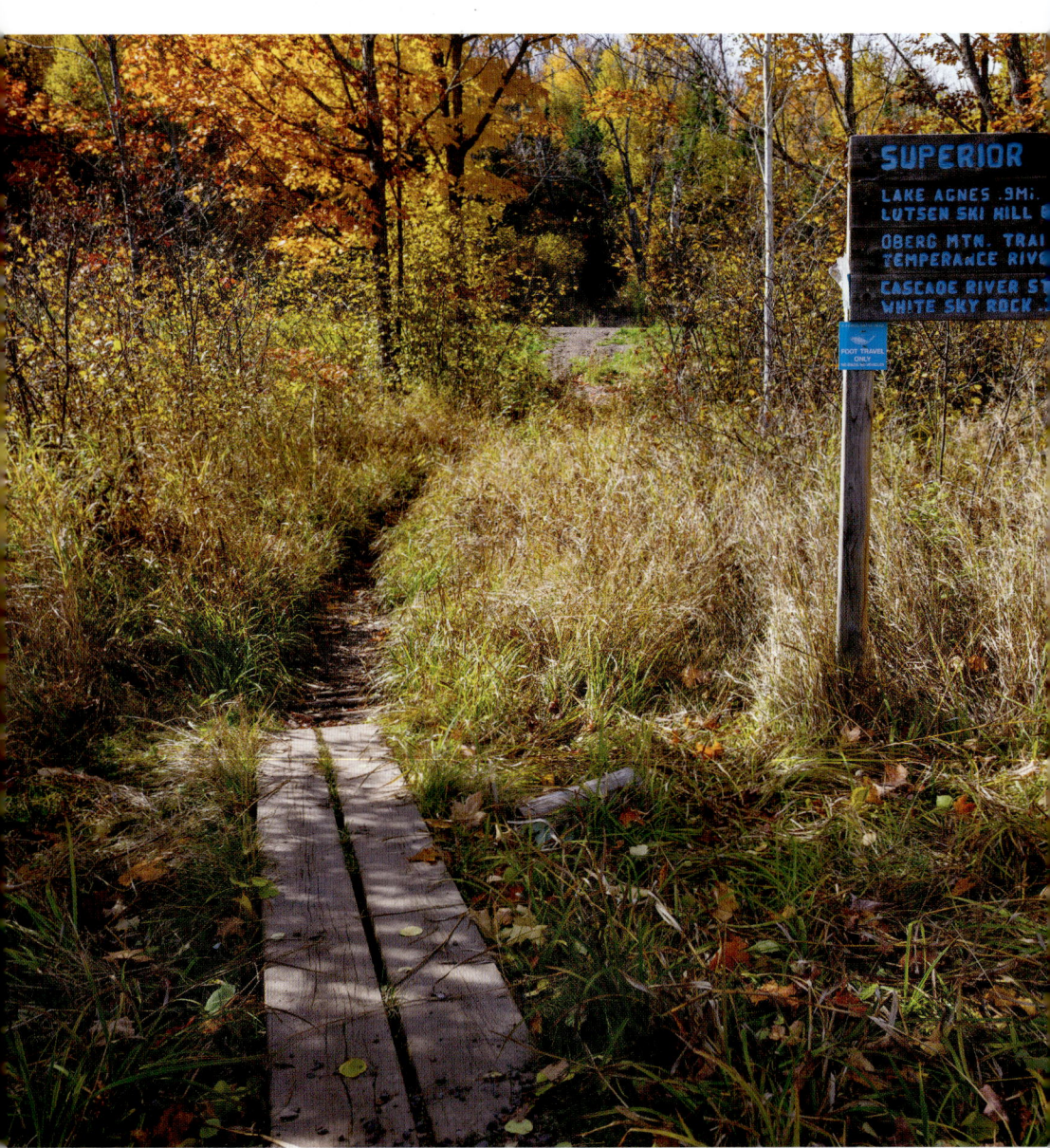

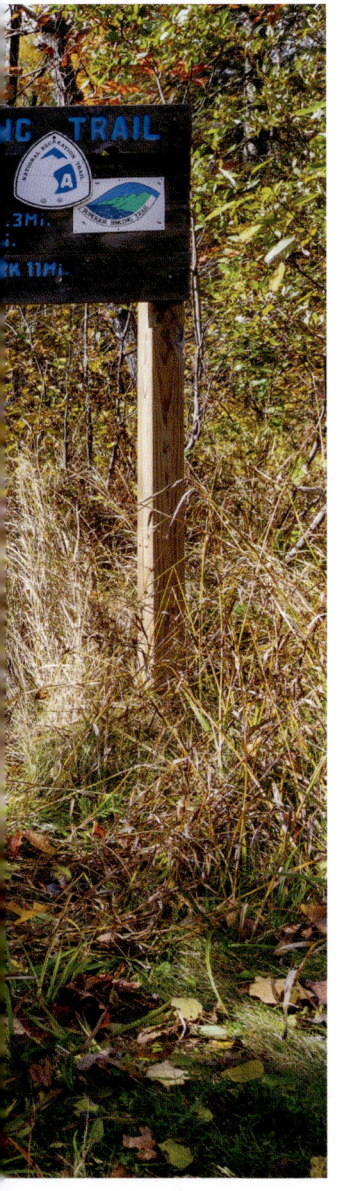
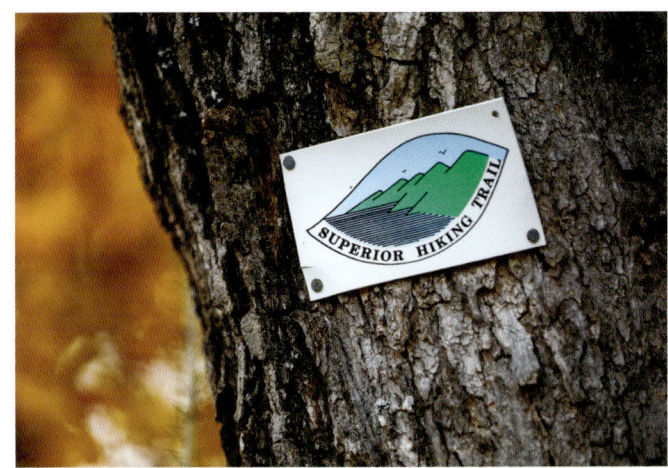

SUPERIOR HIKING TRAIL

Modeled after the Appalachian Trail, the 310-mile Superior Hiking Trail extends from Jay Cooke State Park, just southwest of Duluth, to near the U.S.-Canada Border, hugging the ridgeline above Lake Superior and passing through seven of the eight North Shore state parks. Promoted and managed by the 3,200-member non-profit Superior Hiking Trail Association, construction of the footpath began in 1987 and was substantially complete by 2013. It is used by both day- and thru-hikers and contains 93 backcountry campsites to permit long-distance treks. The well-maintained trail has received several accolades, and as of 2019, plans are underway to incorporate the trail as a segment of the much longer North Country National Scenic Trail, which extends from North Dakota to New York.

GITCHI-GAMI STATE TRAIL

Currently under construction, the Gitchi-Gami State Trail will stretch 89 miles from Two Harbors to Grand Marais when completed, connecting five state parks. As of this writing, six non-contiguous sections of the trail exist, totaling 29 miles. The longest completed trail section extends 14.6 miles from Gooseberry Falls State Park to the town of Beaver Bay. As a paved, non-motorized trail, it specifically caters to bicyclists, skaters, walkers, and joggers. Most of the trail follows abandoned Highway 61 right-of-way, but some segments bring users close to Lake Superior or other scenic locations.

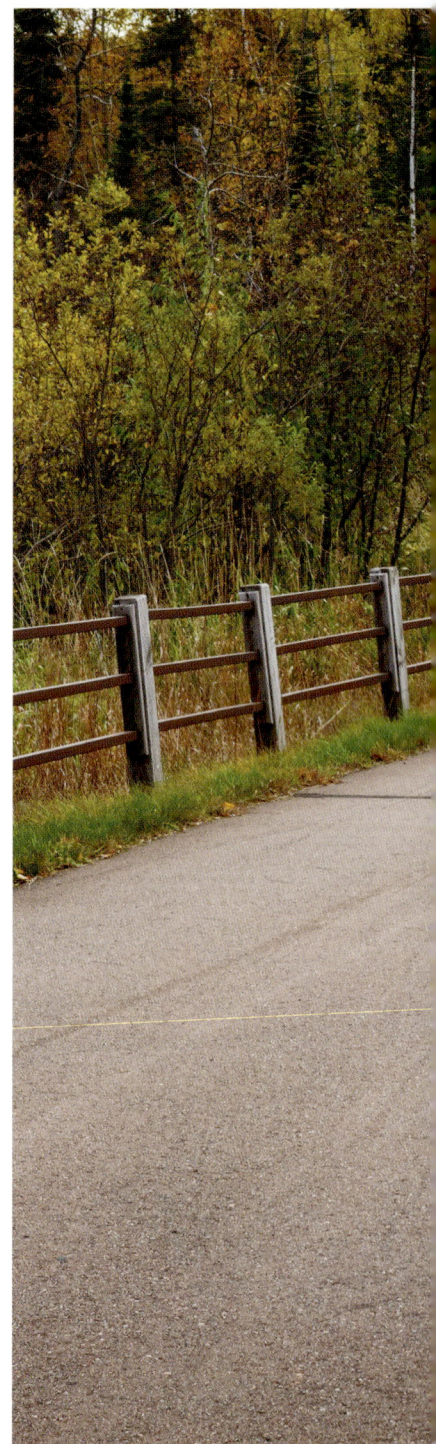

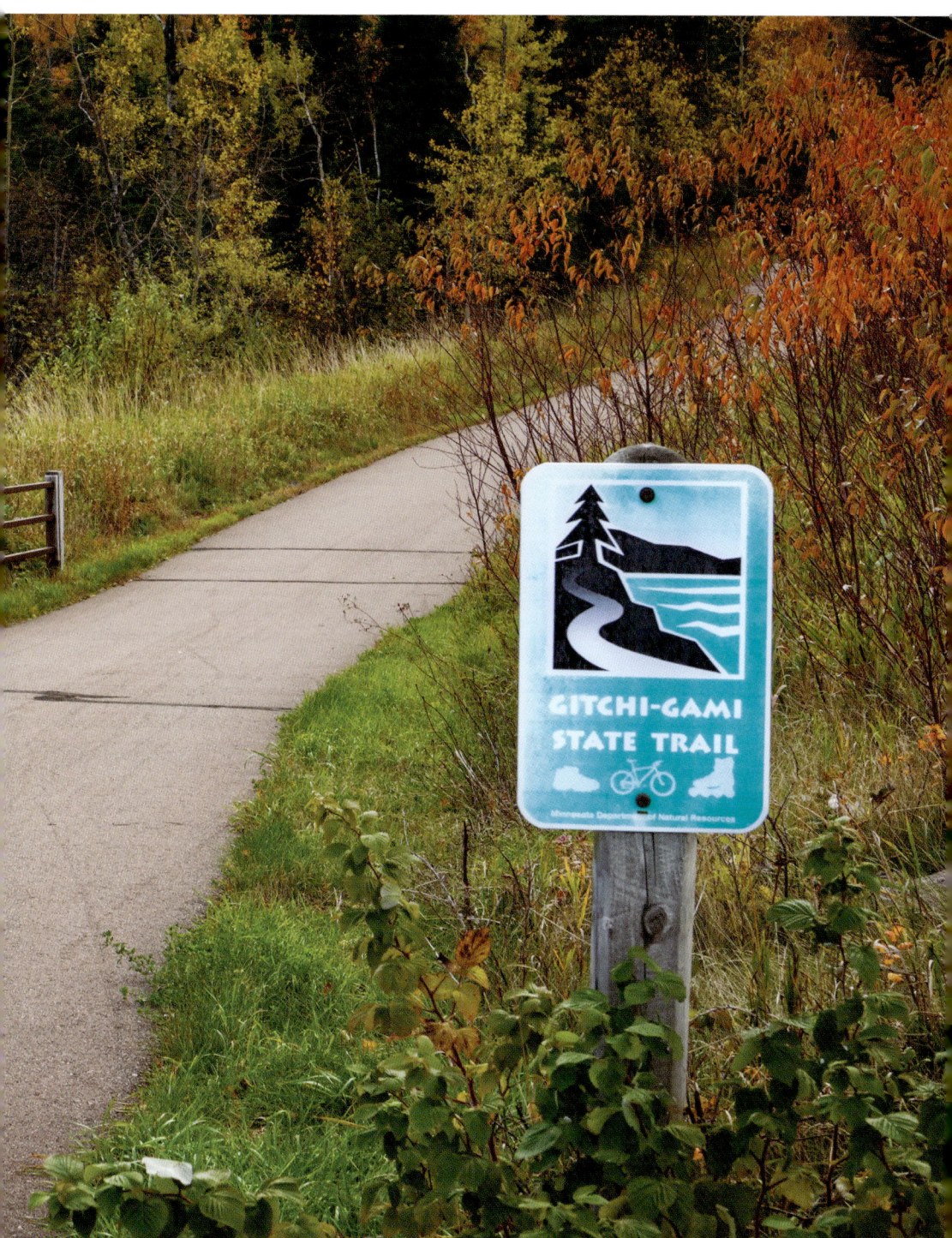

PAGE	NAME	SITE INFORMATION
8	JAY COOKE STATE PARK	780 Highway 210, Carlton, MN 55718; 218-673-7000; www.dnr.state.mn.us/state_parks/jay_cooke/index.html
10	SPIRIT MOUNTAIN	9500 Spirit Mountain Place, Duluth, MN 55810; 800-642-6377; www.spiritmt.com
11	THOMPSON HILL WELCOME CENTER	8525 W Skyline Parkway, Duluth, MN 55810; 218-723-4938; www.exploreminnesota.com/where-to-go/cities-towns/2541/thompson-hill-welcome-center
12	LAKE SUPERIOR ZOO	7210 Fremont Street, Duluth, MN 55807; 218-730-4500; www.lszoduluth.org
14	SKYLINE PARKWAY	218-730-4300; www.duluthmn.gov/parks/parks-listing/skyline-parkway
15	JOHN A. BLATNIK BRIDGE (VIEWPOINT) AND INTERSTATE FISHING PIER	1500 Port Terminal Road, Duluth, MN 55802
16	ENGER TOWER AND PARK	Enger Tower Drive, Duluth, MN 55806; 218-730-4300; www.duluthmn.gov/parks/parks-listing/enger-park
20	BAYFRONT FESTIVAL PARK	350 Harbor Drive, Duluth, MN 55802; 218-722-5573; bayfrontfestivalpark.com
21	GREAT LAKES AQUARIUM	353 Harbor Drive, Duluth, MN 55802; 218-740-FISH (3474); glaquarium.org
22	THE DEPOT	506 W Michigan Street, Duluth, MN 55802; 218-727-8025; www.duluthdepot.org
23	NORTH SHORE SCENIC RAILROAD	506 W Michigan Street, Duluth MN 55802; 800-423-1273; www.northshorescenicrailroad.org
25	DULUTH ENTERTAINMENT CONVENTION CENTER/ AMSOIL ARENA	350 Harbor Drive, Duluth, MN 55802; 218-722-5573; decc.org
26	VISTA FLEET	323 Harbor Drive, Duluth, MN 55802; 218-722-6218; www.vistafleet.com
27	S.S. *WILLIAM A. IRVIN*	350 Harbor Drive, Duluth, MN 55802; 218-722-7876 or 218-623-1236; decc.org/william-a-irvin
28	CANAL PARK	Canal Park Drive, Duluth, MN 55802; canalpark.com
29	AERIAL LIFT BRIDGE	601 S Lake Avenue, Duluth, MN 55802; www.dot.state.mn.us/historicbridges/L6116.html
31	MINNESOTA POINT	5000 Minnesota Avenue, Duluth, MN 55802; 218-722-4745; www.duluthmn.gov/parks/parks-listing/park-point
35	THE LAKEWALK	Bayfront Park to Brighton Beach, Duluth, MN 55802; 218-730-4306; www.duluthmn.gov/parks/parks-listing/lakewalk
37	DOWNTOWN DULUTH	Superior Street, Duluth, MN 55802; 218-727-8549; www.downtownduluth.com
38	HISTORIC OLD CENTRAL HIGH SCHOOL	215 N 1st Avenue E, Duluth, MN 55802; 218-728-2904; www.isd709.org/community/historic-old-central-high-school
40	FITGER'S	600 E Superior Street, Duluth, MN 55802; 218-722-8826; fitgers.com
40	LEIF ERIKSON PARK	1301 London Road, Duluth, MN 55805; 218-730-4300; www.duluthmn.gov/parks/parks-listing/leif-erikson-park
43	DULUTH ROSE GARDEN	15 S 13th Avenue E, Duluth, MN 55802; 218-730-4300; www.duluthmn.gov/parks/parks-listing/rose-garden

44	GLENSHEEN HISTORIC ESTATE	3300 London Road, Duluth, MN 55804; 218-726-8910; glensheen.org
45	HAWK RIDGE NATURE RESERVE	3980 E Skyline Parkway, Duluth, MN 55804; 218-730-4300; www.duluthmn.gov/parks/parks-listing/hawk-ridge
46	LESTER PARK	61st Avenue E & Superior Street, Duluth, MN 55804; 218-730-4300; www.duluthmn.gov/parks/parks-listing/lester-park
49	KITCHI GAMMI PARK (BRIGHTON BEACH)	6000 Brighton Beach Road, Duluth, MN 55804; 218-730-4300; www.duluthmn.gov/parks/parks-listing/brighton-beach-park-kitchi-gammi
51	MCQUADE SMALL CRAFT HARBOR	9628 Congdon Boulevard, Duluth, MN 55804; 888-MINNDNR (646-6367); www.dnr.state.mn.us/water_access/harbors/mcquade.html
54	STONEY POINT	Stoney Point Drive, Duluth, MN 55804
54	PIERRE THE VOYAGEUR	933 Stanley Road, Two Harbors, MN; 218-834-3847
56	TWO HARBORS ORE DOCKS	Waterfront Drive, Two Harbors, MN 55616
57	*EDNA G* TUGBOAT	Waterfront Drive, Two Harbors, MN 55616
59	TWO HARBORS LIGHTHOUSE MUSEUM	1 Lighthouse Point, Two Harbors, MN 55616; 218-834-4898; www.lakecountyhistoricalsociety.org/museums/view/two-harbors-light-station
60	DULUTH AND IRON RANGE RAILROAD DEPOT MUSEUM	520 South Avenue, Two Harbors, MN 55616; 218-834-4898; www.lakecountyhistoricalsociety.org/museums/view/depot-museum
61	3M BIRTHPLACE MUSEUM	203 Waterfront Drive, Two Harbors, MN 55616; 218-834-4898; lakecountyhistoricalsociety.org/museums/view/3m-museum
62	HIGHWAY 61 TUNNELS	Highway 61, mile markers 31 and 34
64	LUPINES	Best patches of flowers found along Highway 61 near Castle Danger (southwest of Gooseberry Falls State Park) and along Caribou Trail near Lutsen
67	GOOSEBERRY FALLS STATE PARK	3206 Highway 61 E, Two Harbors, MN 55616; 218-595-7100; www.dnr.state.mn.us/state_parks/gooseberry_falls/index.html
70	IONA'S BEACH SCIENTIFIC AND NATURAL AREA	Highway 61, mile marker 42; 218-300-7871; www.dnr.state.mn.us/snas/detail.html?id=sna01000
71	SPLIT ROCK RIVER	Highway 61, between mile markers 43 and 44; 218-595-ROCK (7625); www.dnr.state.mn.us/state_parks/split_rock_lighthouse/index.html
72	DAY HILL	(Trailhead within state park campground) 3755 Split Rock Lighthouse Road, Two Harbors, MN 55616; 218-595-ROCK (7625); www.dnr.state.mn.us/state_parks/split_rock_lighthouse/index.html
74	SPLIT ROCK LIGHTHOUSE WAYSIDE REST OVERLOOK	Highway 61, mile marker 45; 218-595-ROCK (7625); www.dnr.state.mn.us/state_parks/split_rock_lighthouse/index.html
75	PEBBLE BEACH	(Trail begins at state park trail center) 3755 Split Rock Lighthouse Road, Two Harbors, MN 55616; 218-595-ROCK (7625); www.dnr.state.mn.us/state_parks/split_rock_lighthouse/index.html

#	Name	Address/Directions
76	**SPLIT ROCK LIGHTHOUSE**	3713 Split Rock Lighthouse Road, Two Harbors, MN 55616; 218-595-ROCK (7625); www.dnr.state.mn.us/state_parks/split_rock_lighthouse/index.html
77	**LIGHTHOUSE KEEPERS' HOMES**	3713 Split Rock Lighthouse Road, Two Harbors, MN 55616; 218-595-ROCK (7625); www.dnr.state.mn.us/state_parks/split_rock_lighthouse/index.html
78	**BEAVER BAY**	Highway 61, between mile markers 50 and 52; www.beaverbaymn.com
79	**BEAVER RIVER**	Highway 61, between mile markers 51 and 52
82	**SILVER BAY MARINA**	99 Beach Drive, Silver Bay, MN 55614; 218-226-3121; silverbay-marina.com
83	**ROCKY TACONITE**	83 Outer Drive, Silver Bay, MN 55614; 218-226-4408; www.silverbay.com
84	**BLACK BEACH**	Highway 61, approx. 0.4 mile north of the only stoplights in town, then right on Mensing Drive. Follow signs to Black Beach
85	**BEAN AND BEAR LAKES**	From Highway 61, follow Outer Drive (becomes Penn Boulevard) for 2.2 miles to Superior Hiking Trail trailhead on right. Known as the Twin Lakes Trail, the route passes Bean and Bear lakes in a 6.8-mile loop; 218-353-8800; www.dnr.state.mn.us/state_parks/tettegouche/index.html
86	**PALISADE HEAD**	Highway 61, approx. 2.5 miles north of Silver Bay, look for green sign indicating Palisade Head. Turn right and carefully follow the one-lane, winding road to the top. Trailers and long vehicles are prohibited from traveling the one-lane road; 218-353-8800; www.dnr.state.mn.us/state_parks/tettegouche/index.html
89	**HISTORIC TETTEGOUCHE CAMP**	Follow Highway 1 from Highway 61 for 4.3 miles to Lax Lake Road. Turn left and continue 3.1 miles to parking area on left. From the parking area, hike 1.7 miles on service road to camp; 218-353-8800; www.dnr.state.mn.us/state_parks/tettegouche/tettegouche_camp/index.html
90	**SHOVEL POINT AND SEA STACK**	5702 Highway 61, Silver Bay, MN 55614. Within Tettegouche State Park. Trailhead begins at main park visitor center. Follow the trail 0.6 mile to the tip of Shovel Point; 218-353-8800; www.dnr.state.mn.us/state_parks/tettegouche/index.html
91	**CRYSTAL BAY**	Highway 61, just north of intersection with Highway 1. Park along edge of highway shoulder. A short, steep trail leads to a beach; 218-353-8800; www.dnr.state.mn.us/state_parks/tettegouche/index.html
92	**BAPTISM RIVER HIGH FALLS**	5702 Highway 61, Silver Bay, MN 55614. Within Tettegouche State Park. From the visitor center, follow the park road 1.5 miles to the trailhead parking area. From the trailhead, follow the trail 0.8 mile to the base of the falls; 218-353-8800; www.dnr.state.mn.us/state_parks/tettegouche/index.html
95	**TWO STEP FALLS**	5702 Highway 61, Silver Bay, MN 55614. Within Tettegouche State Park. From High Falls, follow the trail along either side of the river for 0.3 mile to a short spur trail to the falls; 218-353-8800; www.dnr.state.mn.us/state_parks/tettegouche/index.html

96	ILLGEN FALLS	Follow Highway 1 from Highway 61 for 1.6 miles to small parking area on left. Hike short trail to viewpoint above falls; 218-353-8800; www.dnr.state.mn.us/state_parks/tettegouche/index.html
97	FINLAND MINNESOTA HERITAGE SITE	5653 Little Marais Road, Finland, MN 55603; 218-353-7380; finlandmnhistoricalsociety.com/
98	GEORGE H. CROSBY MANITOU STATE PARK	7616 Co Highway 7, Finland, MN 55603; 218-353-8800; www.dnr.state.mn.us/state_parks/george_crosby_manitou/index.html
99	CARIBOU FALLS STATE WAYSIDE	Highway 61, approx. 5.3 miles north of Little Marais; www.dnr.state.mn.us/state_parks/waysides/index.html
100	SUGARLOAF COVE	9096 W Highway 61, Schroeder, MN 55613; 218-663-7679; sugarloafnorthshore.org
102	CROSS RIVER	Parking area on north side of Highway 61 within town of Schroeder, just west of river crossing.
103	FATHER BARAGA'S CROSS	56 Baraga Cross Road, Schroeder, MN 55613
105	TEMPERANCE RIVER STATE PARK	7620 W Highway 61, Schroeder, MN 55613; 218-663-3100; www.dnr.state.mn.us/state_parks/temperance_river/index.html
106	TOFTE PARK	Tofte Park Road, Tofte, MN 55615; 218-370-0763; www.toftemn.com
107	HEARTBREAK HILL AND FALL COLOR BACKROADS	Loop route includes Highway 61, Sawbill Trail, Six Hundred Road, and Temperance River Road; 218-663-8060; www.fs.usda.gov/recarea/superior/recreation/scenicdrivinginfo/recarea/?recid=75017&actid=105
108	CARLTON PEAK	From Highway 61 in the town of Tofte, follow the Sawbill Trail for 2.6 miles to the Britton Peak Trailhead parking on right. It's a 1.6-mile hike from the trailhead to Carlton Peak, following the Superior Hiking Trail; 218-663-8060; www.fs.usda.gov/recarea/superior/recreation/fishing/recarea/?recid=40276&actid=50
110	OBERG MOUNTAIN	Follow Highway 61 approx. 4.7 miles northeast of Tofte to Onion River Road (also look for sign indicating Superior Hiking Trail). Turn left and drive unpaved Onion River Road for 2.1 miles to parking area on left. Trail to Oberg Mountain begins on right, just before entering parking area; 218-663-8060; www.fs.usda.gov/recarea/superior/recreation/hiking/recarea/?recid=41653&actid=50
111	POPLAR RIVER	Follow Ski Hill Road (also known as Cook County Highway 5) through Lutsen Mountains Ski Area to the road's terminus at the Superior Hiking Trail parking area. From the parking area, the hiking trail to the left leads to bridge over Poplar River in 0.2 miles; 218-663-7281; www.lutsen.com/summer/hiking
112	LUTSEN MOUNTAINS	467 Ski Hill Road, Lutsen, MN 55612; 218-663-7281; www.lutsen.com
113	LAKE AGNES	From Highway 61, just east of Lutsen, follow Caribou Trail (also known as Cook County Highway 4) for 3.9 miles to White Sky Road on the right and the Superior Hiking Trail trailhead parking area. Follow the Superior Hiking Trail spur route for 1 mile to Lake Agnes; superiorhiking.org/trail-section/lutsen-to-grand-marais

114	WHITE SKY ROCK	From Highway 61, just east of Lutsen, follow Caribou Trail (also known as Cook County Highway 4) for 3.9 miles to White Sky Road on the right and the Superior Hiking Trail trailhead parking area. Follow the Superior Hiking Trail spur route toward Lake Agnes for 0.1 mile, then veer right at fork, continuing for another 0.2 mile to overlook; superiorhiking.org/trail-section/lutsen-to-grand-marais
117	CASCADE RIVER STATE PARK	3481 W Highway 61, Lutsen, MN 55612; 218-387-6000; www.dnr.state.mn.us/state_parks/cascade_river/index.html
118	FALL RIVER	Follow Highway 61 to river, approximately 2.5 miles west of downtown Grand Marais.
121	GRAND MARAIS	Grand Marais, MN 55604; 218-387-1848; www.ci.grand-marais.mn.us
123	GRAND MARAIS HARBOR	Many views of the harbor from downtown. For access to lighthouse, follow Broadway Avenue from downtown to large parking lot near Artists' Point. Walk past U.S. Coast Guard Station toward trailhead.
124	ARTISTS' POINT	Follow Broadway Avenue from downtown to large parking lot near Artists' Point. Walk past U.S. Coast Guard Station toward trailhead.
125	BEAVER HOUSE	3 E Wisconsin Street, Grand Marais, MN 55604; 218-387-3349; www.facebook.com/pages/category/Sports---Recreation/Beaver-House-1439599763008641
127	GUNFLINT TRAIL SIGN	Highway 61 and Second Avenue W, Grand Marais, MN 55604
128	PINCUSHION MOUNTAIN	1 Pincushion Drive, Grand Marais, MN 55604; 218-387-1750; www.fs.usda.gov/recarea/superior/recreation/recarea/?recid=71223&actid=70
130	MAPLE HILL CHURCH	90 Maple Hill Drive, Grand Marais, MN 55604; 218-387-1536; spiritofthewilderness.org
131	GEORGE WASHINGTON PINES	From Highway 61 in Grand Marais, follow the Gunflint Trail (Cook County Highway 12) for about 7 miles to parking area and trailhead on left; 218-387-1750; www.fs.usda.gov/recarea/superior/recreation/wintersports/recarea/?recid=64783&actid=91
134	HONEYMOON BLUFF/ HUNGRY JACK LAKE	From Highway 61 in Grand Marais, follow the Gunflint Trail (Cook County Highway 12) for about 27 miles to Clearwater Road (Cook County Highway 66). Turn right and proceed 2.2 miles to trailhead on left; 218-387-1750; www.fs.usda.gov/recarea/superior/recreation/fishing/recarea/?recid=40303&actid=50
134	KADUNCE RIVER	From Grand Marais, follow Highway 61 northbound for approximately 9 miles to parking area on right. Trail begins on opposite side of highway; www.dnr.state.mn.us/state_parks/waysides/index.html
136	SUPERIOR HIKING TRAIL LAKEWALK	Trail intersects Highway 61 between mile markers 120 and 121 and mile markers 121 and 122 (approximately 11 miles northeast of Grand Marais). Park on the highway shoulder near either trail junction; superiorhiking.org/trail-section/grand-marais-to-otter-lake-road
137	JUDGE C.R. MAGNEY STATE PARK	4051 Highway 61, Grand Marais, MN 55604; 218-387-6300; www.dnr.state.mn.us/state_parks/judge_cr_magney/index.html

139	**NANIBOUJOU LODGE**	20 Naniboujou Trail, Grand Marais, MN 55604; 218-387-2688; www.naniboujou.com
142	**HORSESHOE BAY**	From Hovland, follow Highway 61 northbound for approximately 1.8 miles to Horseshoe Bay Road on right; 888-MINNDNR (646-6367); www.dnr.state.mn.us/water_access/harbors/horseshoe_bay.html
143	**HOLLOW ROCK**	7422 E Highway 61, Grand Portage MN 55605; 800-543-1384; www.hollowrockresort.com
145	**GRAND PORTAGE NATIONAL MONUMENT**	170 Mile Creek Road, Grand Portage, MN 55605; 218-475-0123; www.nps.gov/grpo/index.htm
146	**THE GRAND PORTAGE**	170 Mile Creek Road, Grand Portage, MN 55605; 218-475-0123; www.nps.gov/grpo/learn/photosmultimedia/grand-portage-trail.htm
147	**MOUNT JOSEPHINE AND WAYSWAUGOING BAY OVERLOOK**	Wayswaugoing Bay Overlook: From the Grand Portage Trading Post, follow Highway 61 northbound for approximately 3.5 miles to parking area and overlook on right. Mount Josephine Trailhead: Follow Cook County Highway 17 approximately one mile east of Grand Portage National Monument to small parking area on north side of Upper Road.
148	**GRAND PORTAGE STATE PARK**	9393 E Highway 61, Grand Portage, MN 55605; 218-475-2360; www.dnr.state.mn.us/state_parks/grand_portage/index.html
151	**SUPERIOR HIKING TRAIL**	731 7th Avenue, Suite 2, Two Harbors, MN 55616 (Office and Information Center); 218-834-2700; superiorhiking.org
152	**GITCHI-GAMI STATE TRAIL**	1130 11th Street, Two Harbors, MN 55616 (Trail association mailing address); ggta.org

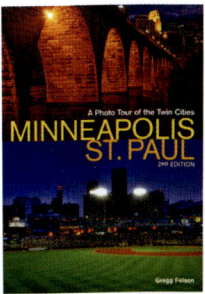

TAKE HOME THE BEST OF THE TWIN CITIES

Add this companion book to your collection. *Minneapolis–St. Paul* is a photo tour featuring 88 of the most popular attractions and events in Minnesota. Renowned photographer Gregg Felsen presents images that reflect the Twin Cities' history and culture.

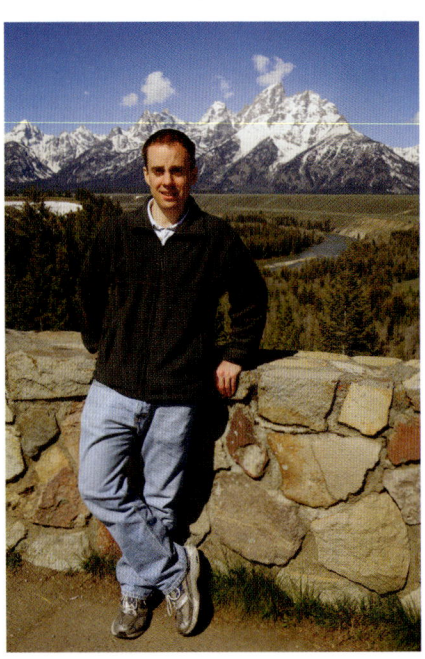

ABOUT THE AUTHOR

A native of central Minnesota, David Barthel has been photographing the natural world for nearly 20 years, specializing in the landscapes of Minnesota's Lake Superior region. Following a brief stint as an electrical engineer, Barthel left the field a decade ago to pursue photography as a full-time occupation, where he blends his technical virtuosity with creative endeavors.

Barthel's work has received numerous awards and has been published in several national and regional magazines, including *Outdoor Photographer* and *Minnesota Monthly*. He devotes much of his time to exhibiting his fine art photography at juried art fairs and festivals throughout the Upper Midwest, where his work is purchased for display in homes and businesses, both locally and around the world.

Barthel currently resides in his hometown of Sauk Rapids, Minnesota. In the rare moments that he is not actively engaged in his photographic pursuits, he enjoys bicycling, traveling, and spending time outdoors and with family.

Learn more about David and view his entire portfolio at www.northshoreimages.com. He is also active on Facebook (David Barthel Photography) and Instagram (@davidbarthelphotography) and may be contacted via email at dbarthel@northshoreimages.com.